THE DIARY OF 1636

TRANSLATIONS FROM THE ASIAN CLASSICS

For a list of titles in this series, see pages 267–272.

THE
DIARY
OF 1636

The Second Manchu
Invasion of Korea

Na Man'gap

TRANSLATED AND WITH
AN INTRODUCTION BY
George Kallander

COLUMBIA UNIVERSITY PRESS   NEW YORK

This publication was made possible in part by an award from the
James P. Geiss and Margaret Y. Hsu Foundation.

COLUMBIA UNIVERSITY PRESS
Publishers Since 1893
New York   Chichester, West Sussex
cup.columbia.edu

Library of Congress Cataloging-in-Publication Data
Names: Na, Man-gap, 1592–1642, author. | Kallander, George L.,
    1967– translator.
Title: The Diary of 1636 : The Second Manchu Invasion of Korea /
    Na Man'gap ; translated and with an Introduction by George Kallander.
Other titles: Pyŏngjarok. English.
Description: New York : Columbia University Press, 2020. | Series:
    Translations from the Asian classics | Includes bibliographical
    references and index.
Identifiers: LCCN 2019057504 (print) | LCCN 2019057505 (ebook) |
    ISBN 9780231197564 (cloth) | ISBN 9780231197571 (paperback) |
    ISBN 9780231552233 (ebook)
Subjects: LCSH: Na, Man-gap, 1592–1642—Diaries. | Korea—History—
    Manchu Invasions, 1627–1637—Personal narratives. | Korea—History—
    Chosŏn dynasty, 1392–1910—Sources.
Classification: LCC DS913.675.N325 A3 2020 (print) | LCC DS913.675.N325
    (ebook) | DDC 951.9/02—dc23.
LC record available at https://lccn.loc.gov/2019057504
LC ebook record available at https://lccn.loc.gov/2019057505

Cover image: Anonymous artist, *Chulgipajŏkdo*, from the series *Pukkwan
Yujŏk Toch'ŏp*. Ink and color on paper, c. eighteenth century, Korea
University Museum
Cover design: Chang Jae Lee

CONTENTS

ACKNOWLEDGMENTS

I would like to thank a number of people and institutions for helping me complete this book. First, I am deeply grateful to Christine Dunbar at Columbia University Press for her willingness to publish the volume. Her professionalism and guidance every step of the way made the publishing process easy to navigate. I extend this gratitude to Kathryn Jorge and Christian Winting, as well as the editorial board and staff of Columbia University Press. Thank you all greatly. Next, I would like to thank several people for commenting on early drafts of my translation. Zhimin Tao, my good friend and former student, provided invaluable suggestions and corrections, and Don Baker, my colleague from the University of British Columbia, helped me understand some of the more convoluted passages. Don also read an early version of the manuscript and provided me with helpful feedback. Another debt of gratitude rests with Yun Chaeyŏng, whose work on the original diary by Na Man'gap, especially the reprint of the original literary text in his book *Pyŏngjarok*, greatly informed this volume. I would like to thank three anonymous reviewers who provided instrumental comments and corrections to the introduction and translation. Their insights have strengthened this work—again, thank you very much. Thank you too to Adriana Cloud and Tracy Stober for copyediting my materials and Alex Martin for creating the maps.

Many colleagues, friends, and locations have helped me along the way. I am forever indebted to my former advisor at Columbia University, Gari Ledyard, as well as to the late JaHyun Kim Haboush for her work in Chosŏn history and for always inspiring me. I am humbled to have had the chance to work with both of them. I am very grateful to Michael Pettid at Binghamton University for his support, feedback, and good friendship. I would like to thank Norman Kutcher, my friend, colleague, and chair of the History Department at Syracuse University. His guidance on scholarship and life has always been invaluable. Syracuse University and the Department of History are great places to live and work. Both nurture an academic environment that encourages scholarship on the world from which I have benefited. Thanks to Suyoung Son for giving me a chance to present parts of the work at the Wason Conference held at Cornell University.

I owe special gratitude to my wife, Amy, and our two daughters, Mona and Sabrina, for their patience and support while I worked many days and late nights and traveled on research trips to complete my manuscript. Finally, I thank Seoul and upstate New York for being so inspirational.

A number of libraries and their staff helped me complete this project by providing access to primary and secondary source materials that took time to track down. These include Janseogak Library at the Academy of Korean Studies in Bundang; the Center for Korean Classics Collection at Yonsei University (Seoul); Kyujanggak Library at Seoul National University; the National Assembly Library in Seoul; C. V. Starr East Asian and Butler libraries at Columbia University in New York City; the Wason East Asia Collection and Library Annex at Cornell University; and the Interlibrary Loan staff at Syracuse University.

This work was generously supported by the Academy of Korean Studies (Korean Studies Promotion Service) Grant funded by the government of the Republic of Korea (Ministry of Education) (AKS-2013-KCL-2230001). AKS is a vital educational and research institution that helps advance the field of Korean studies in Korea and around the world. Their backing, understanding, and patience while I completed this complicated project are greatly appreciated. I also extend my deep gratitude to the Geiss Hsu Foundation for supporting the publication of my book. Additional assistance came from the W. Terry Pigott Faculty Research and Development Fund provided by the Department of History, Syracuse University. Early research was carried out with the help of the East Asia Program at the Moynihan Institute of Global Affairs and Appleby-Moshur travel grants from the Maxwell School, Syracuse University. Without all of this support, this book would have been impossible to complete.

FIGURE O.I

Map of Northeast Asia: Chosŏn Korea, Ming China, Manchu Qing, and Tokugawa Japan, c. 1636.

INTRODUCTION

George Kallander

In the first half of the seventeenth century, Korea was swept up in the shifting geopolitics of Northeast Asia. At the end of the sixteenth century, thanks to the assistance of China, Korea successfully defended the peninsula against invasion from Japan, but China paid a heavy price for the help it provided Korea as this endeavor, along with other costly expenditures, weakened China militarily and economically. At this crucial transition point in East Asian history, the Chosŏn dynasty (1392–1910), a politically stable and culturally vibrant kingdom that was among the most enduring dynasties in the world, ruled the Korean peninsula, while the Ming, one of the most powerful and long-lasting dynasties in Chinese history, ruled China. In accordance with the tributary system that had long governed the diplomatic relationship between China and Korea, Korea accepted subordinate status and paid tribute to China as a "superior." Yet Ming's weakening state eroded its superior status and created a vacuum into which stepped the Jurchen, a tribe residing in Northeast Asia that had ruled China in the past. Uniting under Nurhachi (1559–1626) and adopting the name "Manchu," these mounted warriors would battle the Ming for domination of China, capture the capital of Beijing in 1644, and found the Qing dynasty (1644–1912).[1]

Before advancing toward Beijing, the Manchu went south to deal with Korea. The second Manchu leader, Hung Taiji, attacked across the Chosŏn frontier in 1627, demanding that Chosŏn's King Injo sever diplomatic relations with the Ming. While this move forced Chosŏn to formally ally with the Manchu, the Chosŏn dynasty never fully accepted the Manchu as a replacement for the Ming and continued their support of China. King Injo even openly refused to honor the promise he had made in 1627 to be loyal to the Manchu and rejected official communication from them. He also allowed Ming generals into Korean territory and welcomed Ming envoys at his court, which exacerbated the situation. To punish the Chosŏn dynasty for breaking their oath, a much more formidable Manchu army attacked the peninsula in 1636–1637. In contemporary North and South Korean historiography, the first attack is known as the "invasion of the cyclical year 1627" and the second as the "invasion of the cyclical year 1636–1637."[2] These attacks were seismic events in Chosŏn history, with long-term consequences. They fortified anti-Manchu sentiment, stimulated proto-national consciousness, and began a process that would turn Koreans away from the over-glorification of Chinese civilization to focus their attention on cultural developments in Korea.[3]

Narrating Korea's Manchu Experience: Na Man'gap and *The Diary of 1636*

The Diary of 1636 (*Pyŏngjarok*) is one of the best-known Korean accounts of the second Manchu assault (the invasion of the cyclical year 1636–1637).[4] Written by a demoted member of the court who was living in exile and was a keen observer, Na Man'gap's *Diary* details the unprecedented domestic and international crises faced by the Chosŏn dynasty. At roughly forty-three thousand characters, Na Man'gap's work is the longest known nonofficial source on the Manchu invasion. Na wrote the first half of the diary during the attack, as a day-by-day narrative of events he witnessed directly. These include the Manchu demands that Korea honor the 1627 oath of allegiance, the debate at the Chosŏn court over war or peace, the Manchu military attack and Chosŏn resistance, King Injo's retreat to Namhan Mountain, the siege of the fortress, the negotiations, the surrender of Chosŏn, and the political and military consequences of defeat. In the second half of the diary, which he most likely composed and edited between 1641 and 1642 from oral stories and written documents collected after 1637, Na added political nuance and commentary, sometimes praising, sometimes criticizing those who fought on the battlefield or argued at the court over loyalty to the king. He also offered moralistic tales of individual bravery or deception. Here, Na narrates the war and its aftermath in the areas outside of Namhan Mountain Fortress, including the capture of Kanghwa Island—where Crown Princess Consort Minhoebin (1611–1646), who was the wife of Crown Prince Sohyŏn (1612–1645), and other members of the royal family and the elite had fled. Also included are stories of military campaigns along the northern and western regions of Chosŏn, the Manchu treatment of prisoners of war, and the post-invasion debates over Manchu collusion and the proper Confucian etiquette demanded of Koreans in times of war. The diary is of particular interest because of Na's training and his detailed attention. At one point in his career, he served as a diarist for the Office of Royal Decrees (Kŏmyŏl), and he used his professional skills when writing the diary.

There are multiple Korean records of the Manchu wars. One well-known source is the *Veritable Records of the Chosŏn Dynasty* (*Chosŏn wangjo sillok*; hereafter referred to as *Sillok*), which provides the official government court records of daily affairs, alongside a collection of the major debates, discussions, decisions, and actions of the king and his bureaucracy. Other primary sources include the *Records of the Royal Secretariat* (*Sŭngjŏngwŏn ilgi*) and the *Records of the Border Defense Command* (*Pibyŏngsa tŭngnok*)—official government chronicles that frequently reflect *Sillok* materials. Beyond the court, the trauma of the Manchu attacks compelled witnesses to record their involvements, and a number of diaries navigate the experiences of those who lived through these events as they attempted to make sense of the chaos of war.[5] For instance, the *Collected Works of Nagŭm* (*Nagŭm munjip*), by Nagŭm, the brush name of To Kyŏngyu (1596–1636), describes the period from the 1627 attack through 1636. One of the scholarly officials who attended the crown prince on the 1627 retreat south, To Kyŏngyu was serving the government when he was struck by a bullet and killed during the second attack. The work he left behind was not published until 1906, after it had emerged as a valuable resource for researchers. Mun Chaedo (1575–1643), a military officer who fought in 1627 and 1637, wrote *Namhan Recorded by Hand* (*Namhan surok*), a piece about his experience of the first attack, compiled in the *Collected Works of Hyu Hŏn* (*Hyu Hŏn munjip*). The official Sŏk Chihyŏng (1610–?) composed the *Historical Records on Namhan* (*Namhan haewirok*) and *The Diary of Namhan* (*Namhan ilgi*). Another valuable resource is the diary by Nam Kŭp (1592–1671), known by such titles as *The Diary of Namhan Mountain Fortress* (*Namhan ilgi*), *The Record of 1636* (*Pyŏngja ilgi*), and *The Diary of Nalli* (*Nalli ilgi*). Nam managed the palace kitchen (*saongwŏn pongsa*) and accompanied King Injo to Namhan Mountain Fortress in 1637. His diary covers a period of four months, including various events on Kanghwa Island and the activities of important scholars and officials. At least two other diaries were written by people living outside the capital: *Record of Kanghwa Island* (*Kangdorok*), a short anonymous description of the Manchu assault of the island, and *The Diary of Kanghwa Island* (*Kangdo ilgi*) by Ŏ Hanmyŏng (1592–1648), which provides insights on Chosŏn reactions to the attack and the defenses of the island. Taken together, these sources portray a transitional moment for politics and society in the Chosŏn dynasty from inside and outside the circles of power.

Na Man'gap's *Diary of 1636* is an important source of unofficial history, or *yasa*, a notion Na humbly dismissed. Distinct from the didactic or sterile dynastic records that chronicled the daily matters of the bureaucracy, *yasa* is described by the historian Kim Kyŏngsu as historical sources that record an author's personal views, often about contentious issues and events of the day.[6] Chosŏn-era writers certainly accepted Na's diary as an unofficial history. For instance, the scholar Yi Kŭngik (1736–1806) included it in his section of *yasa* when composing his historical compilation of the Chosŏn dynasty.[7] This makes it clear that the diary circulated among a handful of scholars, although the reception of the work immediately after Na's death in 1642 is uncertain. As he was out of favor with the court when he wrote it, Na had the freedom to explore events without fear of political retribution and could thereby offer an alternative view from the official sources. Not all diaries were considered *yasa* by Chosŏn-era scholars. Most likely a number of factors contributed to the privileging of some over others: the nature of the events covered in the work, the official position of the writer in the government and his political reputation, the literary quality of the writing, and the passing of time. As sources disappeared, and those who witnessed the events passed away, the works that remained became important for the retelling of the past. Na's position at Namhan Mountain Fortress as witness to the invasion, and his deep familiarity with the political and military situation, contribute to the significance of his diary.

Na may have also underestimated the extent to which the diary could serve as a source for Manchu and Chinese history. The work describes the early period of Manchu development and expansion around the activities and personalities of key Manchu figures— such as Hung Taiji and his family members who accompanied him to Korea, and top Manchu generals Ingguldai and Mafuta—who appear frequently throughout the diary. Of course, New Qing History contests the notion of "Manchu" identity today, especially regarding the formative period in the early decades of the seventeenth century.[8] Na did not use the term "Manchu." He refers to them politically as the Jin and the Qing dynasties and, less cordially, as the enemy or barbarians. Still, he describes a time when the Manchu struggled with identity—when to act more Confucian and when to act more Jurchen—as they moved beyond their homelands and collided with other groups, most importantly the Ming Chinese–oriented worldview of the Chosŏn. The diary shows some key concepts that appear to be unique or specific to their Jurchen or Manchu culture, such as the forced intermarriage of the Manchu and Korean elites, the stealing of horses, and the interior arrangement of Hung Taiji's military tent. However, it also reveals that, as early as 1636, the Manchu began deftly adopting Confucian rhetoric and concepts in their diplomatic correspondence with the Chosŏn dynasty, whether or not they actually believed in them.

Along with this was Hung Taiji's insistence that Korea erect a victory monument, the Samjŏndo stele, near the main battlefields outside of Seoul. Composed in Manchu, Mongol, and literary Chinese, the writings etched in this stele were an early usage of what Pamela Crossley dubs the "imperial simultaneous," that is, messages composed in several languages as a "simultaneous expression of imperial intentions in multiple cultural frames."[9] The Manchu empire was divided into constituencies that included various groups and tribes based on language, lineage ties, and geographic proximity under the umbrella of the early khan's leadership. This concept of inclusion extends to interaction with the Chosŏn dynasty. Korea was an integral part of Jurchen-Manchu expansion and imperial identity. To create emperorship, the khan needed recognition by the Korean court and the inclusion of the Chosŏn dynasty into his expanding empire. The Manchu achieved this in the 1627 agreement with the Chosŏn, but King Injo's withdrawal from this arrangement demanded action. Breaking the peace was not only a military threat, it was also an ideological danger to the Manchu emperorship. Allowing the Chosŏn dynasty to break away challenged the entire order and posed a threat to Manchu expansion into China.

Harder to tease out is whether key Korean figures who cooperated with the Manchu before 1636—and those who defected to the Manchu side—actually considered themselves Manchu. Unlike the amorphous area north of the frontier, by the seventeenth century, the Chosŏn dynasty had a defined frontier along the Yalu and Tumen rivers, combined with a distinct political identity extending back several hundred years at least. Those living south of the rivers were subjects of the Chosŏn dynasty. Those who lived across the rivers to the north were Jurchen, Khitan, Mongol, and Han Chinese. Those Koreans who moved across the northern border appeared to have other political identities. Apparent from Na Man'gap's diary is that the conflict around the frontier had forced people to move as refugees or as war captives back and forth to the Korean peninsula. Did Chosŏn people become part of the Qing empire as Manchu or did the Chosŏn court consider those who traveled to the peninsula subjects of the dynasty? This is hard to know as their histories have largely been neglected. Those individuals noted in sources such as the *Sillok* tended to have language skills, education, or wealth that allowed them to move across political and linguistic borders. Na Man'gap describes some of these people in his diary. As will be shown below, the Manchu, in the early decades of the seventeenth century, captured a number of Chosŏn military men who had fought with the Ming in the northeast regions. Some of these men remained in Jurchen-Manchu lands, learned to speak Manchu, and later served as envoys between the Qing and Chosŏn courts. Judging from Manchu acceptance of the Chinese and other tribal people, as the Manchu created their empire, it would not have been a stretch for them to extend this process of assimilation and border crossing to those born on the Korean peninsula. There probably were Koreans who moved across the frontier and took Manchu identities. Na's diary serves as a supplement to the works of New Qing history scholarship by helping to untangle issues of identity in the early period of the Manchu empire.

In Chosŏn times, Na Man'gap had gained some popularity because of his disputes with the court, his exile, his return to his hometown, and his death in the countryside.[10] Na was part of the Korean elite, or *yangban*, with a family origin (*pon'gwan*) of the village of Anjŏng, and his clan had developed strong ties to the bureaucratic class in the capital (*sadaebu*). Na Man'gap's courtesy name (*cha*) was Mongroe, and his brush name (*ho*) was Kupo. Born in Naju, South Chŏlla Province, Na Man'gap was the only son of Na Kŭp (1552–1602), who served as the first tutor in the Crown Prince Tutorial Office (Seja Sigangwŏn Podŏk), and the grandson of Nam Yunch'im (1527–1578), who became a third proctor (*hagyu*) at the Royal Confucian Academy (Sŏnggyun'gwan).[11] Na's father, Na Kŭp, was a talented artist and poet. His contemporary, Yi Sik (1584–1647), described Na Kŭp's poetry as equal to that written by poets of Han dynasty China. Though Na Man'gap lost the collection of his father's essays in the waters around Kanghwa Island when escaping the mainland with King Injo at the time of the 1627 Manchu attack, he was able to preserve his father's poetry.[12] Na Man'gap's mother was the daughter of Kim Hosŏn (of the Kwangju Kim family); Kim Hosŏn served as the bailiff for the Seoul magistrate (*hansŏng ch'amgun*). Na himself married the daughter of literato Chŏng Yŏp (1563–1625), an illustrious official respected by King Injo. These social and political connections of his in-laws accelerated Na Man'gap's career, affording him greater opportunities at the court. Little is known about Na's formal education, but, as the only son, he brought fame to his clan when he passed the *chinsa* (licentiate) exam in 1613 at the age of twenty-one, which qualified him for civil office, and he entered the elite Royal Confucian Academy in the capital.

In 1614, to consolidate power, King Kwanghaegun (r. 1608–1623) orchestrated the killing of his half-brother, Prince Yŏng-ch'ang (1606–1614) and imprisoned Queen Inmok (1584–1632), the former queen consort of his father, King Sŏnjo (r. 1567–1608), on Kanghwa Island. The queen was confined for a total of ten years. Na Man'gap, like many other scholar officials, renounced his post in protest of the fratricide and the treatment of the queen and returned to his hometown to live with his mother. Dethroned in a coup that brought King Injo (r. 1623–1649) to the seat of power, Kwanghaegun was banished to the distant island of Cheju.

Na returned to government service and moved through a number of positions, first as the third diarist (*kŏmyŏl*) in the Office of Royal Decrees and then as the ritual caretaker for the royal tomb of Queen Konghye (?–1474), the wife and queen consort of King Sŏngjong (r. 1469–1494). This was most likely an honorary post without many duties. Later Na was promoted to the position of "gentleman for virtuous service" (*t'ongdŏngnang*). In 1624, he acquired the job of writer (*such'an*) after passing the third tier (*pyŏnggwa*) of the Royal Visitation Mun'gwa Examination (Alsŏng Mun'gwa), after which he held a variety of higher posts, including positions in the powerful Censorate Office.[13]

Na gained the attention of King Injo, and their relationship had both its privileges and its challenges. At the time of the 1627 Manchu attack, Na was the chief administrative officer (*chongsagwan*) accompanying King Injo when the court retreated to Kanghwa Island. He continued to serve in important government positions after the Chosŏn surrender and returned to the capital, most likely because of the royal favors he had earned during the first war. Despite or because of these connections to the king, he was not immune to the strife of court politics. Factionalism permeated court and bureaucratic life in the seventeenth century. Na collided with the powerful official Kim Yu, the leader of the Westerners, a political group with many members in high bureaucratic positions.[14] Kim began attacking Na first in 1625 and again in 1629. After a lengthy debate at court over a variety of charges against Na, including unfilial behavior and immorality in office, King Injo reluctantly agreed to exile him. Hints in court discussions also suggested that Na's life had been threatened by other members of the court who perceived him to be a criminal.[15] Shifting power constellations facilitated Na's pardon and return to government service in 1631. He served as a third censor counselor (*hŏnnap*) of the Censorate Office before being promoted to the magistrate of Hongju (Hongsŏng, South Ch'ungch'ŏng Province) in 1634 and then to minister in the Ministry of Justice (Hyŏngjo ch'amŭi) in 1635.

Na had taken too many liberties with King Injo, for example, when he submitted a lengthy petition criticizing the myriad problems facing the dynasty, including the decline of virtuous debate and the rise of vulgar discussions at the court. The audacity of such a petition was met with royal disapproval, and he received his second dismissal from the court.[16] This misstep was forgotten in the context of growing tension between the Ming and the Qing when the Manchu invaded, and Na soon returned to King Injo's inner circles. After the retreat from the capital to Namhan Mountain Fortress, with the path to Kanghwa Island cut off, Na participated in the defense of the fortress as the chief commissary official responsible for army rations. His earlier experience on Kanghwa Island in 1627, as well as his reputation with supportive *sadaebu* and the king as an upright and efficient government official, provided him unprecedented access to power. Na later served as mediator between the king and a number of government scholar-officials. It was around this time that he began writing his diary.

Na's successes during the second Manchu invasion did not shield him from the intensified political strife in the wake of the 1637 attack. After the peace agreement with the Manchu, Na was accused of misdeeds—while traveling to his mother's funeral in Sŏsan, Na and his slave purchased a military boat from a corrupt navy officer—for which he was exiled to Yŏnghae (near Yŏngdŏk, North Kyŏngsang Province).[17] He was released from banishment for the third and final time in 1639, yet he remained out of favor with the court and spent his remaining days in Yŏngju, where he died in 1642.[18] Upon Na's death, King Injo restored Na's official government titles, but rumors about his actions clouded Na's reputation. Later, some placed blame on King Injo rather than the *sadaebu*, claiming King Injo attacked Na because the king intensely disproved of officials who were shallow and frivolous—a broad assertion made against many officials out of favor with the court.[19] Other scholars claimed these were politically motivated attacks against Na. In 1727, a century after the first Manchu attack, Na's reputation was restored after he was recognized by scholars as an outstanding official (*kwijung chisin*) swept up in the political struggles of the time.[20] The illustrious scholar Song Siyŏl (1607–1689) heralded Na as one whose virtues and devotion to Confucianism were unparalleled. Song concluded that "the people of distant generations will all learn of the grave of Na Man'gap."[21] Only two people of that generation, Song wrote, matched Na: Chŏng Yŏp (1563–1625), a well-respected official, and Kim Sanghŏn (1570–1652), another revered official, of whom more will be discussed below. Kim served the court at the time of both Manchu attacks and took actions that were seemingly offensive to both sides of the battle. Even so, Kim was lionized by both Chosŏn and Manchu officers for his unwavering anti-Manchu sentiment.[22]

Today, two copies of *The Diary of 1636* dating to the Chosŏn dynasty exist; one is housed in the National Library of Korea, and the other resides in the Changsŏgak Royal Archives at the Academy of Korean Studies. The texts are similar in content but with a few stylistic differences.[23] The edition held in the National Library appears to be the most complete and is the version upon which this translation relies.[24] Scholars and the public consider

The Diary of 1636 by Na Man'gap as a reliable primary source, but the authenticity of Na's diary has not gone unquestioned, as his descriptions of events occasionally differ from Chosŏn and Qing government sources.[25] In times of war, such narrative discrepancies are not signs of historical deception, but rather of the fluidity of knowledge and the tendency to interpret events as they unfold.[26] Regardless of these debates, both versions of the diary offer unprecedented details and insights into early seventeenth-century politics during a transitional period in Korean and Northeast Asian history.

Na Man'gap's diary is composed of eight sections, including a brief epilogue. Each section of the diary has its own rhythm, style, and complexity. He wrote one section during the war, but the other sections were composed and edited after 1637. Each section appears to be intended for a different purpose. *The Diary of 1636* can be read as a narration of the Manchu invasion of Korea and the political and social aftermath of a premodern society at war. However, much is happening below the surface of the text. As a deft writer, Na subtly, and sometimes not so subtly, critiques the contemporary politics of the Chosŏn dynasty through the structure, tone, and context of his stories. Na's critiques range from the decision to go to war to the acrimonious environment of political retribution in which many officials were expelled from the center of power, including himself. Na Man'gap describes how the outcome of the attack redefined the relationship between the center and the periphery—those who held power in the court and those who resided in the countryside and did not. He was in contact with people in Seoul even during his exile and after his move to the countryside, demonstrating that exile did not necessarily mean political and social isolation, at least in Na's case. Instead, he continued to hear the latest news from the capital and receive details from beyond the frontier. As he was gently agitating against the outcome of the war and the fall from power of many officials, including himself, he reminds readers of the rippling impact the invasion had on power relations in Northeast Asia. The war disrupted ties between dynasties and fractured loyalties at all levels. Korea redirected relations to Mukden (K. Shimyang, C. Shenyang), the Manchu capital, and away from Beijing, challenging Chosŏn loyalty to the Ming. Ming Chinese soldiers switched sides and fought for the Qing. Mongols joined the invasion force. Chosŏn military men supported the Manchu. Korean officials split between pro-peace and pro-war, and even a handful of expatriate Japanese fought alongside Chosŏn. Loyalty was a fluid concept.

The first section of *The Diary of 1636*, "Early Complications," serves as a preface with its short description of the major incidents that preceded the invasion. To Na, the Chosŏn diplomatic snub of a Qing emperor's letter in the spring of 1636 was problematic. One is struck by the way conflict with the Manchu appeared inevitable because public opinion favored war. Perhaps this inevitability was part of Na's narrative strategy: he blames the outbreak of conflict partly on unnamed officials, in order to further exonerate the king. Also striking is the fairly balanced description of the events, particularly concerning the Manchu. Na seems unwilling to fully blame Manchu leaders for the events and instead points a finger at inept Chosŏn envoys. Few, if any, allusions appear to the Korean decision to break the 1627 agreement, a move that chilled relations with the Manchu. Na recounts the words of politicians and government agencies that criticize the Manchu, deftly withholding his own judgment while recording the support of others who advocated either war or peace.

"Daily Records After Urgent Reports from the Frontier," the second section, is the heart of the diary. This section, the longest and most straightforward, is a day-by-day narration of the invasion, beginning in the middle of the twelfth month of the *pyŏngja* year (solar date January 7, 1637) with the surprising news of the Manchu strike across the frontier. It ends roughly five weeks later, at the start of the second lunar month of the *chŏngch'uk* year

(February 1637), with the departure of the crown prince to Mukden, the return of the king to the capital, and the withdrawal of foreign troops from the dynasty. Na most likely wrote this part during the siege of Namhan Mountain Fortress and edited it later while in exile. His tone is supportive of Chosŏn efforts but, interestingly, he included events from multiple perspectives. Present at many of the key conversations over war strategies and debates over peace, Na was certainly well positioned to witness and record these events. He hoped to appear objective, especially during the heated exchanges between officials at the court in Namhan Mountain Fortress. This seems to be a strategic move. Na briefly describes some of his roles in the fortress—managing the rations for the troops, for instance, or supporting relatively benign decisions such as rewarding Chosŏn soldiers for killing enemy troops. Apart from these few instances, Na is largely a quiet observer throughout the invasion. He understood that rivalries and personality conflicts among officials were exacerbated by the life-or-death situation of the siege. While relatively safe in the fortress, the inhabitants were subjected to constant artillery fire and the possibility of Manchu capture. Na remained acutely noncommitted in his support of the war while reporting on the dangers around him, especially the food shortage and the actions of those in the fortress. He chose to wait and watch most of these debates play out. One of the final conversations he records in this section is held with the crown prince before the departure of the king's son to Mukden, a heartbreaking farewell that reinforced the humiliation of the Chosŏn dynasty. Na hints that defeat was avoidable. In considering the aftermath, he attributes the loss to a number of factors, from an army suffering from low morale and poor leadership to a single corrupt official, Kim Kyŏngjing, whom Na and others blamed for the fall of the country. This was an exaggeration to say the least, but a relatively safe accusation in the postwar environment that sought to assign blame.

Na acknowledges a number of Koreans for their exploits on the battlefield in "Record of Loyalists Everywhere," the third section. Some of these troops fought well, such as the arquebus (the precursor to muskets and modern-day rifles) teams and individual commanders and everyday army units from all levels of the national and local military. Others found short-term success on the battlefield but ultimately lost ground to the invaders and were killed or captured, or they fled. Here, Na identifies Koreans who, having fought and died defending the country, were still criticized and punished by the court and other officials for their apparent failures. Na writes about the heroic actions by Korean soldiers under the constant threat of government punishment. Some of these units performed admirably. One company commander and his troops, for instance, defeated in battle the brother-in-law of Hung Taiji, a significant achievement, but ultimately the Korean soldiers scattered, a loss for which this commander was summarily removed by the court. In another instance, Na subtly critiques the court for dismissing a commander who, after successfully rallying his troops to fight the Manchu, retreated because he had exhausted his arrows and other supplies. In yet another incident, Na describes a moment when a commander, after initially defending a mountain fortress, fell twice for a Manchu-and-Mongol military ruse—the enemy feigned retreat and withdrew their troops, pulling the Korean forces into a trap, where they counterattacked. Short on supplies in his fortress, the commander attempted to resupply his troops, but the enemy struck again, capturing him and his horses. Throughout this section and in other parts in the diary, Na describes logistical issues as an underlying reason for military losses. He suggests that the Chosŏn Army was inadequately supplied in many of these battles—an understandable critique coming from Na, who tended to the rations and supplies during the siege at Namhan Mountain Fortress. While loyal to the king, these troops and their commanders were eventually defeated and their actions criminalized by the court.

This same theme of loyalty appears in the fourth section of the diary, "Kanghwa Island Records." In this section, Na turns to the personalities and events of Kangdo (Kanghwa Island). Traditionally a safe haven for the royal family and the capital's elite during foreign invasions, Kanghwa Island became a military snare in 1637. The Manchu, crossing the water to Kanghwa with relative ease, overtook the defenders, and the island fell quickly before the surrender of Namhan Mountain Fortress. In one of the most dramatic sections of the diary, Na narrates scenes from near Kanghwa Island during the Manchu attack. High and low, men and women, all faced hardship as they escaped Seoul, traveled west, and gathered at the coast hoping to reach the safety of the island. A chaotic moment at the harbor is particularly gripping. The rapid Manchu strike against the capital threatened the refugees, including the crown princess, who, calling out from her palanquin, openly chastised Kim Kyŏngjing, the official responsible for the evacuation. In this dramatic entry, Na juxtaposes this scene of the crown princess carried by servants with the thousands of commoners traveling by foot and amassing along the shore, all fearing the rapidly approaching enemy cavalry. Moments like these fortified the concept of status. Those with official positions and ranks reached the island, while the masses were left behind to be killed or kidnapped into slavery by the Manchu.

Na's descriptions of Kanghwa Island reinforced tropes of Confucian loyalty: faithful troops dying to protect the royal family; scholar officials committing suicide in the name of the king rather than surrendering to the enemy; mothers and daughters killing themselves to preserve their chastity when threatened with Manchu capture and forced concubinage or sexual violence. Na's understanding of loyalty is gendered, as he names the husbands of many wives who killed themselves (women's names were not used in public works of this nature). "There were countless numbers of women who died to maintain their chastity," Na writes.

"It is regretful that all of them cannot be known." Their deaths are a distressing part of the Confucian code of female chastity, here amplified by foreign invasion. For instance, the wife and daughter of official Yi Min'gu, failing to commit suicide, were captured by the Manchu. For Na, the descent of women of high, virtuous birth and marriage to barbarian men was shameful. Na's words tell a cautionary tale. Women who did not take their lives threatened the reputation of the family, and such actions must be recorded for posterity. The "Kanghwa Island Records" section also highlights some of the insecurities women confronted in early modern Korea. Not only were they vulnerable during war, but they were also threatened from within society by laws and social norms that subordinated them to their husbands and their husband's families.

In "Records of Several People Who Rejected Peace and Died Righteously," the fifth section, Na narrates the aftermath of the war and the consequences for Chosŏn officials the Manchu blamed for resisting peace. Stories of Hong Ikhan and O Talche, whom the court dispatched to the Qing as punishment, are told through petitions—letters scholars composed for the king—and notes Hong and O wrote while in Manchu captivity. Na humanizes these two officials by including the poetry they composed while imprisoned by the Manchu, emotional works that spoke of their sadness for the country and their longing to reunite with close family. These examples of dedication and self-sacrifice are reinforced in Na's description of Yun Kye. Yun was an official who, having challenged the Manchu, was killed and his body dismembered, a detail that underscored the brutality of the Manchu retaliation. The Manchu violated their victims' bodies— female bodies with sexual possession as well as male bodies through decapitation, both acts an affront to Confucian norms that demanded respect of the body as a gift from one's parents. Despite such gruesome accounts, Na appears sympathetic to the Manchu in other passages. In one, he compares them more favorably to the people of Korea. They are curious and courteous in their demeanor, he insists, and admire Chosŏn officials for their steadfast refusal to surrender.

The sixth section of the diary, "Miscellaneous Notes Concerning What Happened After the Upheaval," begins in the early months of 1636 with the dramatic exile and death of the deposed King Kwanghaegun. Here, Na implicates a number of army officials who used their proximity to a top military commander at Namhan Mountain Fortress to advocate for the killing of the ousted king. More than just a story about the affairs of these army officers, the incident with King Kwanghaegun serves as a foil to critique the shifting political allegiances and loyalties of soldiers and officials not just in Korea but throughout Northeast Asia. With the exile and death of King Kwanghaegun as a backdrop, Na traces the Manchu demands after the peace settlement in 1637. Submission to the Manchu meant frequent requests from Mukden in the form of letters and the repeated visits of the Manchu, Mongols, and pro-Manchu Chinese envoys. Some of Hung Taiji's representatives demanded that the Chosŏn military support them in campaigns against the Ming, Na explains, while other Manchu envoys inspected Namhan Mountain Fortress to ensure that Korea did not rebuild its defenses. Namhan Mountain held strategic and symbolic meaning for Chosŏn and the Qing. The Manchu, looking upon the mountain as a symbol of Korean resistance, prevented the court from rebuilding its defenses. Aware of this legacy, the only new structure the Manchu allowed the Chosŏn to erect— and in fact demanded it—was the Samjŏndo stele nearby. Na does not hold back his disdain for this monument.

Striking are the repercussions the war had on the Chosŏn dynasty, most significantly the new political, military, and social connections forged with the Qing. Na relates a number of stories about the aftermath of the war and people responding to the large geopolitical shifts around them. Na suggests the invasion had a far-reaching impact on Koreans and non-Koreans alike. These notes end with a discussion about a number of scholars the court exiled because of their anti-peace alignment and later tried to rehabilitate, hinting back to the opening of the section and the removal of King Kwanghaegun, who never returned to power and died in exile.

In the seventh section, "Record of Ch'ŏngŭm's Slandering," the diary turns to the toxic factionalism in Korean politics after peace was secured. Na frames this section around the post-invasion environment in which the country sought to assign blame for the events of 1637. Na juxtaposed the actions of his compatriots laid out in the earlier sections with the events following the war. Despite the disastrous outcome of the conflict, the court promoted many people—whether dead or alive—who took part in it, while punishing others. Here Na issues a gentle rebuke of these people, suggesting that they did not deserve promotion. Na devotes this section to Ch'ŏngŭm, the brush name of Kim Sanghŏn, comparing him to those who accepted rewards and honors. Na mentions Kim a minimum of 130 times in the diary, more than any other individual except for King Injo. Na indirectly praises Kim Sanghŏn, particularly his refusal to accept rewards and advancements for actions that harmed the country. Na discusses how others attacked Kim because of his failure to perform the duties expected of Confucian officials at times of war and for not making better policy decisions to save the country from military defeat. Na goes to great lengths to transcribe the petitions of dozens of officials who argued for and against punishing Kim Sanghŏn. Many of the arguments were based on Confucian principles of duty to king and country. In passionate language, officials lament the long-lasting effects of Kim's actions, while others defended his deeds as less offensive than those of many others during that time.

Na composed the eighth and final section, "Humiliation Received from the Qing," in 1642, just before his death. Despite his exile and subsequent retirement, he continued to receive information from Seoul and copies of petitions from the highest levels of the state about the ongoing interactions along the frontier and even from outside the country. This section includes Na relating the story of Chosŏn officials dispatched to the Manchu as punishment for rejecting peace, including Kim Sanghŏn. Kim's plight reveals some important aspects of the post-invasion realities Korea confronted. One was the relationship forged between the Manchu and Chosŏn courts, a humiliating tributary relationship in which the Manchu had many demands—such as the dispatch of hostages. It was an arrangement that weighed heavily on the state and the minds of government officials. Na also briefly describes personal diplomacy, a new form of person-to-person relations that turned humiliation into opportunity. Na relates how Kim Sanghŏn developed real connections with Manchu individuals who had come to respect him for the way he fearlessly confronted punishment and possible death.

Another Chosŏn official who encountered new political opportunities was Pak No. Pak was sent to Mukden and became close friends with Ingguldai and Mafuta, two Manchu generals. Such personal bonds between the Manchu and Koreans hinted at the possibility for more collegial relations between the two courts. These personal relations also held the potential to transform the Manchu. Remaining steadfast to the moral principles of Confucianism, Kim Sanghŏn won over the Manchu. Kim's story was unfinished when Na passed away; Na was unsure if Kim would return to Korea or die in foreign lands. Na believed that, despite the humiliation of defeat and the hardships and suffering under the Qing, in time Chosŏn would convince the Manchu of the superiority of Confucian norms and win them over. This optimistic message of respect and coexistence was obscured by the tragedy of defeat, but it was true that the transformation went both ways. Through these new relationships, some Korean officials realized that the Manchu were more trustworthy than once believed. The close relations formed with the Qing leadership opened up new opportunities for travel and experiences of foreign lands. Another benefit was the prestige from relationships—and even intermarriage—with Manchu of influence.

Even though section two of the diary—the main and longest section—is a straightforward description of the invasion, Na Man'gap's work is more than just a chronicle of the attack. Na felt compelled to write the seven additional sections to set the record straight and shape a particular legacy of the war. In them, he details the actions of officials who advocated for war or for peace. This includes attaching names to many of the politically sensitive royal petitions he transcribed or summarized. As mentioned above, Na Man'gap spends much energy discussing Kim Sanghŏn, the official criticized after the war and accused of misconduct over the question of his loyalty to the king and the crown prince. Kim was a central figure in 1637 who held a number of key posts. He was a scholar official who, like Na, accompanied the king to Namhan Mountain Fortress. However, unlike Na, who held a secondary role at the court, Kim was a leading official who went to great lengths to express his resistance to peace by tearing up a draft of the royal surrender letter to the Manchu, engaging with Qing envoys in the enemy camp, attempting suicide (he was saved only by Na), and, after the truce, leaving his post to seek out family members in the countryside. Eventually he was dispatched to the Manchu as a prisoner. Na openly defends Kim by calling the attacks against him slander. By naming names here, Na settled scores against those he felt had gone too far in attacking Kim over his loyalty.

Duty and obligation are some of the most telling subtexts of this final section of the diary. Where does one's responsibilities rest? Especially at times of war, should they be focused on a sense of national obligation and the protection of the country and the king? At other times, when the threat to the country has passed, are one's obligations defined by filial loyalty to parents, family, clan, and village? The Manchu invasion pushed this age-old theoretical debate into practice, and Na's work highlights the slipperiness of loyalty. In some sections he spotlights the scholars and soldiers who fought for and, in some cases, died for the king. In other sections, he admires officials who demonstrated their loyalty to the Ming by committing suicide rather than shifting allegiance to the Qing. But, according to Na's narrative, many more officials remained alive than were taken captive. Na relays how pro-peace officials shifted their loyalty from the Ming to the Qing and how Na and other officials had questionable loyalty as well. Decades earlier, these individuals had not remained loyal to the ousted King Kwanghaegun, and most of them remained loyal to King Injo despite the king's capitulation to the Manchu and his rejection of the Ming.

Questions can be asked about Na's own loyalty. Na's actions during and after the invasion did not amount to a great deal. While he recorded the loyalty of his colleagues, some as righteous literati negotiating with the enemy outside the walls of Namhan Mountain Fortress and others nobly fighting enemy troops, he was not among them. He remained within the protective walls of Namhan Mountain Fortress. Even when the court appointed him officer in charge of provisions (*kwallyangsa*), there was little for him to do: food supplies were low, and acquiring more was impossible because of the Manchu siege. In his diary, Na depicts himself as a pragmatic realist who presented the opinions and actions of those on both sides of the debate over war or peace with the Manchu. From the viewpoint of his contemporaries, however, his actions and words may have seemed opportunistic, even cowardly—he never expressed any of his own strong views in the early days of the invasion, but he was willing to criticize others in hindsight. He was someone swept up in the course of events, unable, or unwilling, to take much action or put his life at risk to protect the king and the country. This was his real weakness; he was unable to act decisively and make hard decisions during the war. When he composed the later sections of the diary, he was tarnished by accusations of impropriety in the aftermath of the conflict. By defending Kim Sanghŏn's questionable loyalty, Na belatedly took an active stance, while during the actual moment he had mostly been an observer. His inaction at a time of national crisis allowed him to document the events around him. Writing was a way for Na to shape his own legacy and defend himself.

Military and Political Affairs in the Late Sixteenth Century

The Chosŏn court and central bureaucracy in Seoul governed matters of the state through a Confucian lens. Confucian doctrines paid little attention to war or the importance of a well-funded military and were so influential in the fifteenth century that Chosŏn saw little need to defend itself. Theoretically, the ruler held full power over the kingdom atop the social hierarchy. For the first one hundred years of the Chosŏn dynasty, stalwart kings checked bureaucratic power, but, beginning in the sixteenth century, the bureaucracy grew cunning and made decisions based on allegiances, exerting greater control over the rulers. Kings could not stop these political competitions. Those who tried to exercise too much control over the bureaucracy were pushed aside. Within the court, rulers often sat and watched as members of the bureaucracy battled each other over matters great and small. Those in the bureaucracy, the *sadaebu*, often exerted real authority because kings depended upon them to run the government. Members of the *sadaebu* were often at odds with one another, which in turn generated political, or factional, strife.

The *sadaebu* was the upper echelon of the elite *yangban* class. Representing only a small percentage of the population, the *yangban* were the scholarly and military elites, who qualified for office if they passed the government examinations. While the *yangban* had certain privileges, such as tax exemptions, most were impoverished and held little power. The *sadaebu*, on the other hand, were the governing group of the court; they continued to succeed in the highest examinations—which gave them access to government positions—and held political control. Below them, the *yangin*, or commoners, mostly poor peasants, were the majority of the population and carried the burden of paying land taxes and providing corvée and military service. The commoners were the ones who were largely responsible for funding the treasury of a government run by scholar bureaucrats—officials who attacked excess and surplus as supporting immoral choices that would harm the livelihoods of the people. The *sadaebu* and other *yangban* should have, in theory, paid taxes, but many *yangban* did not; it was a tradition that increasingly burdened the commoners. At the bottom of the social hierarchy, *nobi*, or slaves, were exempt from taxes or other obligations, but they had no privileges. They were considered "base" and "low" (*ch'ŏn*); their lives were not their own.

The Chosŏn court controlled diplomatic relations with its neighbors, including the Japanese before and after the Imjin War (1592–1598), tribes north of the frontier, and China. Among these networks, the most important relationship was with the Ming dynasty. After the founding of Chosŏn, uncertainty strained relations with the Ming, as the newly formed Chinese dynasty gauged Korea's intentions. Soon after, however, Chosŏn entered a hierarchical tributary relationship—a diplomatic and ritual relationship between Korea and China that demanded a variety of rituals, including the dispatch of an ambassador to Beijing representing the king of Korea who hid his face from the Chinese emperor, kowtowed nine times in front of him, and accepted the graces of China. China also ratified Korean succession and confirmed the king. Other requirements were the acceptance of the Chinese calendar and a tribute of Korean goods. Despite these demands, China usually gave more in gifts, trade, and military assistance than it received on tributary missions, although China never gave human tributes, such as slaves or women, back to

Korea. In time, relations between the two countries strengthened as the *yangban* began to see in the Ming the symbol of Confucian civilization. The relative peace meant that a large standing army to guard the frontier was unnecessary. Instead, a small military adequately protected the Chosŏn court by suppressing local dissents and piracy along the coasts. This lack of interest in military affairs eroded the standing of elite military *yangban* families and further weakened Chosŏn's defenses. Hereditary military clans lost status compared to the scholar *yangban*, and the central government diverted limited resources to nonmilitary matters.

By the sixteenth century, the neglect of the military in the era of relative peace after the founding of the Chosŏn dynasty had weakened the army—a weakness revealed during the Imjin War.[27] Hoping to conquer China and install his son as emperor, the Japanese leader Toyotomi Hideyoshi (1537–1598) invaded Korea, landing 250,000 troops at Tongnae (Pusan) in 1592. These forces captured the capital of Hanyang (Seoul) in three weeks and then continued north, advancing toward Manchuria. The Chosŏn military could not contain the enemy forces as demoralized Chosŏn troops fled and returned to their families. The government could neither repel the invading army nor control internal disorder. When the Japanese reached Seoul, civil insurrection against the state had already broken out; slaves had started fires in the capital, in an attempt to burn the slave registries held in the Board of Punishments building.

King Sŏnjo and other government officials retreated north, dispatching a message to the Ming to ask for assistance and warn them of the invasion. Initially, the Ming court did not fathom the gravity of the situation; some believed Japan incapable of conquering China, while others were wary of a unified Korean and Japanese attack—Japanese pirates had previously spread rumors to this effect. The Chinese government delayed sending troops for several months. During this deliberation, King Sŏnjo was forced to withdraw north, to the border town of Ŭiju, the farthest point a monarch could retreat to without violating the Confucian belief that the king must not leave Chosŏn territory. With King Sŏnjo determined not to cross the Yalu River until the last moment, a Chinese envoy traveled to Ŭiju to ascertain the veracity of the situation. Unfortunately, the Ming army was stretched thin, engaged in wars against the Mongols to the north and in distant Burma and Thailand to the south. One Ming military contingent stationed in Manchuria protected the northeast passage into China. The Manchu leader Nurhachi offered to defend the Ming. He secured this region for the Chinese, which allowed Ming forces to advance into Korea, battling the Japanese at P'yŏngyang. The arrival of Ming troops and Manchu support prevented the Japanese from advancing further, and the war began turning into a stalemate.

Ultimately, the regular stationing of Ming troops was crucial to the survival of Chosŏn. Official Ming military support strengthened King Sŏnjo by demonstrating the extent of his political backing from his strong neighbor, the legacy of which would influence Korean state structures and military engagement over the ensuing decades through the tributary system. During the war, the Chinese interfered constantly with the Korean government. The Chinese army required a large amount of supplies and logistical support. The Ming generals were sympathetic to the Chosŏn king, but they also pressured the court through Confucian mores. Korea was a Confucian country, hence the relationship to China had to be approached with sincerity. With Korea full of Chinese troops, the Ming generals approached King Sŏnjo directly to discuss matters that concerned their troops, even down to mundane issues of armor. The Ming officials were personable and authoritative in their dealings with the king. King Sŏnjo responded politely, except when he went on strike in protest of heavy-handed Chinese behavior.[28] But subtle influences arose. King Sŏnjo was the only official in Korea the Ming wanted to deal with because doing so would allow them to circumvent the bureaucracy, which gave Sŏnjo a tremendous amount of leverage over the scholarly bureaucrats. Instead of working through scholarly officials, the Chinese generals dictated wartime decisions to Sŏnjo. Beijing debated withdrawing troops, but the Ming remained in Korea until the Japanese retreat following Hideyoshi's death in 1598. Despite the fact that the Ming Wanli emperor did not hold regular audiences with his bureaucracy for twenty-five years, he personally intervened to maintain troops in Korea.[29]

Given the Ming commitment and the Korean resistance, a Japanese victory was unlikely. Still, this was not a major military triumph for Korea, as it was mostly Chinese power that had stopped the Japanese invasion on land. On the eastern and central fronts, Japanese forces often bribed Chinese besiegers with silver, swords, and horses, and the Chinese would hold back until the Japanese retreated south. From the Chinese point of view, this strategy was successful because Chinese lives were saved. The Ming had lost tens of thousands of men fighting in Korea, and the war was politically problematic in Beijing, where politicians were heavily criticized over the decision to go to war, as others questioned the necessity of fighting in Korea. Chinese generals who suffered heavy casualties on the battlefield would be executed. From the Chosŏn perspective, Ming actions did not fit the Chosŏn strategy to destroy Japanese forces in Korea, and Korean officials feared the Japanese might one day return.

The Imjin War raised important political questions about the nature of the Chosŏn military, its communications, and its infrastructural vulnerabilities. For instance, Ŭiju, on the Yalu River, had been a logistical bottleneck during the war, preventing the efficient movement of supplies to the front. In addition, the roads to the capital were not capable of transporting vehicles or carriages. Korea also lacked docks and pier facilities. The outcome of the war inspired the king to consider greater defensive spending on infrastructure. It also solidified a special relationship with the Ming and greater engagement with the political factions in the

Chosŏn court. For the next century and a half, Korean officials showed their appreciation for the Chinese saving them from the Japanese by holding on to the memory of the Ming.

The Chosŏn State and the 1627 Manchu Attack

In the years following the Imjin War, court officials began to improve the economy and build up defenses.[30] This included passing early taxation and revenue reforms. Thousands of Koreans had died in the war, and their loss resulted in a severely damaged agricultural system—the base of government taxation and of the livelihood of the people. Routine farming had ceased for six to eight years, devastating food production. It was imperative to maintain rice paddies, as rice farming is an intricate process requiring constant work to maintain the artificial irrigation system. The entire process deteriorated quickly. Unlike China's canal systems, agriculture in Korea depended upon seasonal rainfall and the release of water from dikes or other waterways. Agriculture relied upon the solidarity of villages, but many of the village workers had been dispersed, killed, removed, or imprisoned in Japan. Rebuilding the agricultural infrastructure was King Kwang-haegun's responsibility, and he did so by implementing tax reforms that increased government revenue to fund military improvements.

The Chosŏn court argued it should be able to undertake defensive buildup alone without having to rely on the Ming. King Kwanghaegun, a formidable king and a dedicated and skillful ruler, rebuilt the military, the agricultural system, and the economy in the wake of the Imjin War. Fearing another Japanese invasion, Chosŏn officials were disturbed and encouraged the Ming army to remain in Korea. The Ming agreed to leave three or four thousand troops, who contributed to the efforts to rebuild and train Chosŏn forces until 1601. Further improvements included the establishment of the Institute for Military Training (Hullyŏn

Togam), the key institute responsible for developing and stockpiling explosives, rockets, and firearms, as well as training personnel to use them. The Hullyŏn Togam included an elite unit trained to use state-of-the-art weaponry, funded by King Kwanghaegun.

However, domestic and international issues interfered with the rebuilding process. First, political questions arose surrounding King Kwanghaegun's legitimacy—complicated by his proximity to the Jurchen (aka the Manchu)—that led to clashes with the scholar-official bureaucracy and a coup that culminated in his nephew, King Injo, obtaining the throne in 1623. Kwanghaegun was the son of a secondary wife (*ch'ŏp*), and while this was not always acceptable, the royal family did not consistently distinguish between primary and secondary wives, particularly when there was no son by a primary wife. This was especially true at times of war when ensuring succession was paramount. During the Imjin War, amidst concerns that the king could die without a legitimate heir, King Sŏnjo appointed Kwanghaegun as crown prince, angering one of the political factions, the Westerners (*Sŏin*), who advocated waiting. An opposing faction, the Great Northerners (*Taebugin*), supported the decision. King Sŏnjo eventually had two sons by different wives in 1601, but neither was immediately declared crown prince. However, as the children grew, more people began whispering that Kwanghaegun was illegitimate and that King Sŏnjo's other two sons were the rightful heirs, rumors that threatened Kwanghaegun's kingship. King Kwanghaegun's two half-brothers were assassinated, most likely by Kwanghaegun's supporters, which plunged Kwanghaegun into deep trouble. It was in this fraught political context that the Manchu arrived on the scene.

The Manchu were nomadic tribes whose lives were supported by hunting, trapping, and fishing. Some came from a forest environment, others from the plains. In addition to the Manchu, other Jurchen tribes and some Mongols lived in the region north of the

Chosŏn frontier. Originally of Jurchen origin, one tribe coalesced around charismatic and militarily powerful leaders, grew into a major federation, and gained the notice of the Ming.[31] By the 1590s, Nurhachi, their leader, emerged as a rising military power and, inspired to revive the Jurchen Jin dynasty (1115–1234) heritage, sought to conquer China for its wealth and resources. Exploiting a weakened Ming, Nurhachi expanded his power into Manchuria in the late 1610s. Based on geographic proximity, Korea was an early concern for the Manchu. As their main objective was China, they had to ensure Korea did not become a hindrance. In 1616, the Ming acted against the Manchu and began preparing for a counterattack, requisitioning thirteen thousand troops from Korea, three thousand of which were part of Hullyŏn Togam, the special arquebus group. The number of troops—required because of tributary obligations—put Korea in a delicate situation between honoring Chinese wishes and potentially losing its elite firearms unit in a Manchu victory. In response, Kwanghae-gun developed a scheme to avert total disaster. In 1619, the Korean troops arrived at the front and reported to the Ming generals, but immediately thereafter they surrendered to the Manchu. Thirteen thousand Korean men yielded to the Manchu, while the Ming suffered the loss of forty-five thousand troops.[32] King Kwanghae-gun's policy cunningly honored the Ming request for military assistance while saving Korean lives and placating the Manchu.

The failed Ming campaign had the added effect of defeating Chinese power in Manchuria. After this loss, the Ming could no longer support Korea, a fact Nurhachi keenly understood. In 1621, all the other towns in Manchuria were captured from the Ming, making the situation even more politically tenuous in Korea. Political factions within the Chosŏn court used the threat of an invasion to gain power and vilify competing parties. The Westerners abhorred the thought of peace with the Manchu, considering them barbarians, while the Southerners urged negotiation. King Kwanghaegun, increasingly criticized for authorizing the execution of his two half-brothers and for not supporting the Ming, was exiled to Cheju Island after the 1623 Westerners-backed coup, where he died in 1641. With the Westerners in power, government policy shifted to a pro-Ming stance.

King Injo was a weak king dominated by the bureaucratic officials who had enthroned him—a group of politicians belligerent toward the Manchu and supportive of the Ming. They granted Chinese generals access to Chosŏn territory, which the Chinese took advantage of to construct bases on Korean islands along the northwest coast. The Manchu were uneasy with the Ming presence and sent an army into Korea in 1627. Within days of crossing the Yalu River, the court learned from those who had fled south that the border town of Ŭiju had fallen to the enemy. The *Sillok* version of events depicts a rapid Manchu attack and chaotic Chosŏn response. Reports spoke of great Manchu momentum. As part of the response, the Chosŏn armies in Hwanghae and P'yŏngan provinces, amounting to seventeen hundred troops, were ordered to defend the north. In P'yŏngyang, fifty-eight hundred troops fortified the city and fortress, while archers from surrounding villages entered the castle to defend the city.[33] Manchu troops advanced quickly along the main roads. Many reports of the strength of the Manchu forces reached the court. In the face of this advance, Chosŏn troops appeared to resist engagement.[34] One official criticized the inaction of the troops, reporting, "As the enemy advances, not one person comes forward bravely determined to die."[35] Another complained, "It has been days since the enemy invaded and not one [of our soldiers] has cut the throat of an enemy soldier and claimed a reward."[36]

Several Koreans sympathetic to the Manchu cause joined the attack force. One of the Manchu generals was none other than Kang Hongnip (1560–1627), one of the Chosŏn army leaders who had surrendered to the Manchu in 1619 and was taken captive. By 1620, almost all of the Korean prisoners had been released, but Kang remained. He learned to speak Manchu well and grew sympathetic to the Manchu cause. Later, in 1624, an internal rebellion broke out in the Chosŏn court. Yi Kwal, a powerful and respected military commander whose forces temporarily occupied the capital, led the rebellion and declared himself the ruler of a new dynasty until the government crushed the rebellion, and King Injo returned to Seoul. One survivor of the short-lived rebellion, Han Yu, fled to Manchu territory where he convinced General Kang Hongnip into believing that his family members had been killed by the state, presumably for his defection to the Manchu. In 1627, Kang led Manchu troops to Korea, reportedly to seek revenge against the dynasty, but he later learned that his family had not died, and that Han had deceived him. Han was subsequently beheaded.[37] Another Korean defector was Yi Yŏngbang, a former Chosŏn officer who, like Kang, had participated in the 1619 surrender to the Manchu. To help the Manchu win loyalty, Yi married one of the daughters of Nurhachi's many sons, assuming familial ties with the Manchu. Pak Nanyŏng (?–1636) joined Kang Hongnip on the expedition that assisted the Ming in 1619. The Manchu captured him and held him prisoner. Returning in 1627 with the Manchu army, Pak repatriated to the Chosŏn dynasty and later returned to Mukden several times as the Chosŏn envoy after the 1627 peace settlement. O Sinnam (1575–1632) was another Chosŏn military official captured in 1619. He was held in confinement and returned to Korea with the 1627 invading army, where he took part in the peace negotiations, helping the Manchu. Seeing these men's work with the Manchu as a betrayal to the state, some officials argued for the punishment of their families, but King Injo refused to act against them.[38] Kang was branded a traitor by the Chosŏn government but was rehabilitated later. O Sinnam returned to Mukden as a Chosŏn diplomat in 1630. Such decisions by the court may have been made to placate Manchu anger while making use of officials who spoke Manchu and were well versed in Manchu-Jurchen customs.

During the early days of the assault, the court struggled with basic military decisions and troop deployment. Officials requested that soldiers reposition themselves so as to impede the rapid Manchu advances. One strategy was to cut off the passage across the Imjin River to better defend the capital.[39] The approaching threat compelled King Injo to consider moving to the safety of Kanghwa Island. The army had already retreated to Namhan Mountain Fortress, leaving the capital undefended. King Injo thought it was best for him to defend the fortress, while other officials argued for the defense of such places as the Imjin River or even the capital, but Injo insisted that Namhan was too valuable to lose. With Manchu troops in the country, organization broke down, and decisions were hastily made to address the unanticipated rapid Manchu advance. There was a genuine recognition of the weakness of Chosŏn troops. The court had anticipated this Manchu assault as early as the previous year and had begun stockpiling provisions and reinforcements for the fortress.[40] But these actions failed to stop the Manchu. After hesitating, Injo ordered the military to abandon Seoul and fortify Kanghwa Island and Namhan Mountain Fortress. He also ordered all of the children and wives of the soldiers to withdraw to Kanghwa Island and had the ancestral shrines transferred there as well.[41]

Abandoning the capital not only meant ensuring the safety of the royal line, in particular the crown prince, but also indicated that the military situation was untenable. King Injo feared the crown prince, who was fifteen at the time, was too young to move.[42] He may have resisted taking this step for a number of reasons, such as the potential dangers to the crown prince and the clear sign it made to the population of the court's failure to defend the country, which could spark insurrection. Officials insisted the crown prince should be sent to Koje Island, a remote location off the southern coast, but the king reiterated that his son was too young to travel such a great distance.[43] Officials continued to try to persuade Injo to move south, pressing him to the point that he grew angry at their repeated requests; he finally acquiesced and approved their appeals.[44] The court dispatched the crown prince on the twenty-fourth day after the initial attack.

The flow of information into the court slowed because of the rapid advances of Manchu forces. Lacking information, the court dispatched scouts to ascertain conditions. Reports came back detailing the captures and deaths of top Chosŏn officials. Many troops were wiped out, while others fled; fortresses were captured. The situation was precarious: "It is said that all the common people who are captured have had their throats cut."[45] At one point, the king insisted that the Ming should be notified about the situation and requested the Southern Army (Namgun) and "rocket carts" (hwagi), or cannons, from the Chinese, "like during the Imjin War."[46] This is a good example of the court's reluctance to come to terms with Chosŏn's weak military position. The king's request evinces the misunderstanding of the military situation. Based on the precedence of the Imjin War, part of the Chosŏn strategy relied upon Ming assistance in times of national survival. Injo requesting Ming intervention suggests the court had no other options. Officials such as Yi Sik understood the hopelessness of these requests and bluntly stated, "The situation is not the same [as the Imjin War]."[47]

The decision to leave Seoul took three weeks. On his departure from the capital, King Injo composed a letter of sorrow, blaming his flight on the arrival of enemy troops and partly criticizing Ming general Mao Wenlong for demanding excessive military rations from the common people.[48] While King Injo was deciding whether to abandon the capital, some officials argued for diplomacy. The Manchu demanded peace negotiations, but the court responded slowly.[49] On the twenty-third day, King Injo inquired into the dispatch of the Chosŏn response letter to the Manchu and found that it had not been sent because the debate over the letter was as yet unsettled.[50] A discussion broke out about answering the Manchu demand for a state letter. The official Yi

Wŏnik (1547–1634) suggested that peace be concluded with the Manchu, a proposal supported by Yi Kwi (1557–1627), who argued that the military situation was dangerous and stated that a letter should be composed and sent to the Manchu.[51] Sin Kyŏngjin suggested that a slave (*noja*) be sent with the letter, apparently a ploy to prevent potentially losing a more valuable official. The king accepted this idea, ordered that the Identification Tag Registry Office (Hop'aech'ŏng) be burned (presumably so the Manchu could not identify the slave envoy), and sent the slave to Kanghwa Island with the letter. This rationalization may have been an excuse retroactively inserted into the sources to explain the burning of the office by slaves, as was allegedly done during the Imjin War.[52] Other officials opposed this move. Ch'oe Myŏnggil, for instance, suggested sending a letter written by Chang Man (1566–1629), who argued that the Chosŏn dynasty had served the Ming for two hundred years. "How can we not continue following them?"[53]

The court received a letter from Kang Hongnip that reported the arrival of three Manchu envoys. The direct involvement of Kang, a former Chosŏn official who spoke the same language and held the same customs, must have been part of the Manchu effort to reach a quick and positive settlement with the Chosŏn government. The court deliberated over the letter. King Injo decided that he had to retreat to Kanghwa Island, considering the Manchu Army had already arrived. Only then, after the king was safe, should a representative be chosen to accept the Manchu envoys. Chang Yu suggested that the Manchu envoys should be allowed to cross over to Kanghwa Island and be greeted there, but Injo refused and decided to move to the island the next day.[54]

Talk about opening negotiations with the Manchu dragged on. The court decided to select Yi Chŏnggu (1564–1635) as the envoy to receive the Manchu delegation.[55] Some of the debate revolved around the location of the meeting. Yi insisted, "If the Manchu envoys enter the fortress, then they would have no reason to attack. What about meeting them outside Your Majesty's Temporary Quarters?"[56] Some of the discussion centered on the demeanor of the Jurchen-Manchu representatives. King Injo inquired about their disposition and tone. Chang Yu asked if the court could refuse the representatives if they acted respectfully. The king believed that the location of the site was unimportant. More pertinent was the courteous manner in which Chosŏn should receive the envoys. He decided that Chinhaeryu, the entrance to Kanghwa Island along the shore, was a good site.[57] King Injo proceeded to cross over to Kanghwa Island, passing through Chinhaeryu, where the envoys would soon arrive. Once safely on the island shore, he asked about the Manchu. Ch'oe Myŏnggil replied that they only wanted to know if there would be peace or not. Yi Kyŏngjik opposed this view, however, adding that because the Manchu demanded that Chosŏn officials and the king must kowtow to them, "this was not the way to come to cordial terms with each other."[58] One Manchu envoy appeared, wanting to deliver a diplomatic letter to the court. An official argued that since the previous envoy, Kang Hongnip, was originally from Chosŏn and therefore bowed to the court, there was uncertainty about the reception of this new envoy who was calling himself a Manchu general. The king decided this envoy should be received outside the fortress and not allowed to enter.[59]

The rapid advance of Manchu troops to Seoul and Kanghwa Island forced the court to sever relations with the Ming. As part of this formality, on the third day of the third lunar month, two months into the war, King Injo swore "an alliance of friendship with the Great Jin dynasty," noting that if Chosŏn broke the pledge, and the Manchu troops invaded again, disaster would befall the dynasty.[60] The surrender ritual was elaborate. The oath was made over a sacrificial horse and a black ox presented as ritual offerings.[61] In front of a number of Chosŏn officials and eight Manchu envoys on Kanghwa Island, the court official Yi Haengwŏn (1592–1648) read the oath of allegiance as the Manchu collected the blood of the animals in a vessel in front of General Liu Hai (?–1630), a former Ming military officer who defected and was fighting for the Manchu. At the conclusion of the ritual, General Liu quickly departed, likely satisfied that Manchu efforts in Chosŏn had produced the appropriate outcome.

The Diary and the 1636-1637 Manchu Invasion

Upon recommendation by the Westerners, King Injo reneged on the promises made during the alliance ritual and resumed relations with the Ming once the Manchu troops retreated. In the years after, the Chosŏn court recognized the military disadvantages of the 1627 attack and strengthened key defenses, such as the cavalry, arquebus soldiers, and archers.[62] The government built up defenses along the frontier and moved troops to the west and northwest.[63] Another consequence of the defensive buildup and pro-Ming stance was that, in time, Ming bases returned to Korean territory. All of these developments indicated to the Manchu that Chosŏn had not severed its ties to the Ming.

Na Man'gap begins his diary with the Chosŏn movement toward war and the Manchu attempts to resolve the situation peacefully. The description of Manchu diplomacy is rife with mishaps and misunderstandings. Sensing the 1627 agreement was threatened, the Manchu tenth prince dispatched a letter to King Injo in which he reiterated his desire for peace between the two countries. Peace depended on Chosŏn acceptance of the new Qing reign title and Korea permanently ending relations with the Ming. Believing the Manchu prince broke protocol by sending the letter directly to King Injo, officials at the court refused to present the letter to the king. Na Man'gap shared their attitude and admitted that Chosŏn officials mistreated Qing envoys. A Mongol representing the Manchu was ill-treated on one occasion and, on another, Chosŏn representatives refused to convey a letter to the

FIGURE 0.2

Map of Chosŏn Korea with important locations mentioned in
The Diary of 1636.

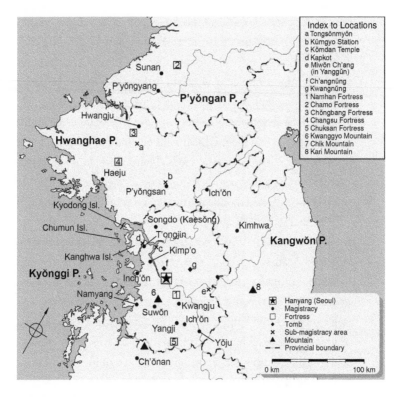

Index to Locations
a Tongsŏnmyŏn
b Kŭmgyo Station
c Kŏmdan Temple
d Kapkot
e Miwŏn Ch'ang
  (in Yanggŭn)
f Ch'angnŭng
g Kwangnŭng
1 Namhan Fortress
2 Chamo Fortress
3 Chŏngbang Fortress
4 Changsu Fortress
5 Chuksan Fortress
6 Kwanggyo Mountain
7 Chik Mountain
8 Kari Mountain

Sunan   ② P'yŏngan P.
P'yŏngyang

Hwangju
     ③
Hwanghae P.   ×a

     ④
Haeju   b
     P'yŏngsan   Ich'ŏn
Kyodong Isl.
     Songdo (Kaesŏng)   Kimhwa
Chumun Isl.   T'ongjin
     d c Kimp'o   Kangwŏn P.
Kanghwa Isl.   f
Kyŏnggi P.   g
Namyang   Inch'ŏn
     6 ▲ ① e× ▲8
Suwŏn   Kwangju
     Ich'ŏn
Yangji
     ⑤   Yŏju
•Ch'ŏnan

✭ Hanyang (Seoul)
• Magistracy
□ Fortress
♦ Tomb
× Sub-magistracy area
▲ Mountain
— Provincial boundary

0 km   100 km

FIGURE 0.3
Detailed map of central Chosŏn Korea, including important locations
mentioned in *The Diary of 1636*.

court from the Qing emperor. A more threatening diplomatic
slight occurred when the Manchu sent a cortège to the funeral
ceremony of Queen Inyŏl *wanghu* (1594–1635). The Chosŏn
court decided to set up the Manchu tent outside the palace compound. They did not want the outsiders near the palace, most
likely because of security reasons, but also because of officials' disdain for the Manchu "barbarians." This entourage included the
famed military commander Ingguldai. Following a tense moment
with Chosŏn royal guards near the Manchu tents, Ingguldai
and his men—fearful of an ambush and infuriated by Chosŏn
slights—rode north toward the Chosŏn frontier. As they left the

capital, they stole horses, a Manchu custom of retaliation after a show of disrespect that was most likely viewed by Chosŏn officials as another example of barbarianism. The letter from the tenth prince and the condolence visit had little impact. By 1636, while some Chosŏn officials advocated peace, many encouraged war. Na described the sentiment of resistance: "Popular opinion called for war and agreed that the establishment of tributary relations [with the Qing] was an erroneous view. There were no dissenters." Voices to resist only grew louder. While the debate at court over peace or war persisted, "the argument for war still dominated."

The incident with Ingguldai marked the end of Manchu attempts at negotiations. In early winter of 1637, roughly fifty thousand Manchu troops crossed the frozen Yalu River and attacked. Unlike in 1627, Korean commanders did not lead the assault. The top Manchu generals, Ingguldai and Mafuta, as well as Emperor Hung Taiji, directed the campaign, indicating the seriousness of Manchu resolve to settle the Korea issue permanently. Like the previous invasion, Manchu troops were unstoppable. The Manchu struck rapidly and within four days reached Seoul. Na Man'gap believed this rapid Manchu advance was made possible because the Chosŏn commander, Kim Chajŏm, failed to heed the fire beacons, giving Manchu troops time to strike south before the court could respond. Even after the forces had crossed the Yalu River, word of the attack was slow to reach the capital as Qing soldiers had by then captured the messengers Kim Chajŏm had dispatched south. Consequently, this delayed King Injo's retreat from the capital, cut off his escape routes, and forced him to Namhan Mountain Fortress, where he, elements of his military, and other officials—including Na Man'gap— retreated. Manchu emperor Hung Taiji anticipated King Injo's attempt to seek safety again on Kanghwa Island, as Injo had done in 1627, and mocked the move as insufficient to save the kingdom.

The rapid strike and delayed announcement of the invasion threatened a quick Manchu victory, provoking a sense of fear. The court, now residing in temporary quarters within Namhan Mountain Fortress, understood the precariousness of the situation. The Manchu blockaded the fortress and, after several weeks, began starving out the defending forces. Confronted by seasoned Manchu troops, Chosŏn resistance dissipated by the day, as did the food and other supplies for the men and their horses. The Manchu surrounded the fortress in most areas, though small bands of Koreans, who were more familiar with the terrain, secreted in and out of Namhan. Chosŏn troops launched small assaults against the Manchu besiegers, finding some success, but the efficacy of these attacks on Manchu lines rapidly diminished. Discussion in the fortress turned to negotiating the best terms of surrender. Chosŏn bureaucrats sent a number of diplomatic letters to Manchu military leaders, hoping to end the attacks, to provide some breathing space for troops defending the fortress, and to probe Manchu intent. The major point of contention that the Korean court hoped to resolve was the embarrassing surrender terms for King Injo and the crown prince. Factions in the court debated various ways to surrender. Early diplomatic letters, written by the anti-peace faction, sought assurances from the Manchu—couched in respectful diplomatic terminology—that the Chosŏn dynasty would continue to exist as a kingdom, the subordinate nature of the relationship between Chosŏn and the Manchu would remain intact, and King Injo and the crown prince would not be required to emerge from the fortress and kowtow before the Manchu. Requiring the king to kowtow was a humiliation, the court argued, which would result in continued animosity against the Manchu, undermining the Manchu hope for complete surrender. The Qing leadership did not back down from their demands. They insisted that King Injo and the crown prince, rather than other officials, emerge from the fortress and surrender. Continued resistance to these terms, the Manchu replied, prolonged the suffering of the Korean people and threatened full-scale warfare against the Chosŏn.

Na Man'gap was privy to many court debates on Chosŏn diplomatic overtures and defensive tactics. These discussions, while seeming to demand quick responses, strung out for days under threat from the Manchu military generals and the blockade of the fortress. The crisis that pushed King Injo into accepting the Manchu demands was the defeat of Kanghwa Island and the kidnapping of the crown princess, other royal family members, and *sadaebu* officials and their families. In the early days of the attack, King Injo and the crown prince hoped to seek refuge on Kanghwa Island. With their route to the island cut off by Manchu troops, the royal entourage proceeded to Namhan Mountain. Dating back at least to the Koryŏ dynasty, kings, queens, and other royal family members retreated to Kanghwa Island when faced with invasions from the north. In 1234, when Mongol armies crossed the frontier to punish Koryŏ for the death of a Mongol emissary and for severing diplomatic ties with the newly rising Mongol empire, the court and the military leadership retreated to Kanghwa Island from Kaegyŏng, the dynastic capital, near modern-day Kaesŏng. On the island, the Koryŏ leadership successfully resisted Mongol demands to return to the mainland and dispatch the crown prince, as well as the sons and daughters of other court officials, to Beijing as an act of surrender.

The Koryŏ court and the ruling military clan, on the other hand, simply refused to leave the island. With limited experience of amphibious warfare, given that their military skills had been developed on the steppe, far from the sea, the Mongols were unable to reach Kanghwa Island and secure complete submission. While the distance between Kanghwa Island and the mainland was geographically insignificant—they were within sight of each other—the seas around the island held some of the roughest and most powerful tidal changes in the region, especially before the introduction of dikes to control tidal surges. That said, with the founding of the Yuan dynasty and with the help of Chinese and Koreans, the Mongols were able to launch two massive seaborne invasions of Japan and one of Java. Most likely, Mongol leadership was content isolating the Korean court on Kanghwa Island without investing time or resources into assembling and launching a full-scale invasion of the island. Instead, the Mongols ruled the peninsula on horseback for decades, leaving behind military detachments and returning with larger numbers year after year, devastating the countryside in an attempt to punish the Koryŏ court. Rather than a Mongol invasion of the island, a coup against the ruling Korean military clan ended the stalemate. In the 1270s, after almost forty years of resistance, the Koryŏ court returned to the mainland and submitted to the Mongols. With the rise of the Yuan dynasty, the leader Kublai Khan demanded the destruction of the temporary royal halls and residences constructed on the island as another act to solidify submission.

The Manchu may have been aware of this history. The 1637 attack against Kanghwa Island demonstrated certain military advancements of the Manchu on Korean territory. The Manchu possessed a better understanding of amphibious warfare and strategies necessary to defeat Korean defenses on the island, including two former Ming Chinese generals who had defected to the Manchu and were experienced in naval warfare. King Injo had retreated to Kanghwa Island in the earlier 1627 Manchu attack, and the court quickly relented to Manchu demands under military and political pressure, without experiencing a Manchu assault on the island. In 1637, the swift Manchu advance down the peninsula prevented the king and crown prince from reaching Kanghwa Island—forcing them to Namhan Mountain Fortress—while during the invasion most of the Westerners retreated to the island. Na Man'gap's diary describes others committing suicide. Kim Sangyong famously blew himself up on a pile of gunpowder. The geographical location and defenses at Namhan Mountain Fortress proved more resistant to Manchu attacks than Kanghwa this time around—the island fell well before the mountain defenders surrendered. As Na Man'gap reported, almost all of the Manchu troops crossed the channel to Kanghwa Island on their initial assault—they "arrived like the wind." Manchu strategy was to circumvent the towns and fortresses on the island and directly attack the royal compounds. Sensing imminent capture, commanders and officials on the island surrendered. The announcement of the capture spurred King Injo to immediately accept the Manchu demands. The suffering of royal family members as prisoners of war must have weighed heavily on King Injo and the crown prince. They also had to consider the added military threat to Namhan Mountain as the capture of Kanghwa Island freed up Manchu forces to concentrate on the fortress.

With Namhan surrounded and Kanghwa Island under Manchu control, King Injo had no other alternative but to concede and accept Qing demands, but now Chosŏn was in a less favorable position than before. The 1627 and 1637 surrenders differed considerably. The 1627 attack was meant to bring Korea into an alliance as a willing, albeit junior, partner. The 1636–1637 invasion punished Korea for reneging on their earlier promise and established a purely subservient relationship. Chosŏn officials were not required to carry out the more humiliating rite where the king was to emerge from the fortress with jade in his mouth while carrying an empty coffin, acts of both humility and courtesy, but the king and crown prince did have to exit the fortress and kowtow in front of the Manchu leaders. Further, the Manchu emperor demanded Chosŏn raise a stele to memorialize the defeat, another humiliating act intended to remind Chosŏn people of the invasion after the withdrawal of the Manchu armies. From the Manchu perspective, Korea was untrustworthy because of their actions— severing the bond of brotherhood formed in 1627 and realigning with the Ming—both of which slowed the Qing advance into China. Part of the 1637 surrender formalities punished Chosŏn by forcing monetary tribute. Korea had to accept a long and onerous list of tributary demands to stop the Manchu army from raiding the country and taking the fortress. Several officials expressed significant anxiety about the economic consequences of the Qing demands.

In addition, as part of the surrender terms, senior-ranking men of the Westerner faction and their families, along with three princes, were taken to Manchuria and held hostage while other prisoners were married into Manchu clans. This hostage-taking ensured Chosŏn obedience to the Manchu. The Manchu used a different lens to view these demands. Hung Taiji dictated that the Korean king order "all the families of ministers inside and outside the court . . . [to] marry ours to make our good relationship solid." Many children of leading bureaucrats were kidnapped and taken to Manchuria as hostages. Many of them suffered tremendously. Some died in Manchu prisons. While some of the Chosŏn princes in Manchuria collaborated with the Manchu, others expressed anti-Manchu sentiment. In the debates about negotiations for the hostages, some members of the court desired a reduction of monetary tributary demands, but the official Kim Yu insisted he would pay, out of his own pocket, a thousand gold pieces to have his wife and daughter released. Other officials were furious by his offer, arguing that his request undermined the argument that the country had little gold to send as tribute payment. To ensure compliance, on this second invasion the Manchu demanded the dispatch of the crown prince and his entourage to Mukden, and Hung Taiji ordered marriage alliances between the Manchu and Chosŏn elite families. Even court minsters were required to enter into these alliances as part of the surrender terms. On the one hand, such demands appear humiliating, as the subjugated people had to provide marriage partners to the victorious Manchu. On the other, in Korea, this pattern of intermarriage had deeper historical roots from well before the 1630s. Marriage was an important element of alliance building among Northeast Asian and Eurasian tribes and polities. From Western Europe to East Asia, ruling members intermarried across large geographical areas. In the case of Korea, Silla and

Koryŏ founders took daughters to help placate defeated regions. The marriage alliance between Kublai Khan of the Mongol Yuan and the Korean Koryŏ dynasty brought the two ruling courts closer together, guaranteeing cooperation and safety, especially regarding military expansion into China.

The Manchu once again raised the importance of marriage alliances to the Chosŏn. The relationship between the Manchu and Korea did not develop as deeply as in the Mongol era, when the crown prince married the daughter of the emperor, lived in Beijing with the imperial family, and raised children there until called to Korea upon the death of his father, the king. Four centuries later, marriage alliances remained a custom for securing peace in Northeast Asia, but the pattern of those alliances shifted away from the royal family to other leading families in Seoul. The daughter of one elite *yangban* was chosen as a concubine for Hung Taiji. She, and her father, helped relieve some of the rice tax tribute the Qing demanded of the Chosŏn. From the Manchu perspective, what Na and others perceived as humiliating surrender rituals, including the dispatch of the crown prince and other powerful officials, were practical acts that would solidify strong relations between the two countries.

The Diary of 1636 also functions as a sourcebook illustrating Chosŏn and Manchu military tactics. The Chosŏn court mobilized able-bodied men to defend the country against the Manchu, including Buddhist monks, Japanese expatriates—presumably captured along the Korean coasts or elderly Japanese soldiers captured during the Imjin War—and slaves. The majority of the Chosŏn army consisted of troops from the capital guard and regional soldiers. All were ill-prepared for the Manchu assault, despite the government program to better train and prepare troops for an anticipated attack. Some units and individuals fought well, as Na narrates, but the Manchu forces, which included large numbers of experienced Jurchen and Mongol troops, overpowered the Korean military within a matter of days. Korea's long coastline proved to be a military disadvantage for the Koreans. Since the founding of the Chosŏn dynasty, the Chosŏn had needed a flexible army to defend the coast against piracy, and therefore having significant numbers of military personnel at the ready to fight massive armies attacking from the north was not part of their strategy. Korea's defenses included the construction of mountain fortresses throughout the country rather than maintaining defensive lines along the frontier. If an invasion took place from the north, the strategy was for as much of the population to retreat to safety within the fortified mountain areas. Once the people were within the fortress, the idea was to have the military wait for the enemy to pass and then emerge from the fortress and attack from the rear. Because ascending these mountains was difficult, defending them was relatively straightforward. Koreans knew their country well and easily entered and exited these mountain fortresses. But this turned out to be a poor strategy as the fortresses were too few and far between and often had insufficient supplies. Part of the attack on Namhan Mountain Fortress entailed encircling it with a wooden barricade. The Manchu added metal plates along the fence whose noise alerted Manchu soldiers to Koreans attempting to cross over the barricades to attack or to escape. The Manchu also dug a moat around part of the perimeter of the fence, which made crossing the siege lines even more time-consuming and dangerous for the Korean troops. Chosŏn countered by setting parts of the barricade on fire in response. Another military tactic the Manchu deployed was a wooden Trojan horse–like cart. Other successful Manchu siege operations involved the repeated attacks over the walls by squads of soldiers, the deployment of heavy cannon fire into the compound, and simply waiting and starving the defenders out.

Written during the siege and expanded in the aftermath of defeat, Na's *Diary of 1636* also contributes to an understanding of crime and punishment at times of war in Chosŏn society. In the face of defeat and the collapse of Chosŏn defenses, the level of punishment the Korean court and military officials unleashed on Korean commanders and foot soldiers was heavy. Flogging was common for crimes such as the failure to carry out military commands. Execution was also ordered when soldiers contradicted or ignored superior officers or attempted to deceive the court. One such story of deception is relayed in the diary. As an example of the way some soldiers deceived the court, Na Man'gap suggested monetary rewards be given to troops who cut off the ears of enemy men to help motivate troop morale. One soldier was executed when officials discovered that a head carried back from the battlefield turned out to be that of a fellow comrade. Also, according to Na, military officers and scholarly officials recurrently had their posts shuffled. Sometimes this was out of necessity, to cover for the death of an officer, for example; at other times it was to provide incentives through promotion or other inducements to men who would agree to attack the Manchu. The positive impact this had on the campaign appeared negligible, and the frequent reorganization of official titles seemed to have the opposite effect and slow military decision-making. In short, the rigid Confucian military and scholarly bureaucracy was unprepared to respond to the shifting military tactics of the Manchu.

Na recounts much of the immediate political fallout from the attack and the surrender during the year 1636–1637. He relates how the Qing did not wish to meddle in Chosŏn internal politics. They permitted the continued presence of Japanese traders at the Japan House in Tongnae, Pusan, for instance, hoping to use the Chosŏn relationship with the Japanese as a means to open communication with Tokugawa. However, the Manchu demanded restitution for the delay in attacking the Ming, calling on the court to punish those Chosŏn officials who had advocated for war. Na Man'gap expressed interest in discussing the anti-peace and pro-peace political factions and made no attempt to hide his disdain for certain officials. Ch'oe Myŏnggil was one such official who was a target of Na's contempt. Ch'oe, one of the central figures of the events of 1636–1637, was the leading voice advocating a practical, realistic approach to the Qing. He was the first to call on the king to dispatch a peace envoy to the Manchu frontlines, an approach that earned him the enmity of those hardline officials advocating war against the Manchu and defense of the Ming. Na Man'gap despised the "rat-like cunningness of Myŏnggil." He also blamed Kim Kyŏngjing, the prosecuting official of the capital who assumed command of Kanghwa Island during the rapid retreat from Seoul. While Kim was corrupt and selfish, Na's accusations were unfair as the defeat resulted from a multitude of military and political decisions before and after the attack. To blame one individual overlooks the complexities of the events. Given the military power of the Manchu, arguing that the Chosŏn dynasty could have survived if it had only maintained its alliance with the Ming is counterproductive. No East Asian polity could withstand the Manchu, not even the Chinese. Of course, it is understandable that those who witnessed and survived the 1637 surrender looked for scapegoats, and Na was no exception in trying to lay blame. Much of the political debate that erupted in the aftermath of the surrender—especially the character attacks against the officials who resisted the Manchu and who, when presented with a copy of the surrender document, tore it up at the court—revolved around blame.

Like in other diaries of the Manchu wars, emotions appear throughout Na's work, especially when describing resistance, surrender, and blame. Diaries like this are conducive to the expression of emotions because of their highly personal nature and their painful subject matter. It appears that in the Chosŏn dynasty conveying emotions was an acceptable form of historical writing. The historiography of emotion is another lens through which to gauge court politics during the Chosŏn dynasty. Hwisang Cho posits that emotional expressions through the written petition system, by the elite and non-elite alike, become a war of words in which the king used the system to help suppress the power of the

Confucian bureaucracy. One drawback was that it would "exaggerate trivial squabbles into serious problems" through the power of emotive language. But if, as Cho argues, "emotional expressions, even if they were excessive, were justified and even honored if they dovetailed with such Confucian values as loyalty and filial piety," then Na's diary perfectly demonstrates these values.[64]

Through the lens of emotion, Na's sense of loss, suffering, and pain surfaces throughout the diary and constructs a narrative of blame to explain the humiliating surrender. The litany of hardships recorded in the diary is extensive: blaming officials for underreported causality figures; listing the officials who exaggerated the reports of victories by Chosŏn forces; and detailing how troops deceived the court by collecting dead bodies of comrades and claiming they were the enemy for rewards. In highly emotive language, Na blames the prosecuting official Kim Kyŏngjing directly and indirectly for his immoral actions on Kanghwa Island. Na wrote in defense of the king, guarding him from accusations of incompetence while blaming anyone other than Injo. Officials emotively asserted that King Injo had no knowledge of their anti-Manchu agenda, most likely an attempt to shield him from blame and hope that this excuse satisfied the Manchu enough to withdraw. The official Yi Sŏnggu clearly blamed Kim Sanghŏn, who destroyed the draft letter of surrender, for the failure of the initial peace negotiations. Yi called on him personally to surrender to the Manchu and accept blame. Kim understood the gravity of his actions. Out of fear of punishment or despair for the Manchu victory, he refused to eat. Na's accusations against all of these "villains" were based on emotions. While the decisions of Kim Sanghŏn and other anti-peace officials brought the Manchu back to the Chosŏn, the actions of other individuals led to the suffering and hardship of the king, his family, and the Korean people.

The Diary of 1636 is a record of the epistolary battle between Chosŏn and the Manchu. The diplomatic correspondence and the exchange of letters during the peace negotiations was not only for practical purposes, such as providing a means to discuss surrender, but it also became a way for both sides to fight with rice paper and brushes. The diary records no fewer than ten letters exchanged during the invasion. Each side attempted to explain its position based on moral Confucian high ground. Chosŏn leaders argued the sincerity of their Confucian heritage and linkages to the Ming, especially regarding the obligation owed the Ming for helping save the Chosŏn dynasty from the Japanese. Chosŏn was a country of scholarship that did not know war, one Korean dispatch argued, while another court letter suggested the main reason for Qing anger emerged from a misunderstanding of history and Confucian dictates. The Manchu responded to such letters forcefully, arguing that the duplicity of the Chosŏn—which they claimed was an un-Confucian characteristic—and the building of military defenses and the capture of land and people along the northern frontier were suggestive of a country knowledgeable of war. The Korean court was adept at deploying Confucian symbolism, including self-denigration and historical references to justify its actions. What may seem surprising is the deftness and complexity of Manchu-Qing responses. Chosŏn may have claimed greater Confucian legitimacy based on its lengthy history of engaging with the Confucian Classics (these were books like *Mencius, Great Learning, Analects of Confucius,* and other works on philosophy and moral values that China, Korea, Japan, and Vietnam adopted for scholarship and governance), but the Manchu, through their interpreters and letter writers, proved an equal of Korea in their written responses. The war on the battlefield, fought also through the exchange of letters, proved challenging for Korea to surmount. The Manchu were as powerful with the brush as they were with the sword.

While this was a major military defeat for the Chosŏn, in retrospect, the invasion of 1636–1637 was not as militarily damaging and saw less material destruction than the Japanese invasions during the Imjin War in 1592–1598—although Na asserts otherwise because of his own experiences in 1637, and he did not witness the war with Japan. Politically, however—and Na's diary speaks to this—the invasion of 1636–1637 was much more destructive. During the Imjin War, the country united against the Japanese, while in the case of the Manchu, the Korean bureaucracy and army split. Many officials remained devoted to the Ming, while civil and military leaders argued that the country should support the Manchu. Compared to the Imjin War, the Manchu wars, while not as physically destructive, were devastating in terms of politics and national morale. The Imjin War did not change Chosŏn politics, though it did wash away all of the earlier objections Chosŏn literati held against the Ming, such as their criticism for Ming support of Wang Yangming Neo-Confucian thought or Korean resentment against Ming tribute demands. The Manchu wars, on the other hand, were so rapid and were conducted with such a small and nimble military—which moved quickly in and out of Korea—that Chosŏn appeared to have been struck by lightning. Unlike the Japanese in the Imjin War, the Manchu stopped once they captured the Chosŏn capital, signaling defeat. These rapid invasions severed Korean contact with the Ming on both occasions. After the first oath of allegiance was broken, the reprisal of the second invasion was more consequential. All of the princes in line for the throne and the sons of leading officials were transported back with the Manchu as hostages. They were released later, but by then these people had established connections and lines of communication with the Manchu, learned their customs and politics, and sometimes even the language. To some, this was a positive result and a way to further communications with the Manchu, but others thought that these hostages were too closely aligned with the Manchu and could pose a threat. What Chosŏn defeat meant for China, Korea's direct neighbor, was evident. The Manchu were an ascending power in Northeast Asia, heralding the end of the revered Ming and the transformation of Northeast Asia and Chosŏn politics and society.

Chosŏn Legacies of the Manchu Wars

In several important ways, the Manchu invasions marked a key date in Korean history, separating "early" Chosŏn from "late" Chosŏn. These included the rise of the vernacular Korean language, calls for economic and military reforms, and shifting political identities in the wake of the Manchu wars. For one, earlier anti-Japanese unity among ruling circles during the Imjin War fractured with disagreement over the response to Manchu imperial aspirations. The Manchu subjugation and the Qing defeat of the Ming had lasting consequences for the Chosŏn dynasty. This event transformed the Korean political landscape, and scholars still discuss its impact today.[65] In heightened ways, the wars fueled political intrigue and struggles in the decades that followed as Westerners continued to exert influence over the court. Westerners' resentment of the Manchu persisted well after 1644, as is evidenced in their cultural affinity to the Ming; they used maps of Ming China and continued to use the Ming calendar for dating, a symbol of the Westerners' rejection of Qing imperial rule. When the Chosŏn government produced a document not intended for public notice, the material was dated in the Ming reign year.

The Manchu's delegitimization of China as a foreign ruler stimulated late Chosŏn distinctiveness. The Manchu rulership of China began turning Koreans away from the over-glorification of Chinese civilization and encouraged them to focus on internal developments instead. Society began opening up and broadening out through culture: artists began depicting a wider segment of society, and groups other than elite male *yangban* began writing their personal stories. Genre paintings of daily life were one example of this. Vernacularization of the written language was another. Very early on, Korea borrowed literary Chinese writing and used it for government documents, scholarship, and poetry, as it was thought to represent a civilized society, one centered in an ancient Chinese past steeped in Confucian learning. While some women learned to use literary Chinese, especially in the houses of the elite, it was a gendered script, mostly used by a small percentage of the male *yangban* who had the time and wealth to learn to read and write it. In general, women were not given the opportunity to learn literary Chinese. After the invention of the vernacular script in the fifteenth century, later known as *Hangul*, Korean monks relied upon it for the translation of Buddhist sutras and poems. Women learned the vernacular and began writing in it, while men learned it but also continued to use literary Chinese. Little had been composed in the vernacular up through the early seventeenth century, but, right around the time of the Manchu wars, this began to change and writers began composing more and more in *Hangul*. Around the same period in Western Europe and other parts of Eurasia, similar patterns of vernacularization appear in novels, a trend that also occurred in Korea.[66] In the late seventeenth and early eighteenth centuries, more and more works in the vernacular were written, such as novels by Kim Manjung (1637–1692), a writer of popular fiction who composed *Cloud Dream of the Nine* (*Kuunmong*) and *Record of Lady Sa's Southward Journey* (*Sassi namjŏnggi*). Both tales take place in China and have complex plots and characters. Other literary works retold the hardships of the Imjin War and the Manchu attacks.[67] This was the beginning of a rich tradition of writing novels in the vernacular and translating popular Chinese literature into the Korean language.

In the wake of the invasion, visible scars on the landscape and the immediate memory of the violence fueled antipathy toward the Manchu. The Manchu Wars hit certain parts of the country harder than others. The north suffered the brunt of the destruction during the 1637 battles, but King Injo's decision to surrender less-ened the military impact on the people and the land. Korean leaders understood the root cause of their defeat to the Manchu—the lack of a national surplus and the cash necessary for military preparations. Scholars found the solution when they began enacting the Taedongbŏp, or the Great Equalization Law.[68] Earlier, King Kwanghaegun had begun implementing changes to the revenue system, which continued in the aftermath of the Manchu attacks. This economic plan for revenue reform enabled the government to collect more money in taxes, permitting economic development and a diversification of the economy. The Taedongbŏp was a heavy but innovative taxation system that led Korea into a period of economic growth in the seventeenth century, in contrast to the economic stagnation of the sixteenth century. As revolutionizing and controversial as the plan was, politicians could not agree on turning it into law, so they began by enacting the reforms in various regions across the dynasty, first in Kyŏnggi Province in 1608 and then in other provinces, until the plan was fully established throughout the Chosŏn territory one hundred years later. Like the pro-war and pro-peace debates in 1636–1637, the law spurred political tensions and disputes. While controversial, the forces the Taedongbŏp reforms unleashed led to steady changes, a prosperous time for the Korean economy, and an orderly eighteenth century.

The policy of deference to the Ming, complicated by the rise of the Manchu and their two attacks on the Chosŏn, fractured relations between pro-Ming officials and those who grew sympathetic to the Manchu. These clashes reached the upper echelons of the Chosŏn polity. At the time of the Manchu invasion, three princes were alive, two of whom grew militarily hostile toward the Manchu. The oldest, Crown Prince Sohyŏn (1612–1645), was disposed to collaborate with the Qing. While outside Korea, he went on expeditions with Manchu generals and accompanied Qing military campaigns. One possibility for his involvement is that the

Manchu hoped to nurture a special relationship with the future king to cement relations between the two countries, connections the Manchu had fostered with Koreans in the past, like Kang Hong-nip and other Chosŏn military men following their surrender to the Jurchen-Manchu in 1619. After the Manchu captured Beijing in 1644, Sohyŏn grew interested in Catholicism after meeting the famous Jesuit Johann Adam Schall von Bell (1591–1666), but little is known about their encounter. When Sohyŏn returned to Seoul in 1645, he brought back religious scriptures, novelty Western items, servants, and eunuchs from the former Ming court, some of whom had converted to Catholicism. Probably the most knowledgeable Korean on Catholicism at the time, Sohyŏn, who was under suspicion for his pro-Manchu ties, died mysteriously six weeks after returning to the capital. All of his Chinese servants were repatriated to Beijing. Perhaps the Westerner faction members felt threatened by the close relationship he had built with the Manchu, and the idea that Sohyŏn was to become king while holding a strong pro-Manchu, pro-Catholic stance was too great a threat to the ruling elite in Seoul.

When Korean princes stirred trouble, the state could do little against their misconduct because of their royal status. For non-royalty, crimes such as treason impacted the whole family. The accused were executed, their wives and daughters were dispersed and made into slaves or commoners, and family property was confiscated. Because officially accusing Sohyŏn of treason was difficult, his punishment may have been carried out in a secreted manner.[69] Crown Prince Sohyŏn died in bed, but very little source material remains as many of the records of the events surrounding his death are missing. The Westerners blamed the Manchu, but most likely the political implications of his potential rulership were so threatening that he was assassinated.

The death of Crown Prince Sohyŏn undercut Manchu designs for closer relations with the Chosŏn court, exacerbating an anti-Qing sentiment that echoed throughout subsequent reigns. King

Hyojong (1619–1659; r. 1649–1659), King Injo's second oldest son, ascended the throne harboring resentment against the Manchu after suffering captivity in Mukden. After relations with the Qing settled and hostages returned to Korea, he and others dreamed of revenge. King Hyojong was not raised as the crown prince—unlike his older brother Sohyŏn—and had not been put through the rigors of training and education, which had provided him greater freedom of mobility while in Manchuria as a hostage. After returning from Manchu captivity, he spoke some Chinese and Manchu and had experienced firsthand countries outside of Korea—an experience that few Korean kings had—the knowledge of which broadened his mind. His reign was stable and politically secure, but he realized the military needed rebuilding to effectively defend the country. As an avid supporter of the military, King Hyojong was intent on using his army to defeat the Manchu and win back Chosŏn freedom from the Qing, who were bogged down in southern China fighting pro-Ming loyalists. Planning to develop the military and exact revenge, he designed a strategy to contact Koreans who were pro–Ming Chinese and coordinated a military campaign against the Manchu in the 1670s, dubbed the "northern strike" (*pukpŏl*). The Korean hostages held from 1637 until 1644— individuals King Hyojong began to mobilize for the strike, including royal princes and Westerner party members—were heatedly pro-Ming and led the charge against the Manchu. While the king thought an attack could be successful, his northern strike never materialized, and his great army never came to be. Hyojong's death in 1659, after a short reign, was not a good omen for the state. As soon as he died, Korea experienced the most devastating political crisis of the seventeenth century.

Ordinary Confucian views held that when the king died, a period of mourning had to take place for a certain number of years, depending on the king's time as principal ruler and his position in the royal family. King Hyojong was not the first son of

King Injo but his second, and this unusual situation spurred a crisis over the question of mourning: how long should the queen dowager, his stepmother, mourn her deceased stepson? The Westerners argued Hyojong should not be granted the full three-year mourning period and instead just one year, but the Southerners argued three years were required. Even though the Southerners were not in power and the Westerners dominated the government at this time, the Southerners still held some influence over the bureaucracy, reasoning that King Hyojong had been a full king and had succeeded as the second son of his father. Some ritual prescriptions stipulated that a second son should have a three-year mourning period. The argument of the illustrious scholar Yun Hyu (1617–1680), the leader of the Southerner party, was overtly political and asserted the legitimacy of the king. Hyojong, he averred, should be honored with a full three-year mourning period—the greater number of years would strengthen the morale of the state. The king, a national figure, was legitimized by heaven itself and through his struggle against the Manchu. The debate, which raged for over a year, ended with the triumph of the Westerners, who won the first round, but their opponents won the second.[70] The victory for the Westerners enhanced their power over Hyojong's royal successor, but resulted in intense political fallout and a determined political struggle for the next thirty to forty years.

While factionalism predates the Manchu Wars of the 1620s and 1630s, the invasions gave these factions new material to argue over. Debates—led by anti-Manchu political groups such as the Westerners over the minutia of Confucian ritual—intensified in the late seventeenth century. Responding to the founding of the Qing, Chosŏn grew more concerned about Confucian norms than other countries, including the Qing. Confucianism extolled, as the greatest virtue, unity with the ruler and, theoretically, called for harmonious behavior over loyalty to a king or national polity. Korean Confucians argued against subjective understanding, such as the Ming-era Chinese scholarship of Wang Yangming (1472–1529), who seemed too individualistic in his Confucian writings. Despite these calls for unity, the debates over Confucian ritual were serious matters. Korean scholarship usually self-critiques these Chosŏn court debates as unproductive issues of "factionalism." The Chosŏn parties' extreme displays of political infighting was representative of the struggle for power and proximity to the king, which had resulted in parties and clans having powerful positions in Seoul. Seoul was home to many *yangban* families competing for a select number of official positions— less than two thousand government jobs were located in the capital, most of which were low-ranking and involved practical work of little political importance. By the seventeenth century, as the dynasty matured, the number of *yangban* claiming to be from powerful clans grew steadily; however, while most of these families had land, they had no prestige. The growth of *yangban* families coincided with increased political bouts of fighting between parties.

The Manchu Wars continued to reverberate through the end of the Chosŏn dynasty. By the nineteenth century, power politics (*sedo chŏngch'i*) shaped the political center, in which the family of the queen obtained a strong dominant position by tracing their legitimacy back to their family's actions in the 1637 anti-Manchu struggle. The wife of King Sunjo (r. 1800–1834) was of the Andong Kim family, the backbone of the Noron, or "Old Doctrine" party, who were intensely anti-Manchu. Because of the martyrs in their family, they had gained political success in the country. A powerful family that grew dominant in Seoul—the base of their national power—and became part of the *sadaebu* central elite, the Andong Kim family began to assert their domination by using their relationship to the throne to control all appointments, especially state council members. This and other politically powerful families were examples of the changing structure of late Chosŏn society.

One of the most visible displays of the Manchu influence on later Chosŏn politics were the shrines constructed for the Ming. The Westerners had suffered much at the hands of the Manchu and took it as a matter of faith that they owed their existence to the Ming for helping the Chosŏn dynasty win the Imjin War. The scholar and leader of the Westerner party, Song Siyŏl, and other Westerners believed that the Wanli Emperor (r. 1572–1620), the Ming leader who had personally intervened to dispatch troops to save Korea, deserved a special shrine. The Mandongmyo Shrine, constructed in 1707 in Ch'ungch'ŏn Province, symbolized the continued reverence Chosŏn held for the Ming while keeping alive the burning memory of the 1637 Manchu invasion. Another shrine, the Altar of Great Gratitude (Taebodan), was erected on the royal palace grounds in 1704. These shrines, built of the Chosŏn's own volition, were displays of Korean dedication to China, established rituals memorializing a foreign power. The Chosŏn state held regular services at both locations from the early eighteenth century through the nineteenth century, when they became the subject of a major political debate. Orthodox Neo-Confucian leaders continued the upkeep of the shrines and the performance of the rituals in the royal palace until 1894.[71] While these shrines and their rituals inhibited the relationship with the Manchu to a certain extent, the Qing dynasty was not overly domineering regarding such symbolism by then, because it had grown to trust the court to follow their lead.

Na Man'gap's *The Diary of 1636* narrates the violent beginnings of what turned into a strong relationship that lasted until the Qing (like the Ming) waged war against Japan, over the Chosŏn, in the Sino-Japanese War (1894–1895). However, unlike the Ming war, this conflict had a very different outcome. The Westerners faction continued to condemn the Qing in an era when the Chosŏn dynasty had prospered and had benefited from the stability Qing rulers had brought to China and the strong economic relationship that had developed with the Qing in the eighteenth century. In reality, the Manchu-Qing no longer threatened Korea. Qing tribute demands were only a fraction of what the Ming had required. The Westerners had no idea what was in Korea's best interest, but convincing them of the benefits of the Qing, as they harkened back to the Manchu Wars of the seventeenth century, was a challenge. By the end of the Chosŏn dynasty, the Chosŏn had built a sensible, civil relationship with the Qing, a relationship that opened Korea to regional and global influences, both good and bad. The Qing capital served as the gateway for Korean contact with the West, including Western science and Catholicism, as well as knowledge of the growing presence of Europeans and other outsiders trading with China. The Japanese defeat of the Qing in 1895 ended the China-centered worldview and ushered in new forces that eventually toppled the Manchu-Qing. The relationship that began with violence in 1637 outlasted the special bond Chosŏn held with the revered Ming by two decades and formally ended with the Chosŏn dynasty in 1910, under the impact of modern forms of violence, imperialism, and colonialism.

Namhan Mountain Fortress

Located twenty-five kilometers south of Seoul, Namhan Mountain Fortress, a place that Na discusses in great detail in his diary, is a popular destination for hikers, bikers, mountain climbers, and sightseers. It is easily accessible through South Korea's subways, buses, and highways, and is frequently mentioned in tourist guidebooks. To the north, the fortress delivers an impressive view of the Seoul cityscape, especially at night—a breathtaking constellation of lights, skyscrapers, roadways, bridges, and various aircrafts flying overhead. It is a view that highlights the peace and prosperity of South Korea today, a far cry from Korea's position in the winter of 1637, when Chosŏn troops clung to the mountain ridges and walls defending the court from the Manchu attacks below.

The most impressive view of Namhan Mountain is from Seoul. Looking south from virtually any spot in the capital that is unobstructed by high-rise buildings, one can see the mountain in the distance, rising nearly 1,650 feet (500 meters) above the city, which explains why this mountain was recognized as an important defensive site. From the earliest indigenous societies on the peninsula, and from the Three Kingdoms era (circa the sixth century CE) to the Koryŏ dynasty (918–1392), the mountain played a defensive role several times. Its importance magnified dramatically when the Chosŏn dynasty established its new capital in nearby Seoul at the beginning of the fifteenth century. In Chosŏn times, writers composed a myriad of essays and poems about Namhan Mountain Fortress, extolling its beauty and defensive nature.[72] Following the Imjin War, King Kwanghaegun expanded and fortified the fortress defenses, a task King Injo extended in 1624. Thick battlement walls, roughly five meters high and twelve kilometers long, encircle an area of more than two hundred million square meters, a suitable space for government and military buildings and the temporary compounds of the court in times of war and invasion. The mountain's height and terrain made it a natural choice for both a defensive position and a quickly reachable hideout for officials in the capital. Even for those who knew the terrain, the journey across the Han River south and up the steep hillsides and rocky crevices was rough, whether one was on foot, on horseback, or in a palanquin. For invading foot soldiers and cavalry units uncertain of the area, the path was formidable. Manchu troops assaulted the fortress but never succeeded in capturing it.

From 1910 to 1945, the Japanese colonial government neglected Namhan, while during the Korean War (1950–1953), stray bombs and shells damaged the fortress. The Park Chung

Hee government (1961–1979) designated the fortress as a cultural heritage site to convey the idea that he and his government were the preservers of Korean cultural memory, thus legitimizing his rule of South Korea. The fortress's popularity as a cultural symbol exploded with the UNESCO World Heritage Site designation in 2014. While summarizing the history of the Namhan area, the application spotlighted the natural beauty of the mountain and its important contribution to the environmental movement.[73] Namhan remains in the popular imagination through works of fiction and films that depict the heroism of Korean defenders—stories and images that have helped to boost national pride and South Korean patriotism—in a time when society has rapidly changed through, and been threatened by, the forces of globalism.[74] While the country transforms around it, Namhan remains steady.

The rethinking of Namhan as a cultural site is part of the long process of reimagining the 1636–1637 Manchu invasion. Na Man'gap's *Diary of 1636* helps in this reimagining by breathing life into events and humanizing the people who fought and died on both sides. The 1637 surrender may have been a humiliating defeat, as critics have argued, but the composition and transmission of *The Diary of 1636* should be celebrated as a victory over the forces that have long since departed.[75] Na's *Diary* highlights the importance of Chosŏn in the minds of rising powers in Northeast Asia and gives voice to the many individuals in the fortress—elite and low status, Korean and Manchu—some of whom were often overlooked in history.

The transformation of historically painful sights into places of domestic and international recognition is one step in reclaiming a traumatic past.[76] The transformation of sites like Namhan Mountain is part of a wider pattern of recreating history to make it economically important as well as providing another symbol of national identity. The identification of heritage sites such as Namhan promotes tourism and turns these areas and even history itself into a commodity to be packaged, sold, bought, and consumed. Simultaneously, such designations raise awareness in the public sphere and among scholars, and thereby promote critical debates among specialists about the role private and governmental groups play in creating heritage tourism.[77] As Lauren Rivera notes, "Management of the past is thus not only a matter of national cohesion but also an international and economic affair."[78] The South Korean government has reimagined the difficult past of the fortress by reframing the debate around patriotism, nationalism, and self-sacrifice. These values are understandably important, given Korea's twentieth-century history with Japanese colonialism, the political division of Korea into North and South, both Koreas' experiences with the United States, China, and the Soviet Union, and the disastrous Korean War (1950–1953). While the 1636–1637 invasion is often viewed negatively, the site of this reputation-damaging event has become an important part of South Korea's national heritage. Reading Na's *Diary of 1636* gives us unique ways of thinking about the mountain and the historical heritage of South Korea and its place in the region and beyond.

Chosŏn Korea

Royal Family Members

King Injo (1595–1649) ascended the throne in 1623, after a coup against his uncle King Kwanghaegun, and aligned with officials from the pro-Ming and anti-Qing Western faction. During the 1637 Manchu invasion, he retreated to Namhan Mountain Fortress. Na Man'gap and others refer to him as "His Majesty," "Your Highness," and "the king."

Crown Prince Sohyŏn (1612–1645) was the first son of King Injo. He was twenty-four years old at the time of the second Manchu invasion. He was present in Namhan Mountain Fortress with his father. Following the surrender, the Manchu commander Mafuta demanded Sohyŏn's dispatch to Manchu lands, where he was held until 1645. After returning to Chosŏn, he died in bed, most likely assassinated for his pro-Manchu sentiment.

Crown Princess Consort Minhoebin (1611–1646) of the Kang clan married Crown Prince Sohyŏn in 1627, the year of the first Manchu attack. In the 1636–1637 retreat from the capital, she escaped to

Kanghwa Island along with other royal family members and leading elites. With the surrender, she followed her husband to Mukden, where she remained until 1645. After her husband's death, she was accused of trying to poison King Injo and was executed.

Queen Dowager Inmok (1584–1632) married King Sŏnjo in 1602. Her son, Prince Yŏngch'ang, was killed by King Kwanghaegun in 1614, while she and her daughter, Princess Chŏngmyŏng, were imprisoned.

Queen Inyŏl wanghu (1594–1635) married the future King Injo in 1610. Events at her funeral service precipitated the second war with the Manchu.

Grand Prince Inp'yŏng (1622–1658) was the third son of King Injo and Queen Inyŏl and the younger brother of Grand Prince Pongnim. He retreated to Kanghwa Island during the 1636–1637 invasion.

Grand Prince Pongnim (1619–1659) was the second son of King Injo and Queen Inyŏl and the older brother of Grand Prince Inp'yŏng. He was captured by the Manchu during the fall of Kanghwa Island.

King Kwanghaegun (1575–1641; r. 1608–1623) was the second son of King Sŏnjo and the uncle of King Injo. Following the 1623 coup that deposed him, he was exiled to Cheju Island, where he was most likely poisoned.

Prince Hoeŭn (Yi Tŏgin; ?–1644) was a very distant relative of King Injo through King Sŏngjong (r. 1469–1494). He served as an envoy to the Manchu and was rewarded for helping to reduce the tribute levy to the Qing. His daughter became an imperial consort to Hung Taiji.

Officials at the Chosŏn Court

Chang Sin (?–1637) was a scholar official who was present on Kanghwa Island during the 1636–1637 invasion and defended the island against the Manchu. The court punished him for his failure to protect the island and forced him to consume poison.

Ch'oe Myŏnggil (1586–1647) rose to importance in the government during the 1623 coup that brought King Injo to power. He served on Kanghwa Island during the first Manchu attack and argued for peace with the Manchu in 1636–1637, a view that earned him the gratitude of Hung Taiji. He frequently carried letters back and forth between the Manchu camps and the Korean court during the invasion.

Chŏng Myŏngsu (?–1653) was a Korean serving the Manchu as a go-between and an interpreter. Chŏng first appears in the *Sillok* in 1633. He frequently traveled between Chosŏn and the Qing.

Chŏng Noegyŏng (1608–1639) was an official accused of cheating Hung Taiji out of tributary items promised to the Manchu Court. King Injo ordered him executed in Mukden.

Chŏng On (1569–1641) was a high-ranking scholar official. He returned to the government from exile and served in a number of top posts following the coup against King Kwanghaegun. Present in Namhan Fortress during the siege, he opposed peace with the Manchu and was later accused of disloyalty against King Injo.

Hong Ikhan (1586–1637) was a scholar official executed by the Manchu, along with Yun Chip and O Talche, as part of the antipeace negotiations group. Later, these men were dubbed the "three loyal scholars" (*samhaksa*).

Hong Sŏbong (1572–1645) was a scholar official who served in the highest positions in the government. He came to power as one of the leaders of the coup that deposed King Kwanghaegun and brought King Injo to the throne. He was present in Namhan Mountain Fortress during the 1636–1637 invasion and, along with a few other top officials, carried letters back and forth between the Manchu camps and the Korean court.

Kang Chinhŭn (?–1637) was a naval official at Kanghwa Island. He was heralded by Na Man'gap and other Chosŏn-era writers for his heroic self-sacrifices.

Kim Chajŏm (1588–1651) was a military commander from the scholar official order who rose to prominence following the 1624 Yi Kwal uprising. Promoted to head general, he was blamed for committing a number of strategic errors in the opening days of the 1636–1637 invasion that contributed to a rapid Manchu victory.

Kim Kyŏngjing (1589–1637), the son of Kim Yu, was vilified by many of his contemporaries and by future generations for his arrogance and selfishness during the defense of Kanghwa Island in the 1636–1637 invasion. Placed in charge of Kanghwa Island, he was later belittled for cowardice and selfishness in defending the island.

Kim Pan (1580–1640) was a scholar official who supported King Injo during the 1624 Yi Kwal rebellion. He served in several posts with Na Man'gap. He was a pragmatic official who avoided factional dismissal and received high honors posthumously.

Kim Sanghŏn (1570–1652) was a scholar official who served during the 1627 and 1636–1637 Manchu invasions. He was stubbornly anti-Manchu, and his actions, and the policies he advocated, prolonged the siege of Namhan Mountain Fortress. As punishment for his resistance, the Manchu khan ordered him held captive in Qing lands, where he was praised for his steadfast refusal to deny his anti-Manchu feelings.

Kim Sin'guk (1572–1657) was a scholar official present at Namhan Mountain Fortress at the time of the 1636–1637 invasion. He served as an envoy for the Korean court by traveling to nearby Manchu camps to accept and present diplomatic letters. He also managed the food supply of the fortress with Na Man'gap.

Kim Yu (1571–1648) was a senior politician with a long career in government and also a pragmatic scholar of fine literary talent who served as a confidant to King Injo. He first called for war with the Manchu but later advocated peace.

Ku Koeng (1577–1642) was a well-respected military official who escorted King Injo to Namhan Mountain Fortress during the 1636–1637 invasion. He supported peace with the Manchu and the punishment of the anti-peace negotiations officials.

Na Man'gap (1592–1642) served in the government of King Injo for a number of years, including at court during both Manchu attacks. He clashed with a number of high officials, especially Kim Yu. Charged with crimes and exiled after 1638, he spent his remaining years writing *The Diary of 1636*.

Pak Hwang (1597–1648) was a scholar official who served in a number of high-level posts. He attended King Injo at Namhan Mountain Fortress during the 1636–1637 invasion and accompanied Crown Prince Sohyŏn to Mukden.

Pak No (1584–1643) was a scholar official who served as an envoy to the Manchu court in Mukden before and after the 1636–1637 invasion. While the close relationship he developed with the Manchu emperor and other military leaders gave him unprecedented access to the Qing and Chosŏn courts, it also earned him the enmity of Korean officials.

Sim Kiwŏn (?–1644) was a scholar official who rose to importance during the 1623 coup that brought King Injo to power. In the second Manchu invasion, the court appointed him defender of Seoul. In 1644, he led a revolt against King Injo for which he was executed, even though the revolt failed. Later, his actions were often mentioned in court sources such as the *Sillok* alongside the failures of Kim Chajŏm.

Sin Kyŏngjin (1575–1643) was an army veteran from the military official order who served during the Imjin War from 1592 until 1598 and in the 1624 Yi Kwal uprising. A trusted commander throughout his career, he escorted King Injo to Kanghwa Island in 1627, and in 1636 distinguished himself as one of the Chosŏn's most reliable officers.

Sin Tŭkyŏn (1585–1647) was the envoy sent to the Manchu over the matter of Kim Sanghŏn. Often dispatched to Mukden, he frequented the Korean court and reported on matters concerning the Manchu.

Yi Kwak (1590–1665) was an envoy dispatched to the Manchu court in early 1636 and was infamous for leaving behind Hung Taiji's letter to King Injo.

Yi Min'gu (1589–1670) was a well-regarded scholar official before the 1636–1637 Manchu invasion. He was awarded honors for his role suppressing the 1624 Yi Kwal rebellion. In the 1627 Manchu attack, he aided Crown Prince Sohyŏn's safe retreat from the capital. After the 1637 invasion, he was punished for failing to escort King Injo to Kwanghwa Island and defend the island with Kim Kyŏngjing. King Injo resisted calls for his execution. In his later life, Yi became well known for his literary talents. He was the younger brother of Yi Sŏnggu.

Yi Sŏnggu (1584–1644) was a high-level scholar official who served during the King Kwanghaegun years. A harsh critic of those who opposed peace, he was present in Namhan Mountain Fortress and supported surrender to the Manchu during the invasion. He was the older brother of Yi Min'gu.

Yu Sŏk (1595–1655) was a passionate scholar official frequently censured for his petitions. He objected to the talks with the Qing. After 1637, he was one of a number of officials who attacked Kim Sanghŏn, for which he was criticized.

Yun Chip (1606–1637) was part of the anti-peace negotiations group. The court later sent him to the Manchu—where he was executed—along with O Talche to appease Hung Taiji.

Yun Pang (1563–1640) was a scholar official who served in some of the highest posts in the central government. He became a target of political attacks and was later exiled and then rehabilitated for the decisions he made during the invasion, such as appointing Kim Kyŏngjing as the strategic governing official for Kanghwa Island and mishandling the ancestral tablets of the state.

Manchu

Hung Taiji or *Abahai* (1592–1643) became the second Manchu leader in 1626 and led wars against neighboring tribes and states, including the Chosŏn dynasty in 1627. After he consolidated his rule over other Manchu princes in 1629, he expanded into Inner Mongolia and the Liaodong peninsula. By the 1630s he had proclaimed himself emperor of the Qing dynasty. Na Man'gap refers to him as the khan.

Ingguldai (1596–1648) was a superior military officer who first gained recognition in 1619 for his fighting abilities. After earning distinctions on the battlefield against the Ming, he served as the official in charge of procuring supplies and food for the army. He traveled to Korea in 1632 to request grain from King Injo and again to attend the funeral of Queen Inyŏl in 1635. He was one of the commanders during the 1636–1637 invasion.

Jirgalang (1599–1655) was a nobleman and the son of Nurhachi's younger brother. He was a military leader who fought against the Mongols in 1625, Korea in 1627, and a Ming-Chosŏn army in 1633. In the 1636–1637 invasion, he was entrusted with the protection of Mukden.

Mafuta (?–1640) was a leading general who campaigned in Korea during the 1636–1637 invasion.

The *ninth prince* was Prince Dorgon (1612–1650). He was the Manchu commander who captured Kanghwa Island. He was the fourteenth son of Nurhachi and the younger brother of Hung Taiji.

Omoktu (1614–1662) was a scholar and warrior who was well trained as a classical official in Mukden. He served as the recordkeeper for the tribute that Korea submitted to the Manchu.

Prince Mingda (dates unknown) was a military leader whom Na Man'gap believed to be Manchu nobility. He befriended Korean army commander Sin Kyŏngwŏn after capturing him on the battlefield.

The *tenth prince* was most likely Prince Dodo (1614–1649), the fifteenth son of Nurhachi, brother of Hung Taiji. He led the campaign in China against the rebel leader Li Zicheng and captured Beijing in 1644.

Chinese

Geng Zhongming (?–1649) was a Ming military officer skilled at naval warfare who defected to the Manchu. Na Man'gap refers to him as "General Geng."

Huang Sunmao (?–1637) was a Ming army officer who brought the message to the Chosŏn court that encouraged Korea to resist the Manchu in 1637.

Kong Youde (?–1652) led a life similar to that of Geng Zhongming. He was a military official adept at naval warfare who defected to the Manchu. Na refers to him as "General Kong."

Shen Shikui (?–1637) was a Ming soldier who occupied Pido Island in northwest Korea.

Zhang Chun (?–1641) was a Ming official captured by the Manchu in 1631. He died of an illness in Mukden.

Zu Dashou (1579–1656) was a Ming officer who defended the Jinzhou Command against a combined Manchu and Chosŏn attack. He was famous for his extended resistance against the Manchu.

TRANSLATOR'S NOTE

Readers of the diary might be overwhelmed by the tangle of official titles Na Man'gap so easily and readily throws around. Titles are fluid. Scholar officials frequently shuffled posts, and modern readers will be tasked to follow all of the official positions that appear. What to make of all these titles? These titles were important to Na. They would have been easily comprehended by officials like himself and other Chosŏn-era readers as they convey status and rank within the Chosŏn bureaucracy. The original literary Chinese expressions for these titles are usually three to five characters in length. Rather than reinvent English equivalents for these titles, I have mostly adopted them from existing comprehensive lists of titles translated by scholars much more capable than me, from such sources as Harvard University's *Korean History Gloss* compilation, Brother Anthony's list of government offices and posts, and the English translation glossaries of the *Veritable Records of King Sejong* from the National Institute of Korean History, all cited in the bibliography. These titles, when rendered into English, are clunky and long, but I have left them in the diary to remain faithful to the original text.

Along with the many names of individuals and the titles, the diary is full of geographical particularities. Most of the action recorded in the diary takes place around the capital, Namhan Mountain Fortress, and Kanghwa Island. Chosŏn and Manchu armies fought mainly in the northwest, but with a few skirmishes in areas to the northeast. Some of these locations are well known to readers today, while the names of other locations mentioned in the diary have been lost. The invasion of 1636–1637 was one battle in a much longer and larger war. While the invasion took place in Korea, other battles before and after the invasion, some mentioned in the diary, were fought on islands and regions along the Chosŏn frontier or north of it in present-day China. Three maps are included to help readers imagine the geographical space of this conflict and visualize the scope of the Chosŏn-Manchu interaction as armies fought, hostages were seized, and envoys dispatched to distant lands. The many references to counties, villages, towns, and regions, all important to Na, are included to assist in charting the conflict.

The dramatis personae does not include all of the nearly one hundred Korean officials mentioned in the diary but focuses on a select few. They are grouped by social status, such as royalty and officials, and territory of origin, such as Chosŏn or Manchu. I fully understand the tension of identifying individuals outside of Korea based on the ethnic term "Manchu," knowing that this expression is newly coined. But this division of the dramatis personae helps modern readers understand that these people were not considered Korean or subjects of Chosŏn. The names of the Chosŏn royal family are listed according to frequency of appearance, while the other groups are listed alphabetically. A brief description of roles and ranks, along with important information gleaned mostly from the *Sillok*, the *Sŭngjŏngwŏn ilgi*, and *The Diary of 1636* itself, helps readers follow individuals through the many sections and interrelated stories of the diary. I relied upon biographies in Arthur Hummel's *Eminent Chinese of the Ch'ing*

Period, along with relevant information from the diary, to complete the brief descriptions of the Manchu; the *Sillok* and *The Diary of 1636* accounts were my sources for the handful of Ming Chinese.

Unless otherwise noted, the months and days in the translation remain faithful to the original. For ease of comprehension and comparison to other world events, the cyclical lunar years have been converted to solar years and placed in brackets where relevant. Thus, the cyclical year *pyŏngja* begins in the early year 1636 and ends in early 1637. I have used McCune-Reischauer to transcribe Korean names and words, and Pinyin for Chinese—the systems most widely adopted in academia and libraries around the world. Finally, I have tried to remain true to the original text, but, considering the arcane language and its often-ambiguous expressions, errors are sure to have arisen. I claim responsibility for any such mistakes in my work.

THE DIARY OF 1636

I n the early spring of the *pyŏngja* year [1636], Military Officer of the Sub-Prefect (*musin tongji*) Yi Kwak and Na Tŏkhŏn, a fifth minister (*ch'ŏmji*), traveled to Mukden as envoys (*ch'unsinsa*).[1] The eleventh day of the third lunar month was the day Hung Taiji of the Manchu Jin dynasty assumed the title of emperor.[2] The Manchu ordered the envoys, against their will, to take part in the congratulatory procession (*panyŏl*), but, risking death, they did not obey. The barbarian official seized Kwak and the others with force, damaging their clothes and caps, but the envoys never surrendered.[3] Among the Chinese people (*Hanin*), there were those who shed tears.[4]

When it was time for Kwak and the others to return to our country, Hung Taiji gave them a state letter. In this letter, Hung Taiji designated himself emperor.[5] Kwak and others took it, wrapped it in a black cloth, secretly put it in a sack, and reached Tongyuanpu.[6] Kwak made an excuse that his horse was ill and that the load was too heavy and left the sack [with the state letter] with the barbarian (*hoin*) guarding Tongyuanpu.[7]

Hong Myŏnggu, the provincial governor of P'yŏngan Province, blamed Kwak and the others for receiving the letter from

Hung Taiji in which he styled himself the emperor and not reprimanding him harshly on the spot. The fact that the envoys secretly left the letter on their way back was actually a conspired excuse to set themselves free of criminal charges. Hong thus requested the sword of Shangfang to sever the heads of Yi Kwak and the others and display them at the frontier.[8]

His Highness [King Injo] sent a royal report (*changgye*) to the Border Defense Command (*piguk*).[9] Kim Sanghŏn, the minister of personnel (*ijo p'ansŏ*), believed that Kwak and the others were guilty, but they did not deserve the death penalty. The Border Defense Command reported back to His Highness and referred only to capturing Yi Kwak and the others and bringing them back. His Highness agreed.

The Border Defense Command was well aware of their innocence. However, all kinds of opinions were then raised, and so they reported it that way. The Three Offices (Samsa) argued that they had to be punished according to the law, without exception.[10] The Confucian scholar (*kwanhak yusaeng*) Cho Pogyang and others petitioned the throne.[11] As for Chief State Councilor (Yŏngŭijŏng) Kim Yu, those of the Young faction (Yŏnso)—who stringently criticized him and advocated war (*chŏkhwa*)—followed him and wanted peace.[12] Among the high officials (*chinsin*), some thought that "although the Jin dynasty claimed the title emperor within their own country, our country only needs to maintain the brotherhood with them taken under oath during the *chŏngmyo* year [1627].[13] They dare to overreach by assuming the title of emperor. How can this event even matter to us? If we do not properly estimate the strength of our military and abandon the oath of alliance with the Manchu, it could incite death and deep misfortune." Even though some truly thought this way, no one dared to open his mouth.

This year, at the end of spring, Ingguldai and Mafuta, two Manchu generals, arrived for the funerary ceremony of Queen Inyŏl. The tenth prince of the Jin dynasty (*sibwangja*) dispatched a diplomatic letter to His Highness.[14] It explained the claim to the title of emperor and stated the hope that peace should not end. It also mentioned the crimes of Yi Kwak and others for not being respectful when attending the congratulatory celebration. This was indeed how the Manchu probed our intentions and attempted to use military force.

This plot was very intriguing. But the court (*chojŏng*) appointed such inappropriate people as Yi Myŏng, Pak No, and others to host the Manchu envoys. Yi Myŏng and the others grew aware of the potential misfortune of this appointment, but they feared offending the common consensus. Whenever they dealt with the barbarian envoys, they always treated them poorly and deliberately slighted them. A Mongol, whom the two generals brought, was a person who recently swore allegiance to the Jin dynasty. He intended to make our country treat him hospitably as he thought this was a land of exaggerated power. But the court did not approve. They treated him in a manner similar to his host barbarians [the Manchu] in order to disappoint him. In addition, the court said that the subordinate [the tenth prince of Jin] could not dispatch this diplomatic letter to His Highness. In the end, the letter from the tenth prince remained unopened.

Once, during the funeral services of Queen Dowager Inmok (Inmok *taebi*), a barbarian general paid a condolence visit.[15] At that time, he was allowed to enter the royal palace and offer sacrifices. But this time, the court offered the excuse that the palace was too crowded, so they separately set up an empty tent across Kŭmch'ŏn Bridge where the Manchu could conduct sacrifices and express their condolences.[16]

Then the wind blew, and the tent lifted up. Ingguldai and the others started to realize the deception and grew angry. Moreover, governmental, arquebus soldiers (*togam p'osu*) were secretly practicing in the rear garden on this day, and they all assembled below the palace gate.[17] At the same time, the royal security guards were rotating shifts. Because the barbarian envoy was at the palace gate, each one grasped his weapon, and all stood behind the flap. When the wind lifted up the tent flap, Ingguldai and the others looked out. They were suspicious of an ambush and departed in haste.

At this time, Third Inspector of the Office of the Inspector General (*changnyŏng*) Hong Ikhan reported to His Highness, petitioning for the beheading of the envoys and others. The Confucian students (*kwanhak*) reported to His Highness the second time, petitioning for the beheading of the envoys.

The barbarian generals and others became aware of these schemes. They also grew suspicious and fearful, so they tore down the city gate and walked out. They scattered, broke into the homes of the villagers, stole their horses, and ran off. Those in the paths and roads who witnessed this were shocked and frightened, and the children at the village gates and alleyways (*yŏhang*) fell over each other in their eagerness to throw stones at them. The capital grew clamorous.

Only then did the court begin to fear. Timidly, the court officials dispatched high-ranking courtiers (*chaesin*); these courtiers proceeded one by one along the road, begging the barbarian generals to stay, but, in the end, they did not return.[18] His Highness issued a royal proclamation to the eight provinces to reject peace. The royal order that proceeded along the western road was seized by the barbarian generals and they came to grasp the extent of its message.

The court thought the event—when Yi Kwak and the others secretly left the letter from Hung Taiji on their way back behind in Zhongdao—had not been publicized, so they made the royal messenger (*sŏnjŏn'gwan*) take to Mansang the letter in which they denounced Mukden.[19] That the court criticized Mukden meant letting the Manchu learn about this event [that Kwak and the others did not purposely bring back the letter]. Afterwards, His Highness repeatedly issued royal edicts of regret, and through selfless loyalty (*ch'ungŭi*), he strove to convey his hatred of the enemy.

From near and far, appeals poured in daily. Every one of them called for war and attacking the barbarians.

Censor General (*taesagan*) Yun Hwang reported to His Highness, requesting the reduction of royal exactions (*ŏgong*), the removal of music from the temple (*myoak*), the burning of the palace (*haenggung*) on Kanghwa Island (Kangdo), and a sole commitment to war.[20] Vice–Minister of Personnel (*ijo ch'amp'an*) Chŏng On reported to His Highness, calling for the military garrisoning of Songdo.[21] Third Minister (*ch'amŭi*) Kim Tŏkham requested the garrisoning of P'yŏngyang. These requests were to excite the military leaders.

At this time, natural disasters and unusual events took place. The rocks of Pup'yŏng and Ansan shifted. The mallards of Yŏngnam and Kwansŏ fought each other. The cranes of Taegu grouped for battle. The frogs of Ch'ŏngp'a went to war. The toads of Chungnyŏng marched in procession. The streams of Yean ran dry. Lightning struck Two Hills (Yangnŭng), and the soil of the capital turned red.[22] About twenty-seven locations shook violently throughout one day in the capital. A great flood suddenly appeared. The road to the east gate was washed out. The three royal palaces (*samgwŏl*) shook simultaneously. A white rainbow threaded the sun, and celestial portents appeared.[23] These events all happened in a single year.

But Chief State Councilor (*yŏngŭijŏng*) Kim Yu, Left State Councilor (*chwaŭijŏng*) Hong Sŏbong, and Right State Councilor (*uŭijŏng*) Yi Hongju were eminent officers at the court. It was not clear if peace negotiations would be successful, so attacking and defense had yet to be discussed. Supreme Commander of War (*ch'ech'alsa*) Kim Yu submitted a petition that said, "If the barbarian enemy launches a deep invasion into the country, the supreme field commander (*towŏnsu*), the assistant supreme commander (*puwŏnsu*), and the provincial high commissioner (*pangbaek*) of Yangsŏ must face collective family punishment (*noryuk*) according to the law."[24] His Highness's instructions were that it would be difficult for the supreme commander of war to avoid serious punishment. Kim Yu originally advocated war, but now, after receiving His Highness's warnings, he advocated peace.

The time for autumn defense preparation (*ch'ubang*) drew near.[25] Ch'oe Myŏnggil requested the dispatch of a peace envoy. Fifth Counselor (*kyori*) O Talche and Section Chief of Personnel (*ijo chŏngnang*) Yun Chip petitioned the throne, demanding the beheading of Ch'oe Myŏnggil. The petition by Third Censor (*hŏnnap*) Yi Ilsang spoke of such things as betraying the Heavenly Court (*Ch'ŏnjo*) and deceiving the people.[26] Popular opinion (*siron*) called for war and agreed that the establishment of tributary relations with the Jin was erroneous. There were no dissenters.

The court showed an ambiguous attitude toward these two views and did not offer a proposal. Then Kim Yu came to agree with Ch'oe Myŏnggil's view. Later, he sent a low-level interpreter (*soyŏk*) to Mukden in order to explore the intention of the enemy.[27] The Three Offices jointly demanded that the interpreter not leave, but they failed to halt the debate, and the interpreter was dispatched by royal decree.

The Manchu Jin [Hung Taiji] spoke to the interpreter, saying, "If your country does not send us a high official and the king's son and agree to peace before the eleventh lunar month, the twenty-fifth day, then I will immediately raise a great army and invade the east by force."

His response letter stated,

> Your distinguished country has constructed many mountain fortresses, but as I pass along the main road toward the capital, can these mountain fortresses block me? Your honorable country puts its trust in Kanghwa Island, but as I ravage along the roads throughout the land, can you turn this small island into a country?[28] Those who argue for war in your honorable country

are Confucian officials, but can they wield their brushes and fend me off?

The interpreter returned and conveyed this message and the written letter. The court intended to dispatch the prime minster (*chaesang*), but the argument for war still dominated, and no one dared to say clearly that the envoy should go. After a long time, the court ordered Pak No to depart, while officials of the censorate (*taegan*) argued strongly against sending him and persisted with their disapproval for a time. They were finally forced to dispatch Pak No, but he had already missed the deadline the Manchu Jin [Hung Taiji] had set.

At this time, Yi Sibaek was the defense commander (*suŏsa*) of Namhan Mountain Fortress (Namhan sansŏng). Sibaek's father Kwi and Kim Yu did not get along with each other. None of the defense issues regarding Namhan was approved by Yu. The soldiers among the troops defending the fortress were all deployed from Yŏngnam. In case of urgency, how could people from such a distance come in time?

Since the time of the ancestral kings of the royal court, they had put in place important towns at strategic locations to ward off the enemy and defend the country. In recent times, Kim Yu and Supreme Field Commander Kim Chajŏm took the lead in pleading for the redeployment [of troops from towns to nearby mountain fortresses]. As a consequence, Ŭiju redeployed to Paengma, P'yŏngyang redeployed to Chamo, Hwangju redeployed to Chŏngbang, and P'yŏngsan redeployed to Changsu.[29] Among them, the relatively close one was roughly thirty or forty *li* away from the main road, whereas it took one or two days to journey to the distant ones. The large towns of the two western regions (*yangsŏ iltae*) had become uninhabited.[30]

At that time, Area Commander (*todok*) Sim Segoe of Kado Island notified the Ming court about the intention of our country to go to war [with the Manchu Jin].[31] In the autumn of that year, the Ming sent Army Inspecting Censor Huang Sunmao to offer praise and honor to our country.[32] When he returned to Kwansŏ, he issued a report to the Chosŏn court.[33] It read, "Despite observing the will of your people and the military preparations of your distinguished country, you will never be able to deal with those Manchu bandits. Do not end up conciliating with the Manchu only because of this praise and honor from the Ming court."

Unexpectedly, Kim Chajŏm was given the important responsibility of supreme field commander (ch'ugok).[34] However, he did not comfort the soldiers. He enslaved the commoners, levying them to build defenses. Moreover, he used punishment to impose his prestige. Gradually, he lost much of the will of the people. He constantly said, "The enemy is certainly not coming this winter." If someone said that the enemy was coming, he would grow infuriated. If someone said that the enemy was not coming, he would be pleased. Therefore, those under him were reluctant to say that the enemy was coming. The time for winter defense preparation had already passed, but the troops that defended the fortresses had not been reinforced even by a single man.

Along the ridge of Yonggol Mountain at Ŭiju are fire beacons [to signal the start of an invasion].[35] Lighting one torch means there is no activity. Two torches mean the enemy has appeared. Three torches mean they have crossed the frontier. Four torches mean they approach for battle. Starting from Yonggol and ending at Chŏngbang, where the commander-in-chief is stationed, the fire beacons seem to reach the capital. Fear would turn into chaos, so any disturbance must be stopped here.

On the sixth day of the twelfth lunar month, two torches were lit, but Kim Chajŏm said, "This just means that the dispatched Pak No must have been greeted by the barbarians. How can this mean that the enemy is approaching?" Hence, he did not notify the king promptly.

On the ninth day of the twelfth lunar month, Kim Chajŏm dispatched the military official (*kun'gwan*) Sin Yong to Ŭiju to examine the situation. The next day, Sin Yong arrived in Sunan, and the enemy's horses (*ma*) were swarming all over the district capital (*ŭmnae*).[36] Immediately, Sin Yong turned around and rode back, reporting this situation to Provincial Governor (*kamsa*) of P'yŏngan Province Hong Myŏnggu. Myŏnggu did not know about the situation of the enemy either, and when he learned about it, he grew alarmed and rode alone to Chamo Fortress. Sin Yong returned and reported what he had witnessed to Kim Chajŏm, but the commander-in-chief scolded him by saying that his nonsense would upset the military situation (*kunjŏng*) and proclaimed he would behead Yong.

Yong said, "The enemy troops will arrive here tomorrow. Do not behead me. Please wait." Before long, the military official (*kun'gwan*) who was sent in pursuit returned again and made an urgent announcement, corroborating Yong's story. Only then did the supreme commander submit a royal report.

Virtually all the enemy troops crossed the river and ignored the fortresses and towns. Arriving like the wind (*p'yop'ung*), they moved directly to call for peace terms (*kanghwa*). All the reports (*changgye*) of the officials at the frontier had been completely captured by the enemy, so the court was unaware of the circumstances along the frontier.

DAILY RECORDS AFTER URGENT
REPORTS FROM THE FRONTIER

I n the *pyŏngja* year [1637], twelfth day, twelfth lunar month, in the afternoon, the official report regarding the Manchu invasion from the supreme field commander [Kim Chajŏm] reached the court. After that, the court began to learn about the urgent threat posed by the enemy's strength. In addition, the court had not known about the swiftness of the Manchu until now.[1]

O n the thirteenth day of the twelfth lunar month, the decision from the court was about departing for Kanghwa Island. The court appointed Kim Kyŏngjing as the prosecuting official (*kŏmch'alsa*) of Kanghwa Island and Yi Min'gu as the district magistrate (*pusa*), and the reappointed (*kibok*) official Sim Kiwŏn was made capital defense general (*yudo taejang*).[2] At first, Right State Councilor Yi Hongju recommended Kyŏngjing. Kim Yu did not know that his own son [Kim Kyŏngjing] was unqualified and so did not interfere with this appointment. After receiving his Highness's instructions, Kim Yu praised his son. Sim Kiwŏn elevated himself from a straw mat and a dirt pillow (*ch'ot'o*).[3] There was not a single soldier under his command. What could be done?

On the fourteenth day of the twelfth lunar month, the enemy troops had already reached the outskirts of the capital. The royal palanquin (*taega*) departed in a flurry. In the afternoon, it left through Great South Gate (Namdaemullu), intending to head toward Kanghwa Island, but the barbarian general (*hojang*) Mafuta commanded several hundred armored cavalry (*ch'ŏlgi*) and had already reached Hongjewŏn. His Highness had to turn back. He entered the fortress [of the city] and governed from a tower in the Great South Gate. High and low [all the officers at the court] hurried around, and there was none who knew what had happened. The elite (*sadaebu*) of the capital held the old by the arm and the young by the hand (K. *puro hyuyu*, C. *fulao xieyou*). The sound of weeping packed the roads.

Minister of Personnel (*ijo p'ansŏ*) Ch'oe Myŏnggil, petitioning His Highness, volunteered to see Mafuta, the barbarian general, but His Highness dispatched Government General (*togam taejang*) Sin Kyŏngjin to go to battle at Mohwagwan. That morning, Military Guard Officer (*togam changgwan*) Yi Hŭngŏp was first dispatched with roughly eighty cavalry units to go and confront the enemy. As they were saying their farewells and leaving, they drank too much of the rice wine bestowed by His Highness and the farewell drinks from their relatives and friends. From the guard officer (*changgwan*) on down, there was no one who was not intoxicated. They arrived at the hills of Ch'angnŭng and climbed toward the frontier. The enemy annihilated them, and only a few survived.

It was a two-day journey to Kanghwa Island. Fearing that enemy cavalry pursued closely, the royal palanquin instead entered Namhan Mountain Fortress (Namhan sansŏng) through Sugumun.[4] Ch'oe Myŏnggil went to see Mafuta and asked how his troops could have crossed the border and invaded so far. Then Mafuta replied arrogantly, "Because your distinguished country disobeyed the oath without any just reason, I have come here to make a peace treaty."

Ch'oe circled back around, entered the capital to stop and lodge for the night, and then reported the intention of Mafuta to His Highness at his residence. Everyone wondered if the rumor about concluding a peace treaty with Mafuta was true. Only His Highness alone considered it not so. Supreme Commander of War Kim Yu, Minister of Military Affairs (*pusa pyŏngjo p'ansŏ*) Yi Sŏnggu, and others asked for a secret meeting. At dawn, under the cover of darkness, they intended for His Highness to covertly enter Kanghwa Island. Director of the Office of Royal Decrees (*taejehak*) Yi Sik asked to go to Inch'ŏn and to sail by sea to moor at Kanghwa Island. While at court, they met to discuss how to move the king [relocating him to somewhere more secure than the mountain fortress]. However, among the old and young who had entered the fortress, there was no one who knew how this could be accomplished.

At daybreak on the fifteenth day of the twelfth lunar month, His Highness left the fortress. After heavy snow fell, the mountain slopes were frozen over. The servants attending the royal palanquin slipped and fell. His Highness dismounted his horse and began to walk, and numerous times he completely lost his footing and fell, hitting his head on the ground. His Highness's royal body (*okch'e*) was not at ease. He turned back to Namhan Fortress.

Government General (*togam taejang*) Sin Kyŏngjin arrived at the fortress from the capital. He was appointed to defend the eastern fortress of Mangwŏltae. Yi Hyŏndal became chief military officer (*chunggun*). Guarding General (*howi taejang*) Ku Koeng was put in defense of the Southern Fortress (Namsŏng). District Magistrate (*pusa*) of Suwŏn Ku Inhu reinforced the troops under his command from his headquarters (*ponbu*). Yi Kwak was reappointed and made chief military officer (*chunggun*); General (*taejang*) of Ch'ongyung Yi Sŏ was put in defense of the Northern Fortress (Puksŏng); Defense Commander (*suŏsa*) Yi Sibaek was put in defense of the Western Fortress (Sŏsŏng); and Yi Chik was made the chief military officer, the supreme commander of war (*ch'ech'alsa*).

The troops protecting Yŏngnam were divided up for the defense of the mountain fortress the previous day, but it was too far away, and they could not arrive in time. The supreme commander of war [Kim Yu] ordered the defense of the capital and divided the battlement of Namhan Fortress. He ordered Magistrate (*moksa*) of Yŏju Han P'irwŏn, District Magistrate (*pusa*) of Ich'ŏn Cho Myŏnguk, Country Magistrate (*kunsu*) Yanggŭn Han Hoeil, and Lesser Prefecture Magistrate (*hyŏn'gam*) Arbitrator (*chip'yŏng*) Pak Hwan to lead some sentries and enter the fortress. However, more than half the soldiers could not arrive. Excluding the divided battlements of the four districts, Magistrate of P'aju Ki Chonghyŏn led several hundred troops, entered the fortress, and assisted those inside.

Inside the walls of the capital, the outer army [from the surrounding region] numbered around twelve thousand men. The civil and military officials (*munmu*) and lesser irregular officials (*san'gwan*) numbered two hundred men. Members of the royal family (*chongsil*) and the Three Medical Bureaus (Samŭisa) numbered approximately two hundred men. The government officials (*hari*) numbered one hundred men. The slaves (*nobok*), who were commanded by attending officials (*hojonggwan*), numbered three hundred. Ch'oe Myŏnggil and Yi Kyŏngjik arrived from Hongjewŏn and said,

Mafuta is set on peace negotiations. He is leading his army and has reached Samjŏndo. The wind is blowing, and the weather is extremely cold. The troops were allowed to enter and lodge in the homes of the commoners. But Mafuta said, "Before a peace treaty is made, we must not enter [the homes of commoners], even though our troops are exposed to the wind and snow." Judging from his appearance and his words, they showed no other meaning.

The court believed Ch'oe's words.

O n the sixteenth day of the twelfth lunar month, after their morning meal, the enemy troops arrived in great numbers and laid siege to the fortress. There was no longer any communication in or out [of the mountain fortress].[5] Because the main forces had not yet arrived, Mafuta used sweet words to deceive us. When the enemy troops first arrived, there were few of them. They had come far on icy roads, so their appearances were like those of ghosts. All of their horses were fatigued. If we had taken advantage of them at this moment, we could have prevailed. Instead, we urgently entered the fortress and divided up the battlements. All the weak generals trembled with fear and did not dare come out to fight.

Mafuta requested the dispatch of the crown prince [Crown Prince Sohyŏn (1612–1645)] and a high-ranking minister (taesin) to Mukden as hostages. The court made Yi—who was the defender of Nŭngbong (Nŭngbongsu)—the prince (kun), while Minister of Punishments (hyŏngjo p'ansŏ) Sim Chip was given the false title of a high minister. They were sent out to the barbarian lines. Sim said, "Throughout my life, I have been loyal and truthful. Even though they are savage barbarians, I cannot deceive them." To Mafuta, he said, "I am not a high-ranking official and have only been given a false title. The Nŭngbong royal clansman is not the crown prince." "Prince" Nŭngbong said, "What Sim Chip says is wrong. Really, he is a high official and I am really the crown prince." Pak No and Pak Nanyŏng traveled toward Mukden. On the way, they were detained by Mafuta and taken to the frontlines.

Mafuta asked Pak Nanyŏng, "What do you have to say about this?" He replied, "What Nŭngbong says is correct." Later, Mafuta learned about this deception. Because of Pak Nanyŏng's lie, Mafuta beheaded him. "Prince" Nŭngbong and Sim Chip turned back and returned to the fortress.

On that day, His Highness had to send Left State Councilor Hong Sŏbong and Minister of Taxation Kim Sin'guk to the frontlines to convey a message. "Between the two royal sons (*taegun*), Grand Prince Pongnim and Grand Prince Inp'yŏng, one will be dispatched.[6] But they reside on Kanghwa Island [Kangdo], hence they have not yet been sent." Then Mafuta said, "If the crown prince does not come, then there cannot be peace."[7] Hong Sŏbong and the others returned with no result.

Day after day, His Highness toured the fortress. On this day, I petitioned His Highness, telling him,

Mafuta the barbarian first requested a peace treaty be made by our dispatching one prince (*wangja*). Now, again he asks that we dispatch the crown prince (*tonggung*). He is deceitful in hundreds of ways. How can this be the real intention of peace? He must be waiting for reinforcements from Mukden. As for their demand of dispatching the crown prince, how can we courtiers bear to hear this? If all of these are carried out, for us as your subordinates, I would rather die than live so humbly. I would rather shatter my head in front of the royal palanquin. Now, if we take advantage of the enemy as they have arrived from a great distance, and they are fatigued and weak, our troops can be dispatched to attack them at this moment, and then we can possibly defeat them. Because the troops of our country resist confrontation, when they see the enemy, they are the first to get cold feet. But if they engage in combat and are triumphant, then all of the soldiers will come to feel that the enemy is not difficult to overcome. One victory leads to another, and their morale will double. In China if a soldier presents one left ear of the enemy, he will be rewarded with fifty *nyang* of silver.[8] This is why the Ming soldiers forgot about their own bodies [sacrificed themselves] while attacking the enemy during the Imjin invasion. Right now, money is scarce inside the fortress, but Yi Sŏ has carried in around eight thousand *nyang* of silver. Now, we can use this money, the ten *nyang* of silver for each left ear of the enemy.[9] For those who refuse the money, we can confer on them the rank of officer to reward their merits. If we recruit troops based on this reward, how could it be that there are none that are brave?

His Highness conveyed his thoughts to the supreme commander of war [Kim Yu]. Kim Yu said, "The soldiers defending the fortress are weak. What if they fight and lose? This is not a safe plan." There were no military generals who were not afraid, only those spending their days with flowing tears and deep sighs. They all thought what I suggested was poorly conceived. But His Highness rejected various counter-proposals and ordered that twenty *nyang* of silver be given for each left ear of a slain enemy to recruit those who would want to earn this money. Everyone vied with one another to enlist. That evening, the left state councilor, along with Kim Sin'guk, Yi Sŏnggu, Ch'oe Myŏnggil, Prince Sinbung, Chang Yu, the official (*sajae*) Han Yŏjik, Vice-Minister (*ch'amp'an*) Yun Hwi, and Hong Pang arrived. They presented a petition asking to dispatch the crown prince to the enemy. Moreover, they asked us to officially submit ourselves as subordinates to the Jin and Emperor Hung Taiji. His Highness did not follow these suggestions.

Minister of Rites (*yejo p'ansŏ*) Kim Sanghŏn heard about this discussion. He went before the Border Defense Command and shouted, "I will sever the heads of those who propose these views. I swear that I cannot live under the same sky with them!"

Kim Yu, beginning to realize his mistake, promptly visited the palace and awaited his punishment. Yi Sŏ was unable to defend the fortress due to an illness. So, Wŏnp'yŏng was assigned to be the deputy general of the royal guard units (*ŏyŏng pusa*). Hwang Chŭp became the chief military officer.

On the seventeenth day of the twelfth lunar month, His Highness came out through the royal gate, ordered all the high and low court officials to assemble around him, and conveyed a sad message to them. He ordered the release of all of the criminals from the serious ones on down. Among all the court officials, there was none that did not cry out bitterly. His Highness said, "If there is anyone who has something inside him aching to be expressed, do not hold it back."

His Highness held an audience with Kwangsu, the son of Sim Aek, and Kwangsu requested the beheading of Ch'oe Myŏnggil for being a criminal of the country. His Highness did not reply. Except for several among the court officials, everyone was afraid. They were at a loss about what to do and grew pale. On the day when he was supposed to enter the fortress, army officer (*pyŏngsa*) Yi Chin'gyŏng made up an excuse that he had fallen from his horse and suffered a stroke (*chungp'ung*). He fell behind and did not enter the fortress. It was well known that people at that time treated entering the fortress as a death sentence.

On the eighteenth day of the twelfth lunar month, the general of the north gate, Wŏn Tup'yo, began mustering the troops he had recruited to battle. They killed six enemy soldiers. Even though they only killed a few, the troops felt like fighting with the enemy with confidence. On this day, I was summoned to the court and was appointed officer in charge of provisions (*kwallyangsa*). In the storehouse, all of the grain, rice, and millet (*p'ijapkok*) I observed amounted to about sixteen thousand *sŏm*.[10] This equaled merely one month of food for approximately ten thousand soldiers. Yi Sŏ was the Namhan Fortress defense commander (*suŏsa*), and he tried hard to store sufficient military provisions. After he fell ill and turned over the position, Han Myŏngok, the magistrate of Kwangju, thought that transporting the provisions into the mountain fortress was a nuisance (*minp'ye*). Instead, he set up an armored storehouse on the bank of the river, and all the military provisions were stored in this granary or in the old city granary. But now enemy soldiers had seized them all. All the provisions in the fortress came from what Yi Sŏ had stockpiled on the previous day. Items such as salt, soybean paste, paper, cotton, weapons, and other miscellaneous items were likewise rapidly prepared by Sŏ to be transported into the fortress. All the essential items depended upon Sŏ's every effort. Compared to all the strategies and plans prepared by other generals, his were barely satisfactory. All the people in the fortress called Sŏ an official who always served for the sake of the state altars. Those who used to point out his weaknesses now called him someone who sacrificed himself for the country. Their praise was endless.

On the nineteenth day of the twelfth lunar month, Ku Koeng, the general (*ch'ongyungsa*), left the fortress, recruited troops, and killed approximately twenty enemy soldiers. The military officer (*kun'gwang*) Yi Sŏngik advanced and fought, gaining glory. His Highness immediately elevated Yi's rank. This day, high winds blew like it was going to rain. Kim Sanghŏn was ordered to sacrifice to the town god (*sŏnghwang*). After this, the wind immediately died down and the rain never poured.

On the twentieth day of the twelfth lunar month, Mafuta dispatched the barbarian interpreter Chŏng Myŏngsu and requested that he conclude a peace treaty.[11] His Highness summoned Kim Yu and asked if he should or should not reply. I was also summoned to give an answer. Kim Yu said, "You should open the gate and dispatch an important official." I replied, "The day when you defend the fortress, do not open the gate. If Your Highness painstakingly negotiates for peace now, then the morale of the soldiers will certainly fall. Your Highness can randomly ask those soldiers in the fortress to glean their replies." His Highness followed my suggestion. He sent a messenger to plant a rumor in the fortress, instead of asking around and collecting answers. Royal Messenger (*sŏnjŏn'gwan*) Min Chinik was ordered to go to Ch'ungch'ŏng Province. He was able to enter the besieged fortress from the rear. His Highness bestowed upon him greater wealth and higher rank. On this day, Min received another order and left the fortress.

On the twenty-first day of the twelfth lunar month, Special Royal Commander (*ŏyŏng pyŏlchang*) Yi Kich'uk led troops out the western gate of the fortress. They killed roughly ten enemy soldiers. Also, from the eastern gate of the fortress, Sin Kyŏngjin dispatched some troops. An attack ensued in which they killed enemy troops.

On the twenty-second day of the twelfth lunar month, Mafuta again dispatched an interpreter, saying, "From this day forward, you do not have to send the crown prince. If one prince and a high-ranking minister can be dispatched, we can conduct peace negotiations." His Highness still did not permit it. The royal guards (*yŏyŏnggun*) from the north gate killed approximately ten enemy soldiers. Sin Kyŏngjin from the eastern side of the fortress also killed roughly thirty people. So far, the killed enemy soldiers numbered one hundred. Among our country's soldiers, deaths did not exceed five or six men. Those injured by arrows amounted to seven or eight. His Highness rewarded with food and drink the military in the court.

On the twenty-third lunar day of the twelfth lunar month, the soldiers of the four garrisons came out of the fortress to engage in battle, and His Highness appeared at the north gate to encourage them to fight. Each one of the four garrisons killed some of the enemy; the garrison at the north gate killed the most. Some of our soldiers were injured, but only a few were killed. Though some were killed in the battle, the barbarian enemy had a rule that first prize would be awarded to the soldier who collected the most fallen comrades from the battlefield. For this reason, dead barbarians [entire bodies] were removed intact with no left ear cut off or collected. At the moment of the battle, it was well known that the same reward would be given to the soldier who killed an enemy as to the one who collected a left ear, since the royal guards collected only the left ear from the enemy and dedicated it to the military government by hanging it high on the top of the military gate, and that was why all the people in the fortress laughed at them [the bodies] who were left out in the cold.

On the twenty-fourth day of the twelfth lunar month, the rain did not let up. On top of the fortress, all the defenders were drenched in the pouring rain, and there was a concern as to whether or not they would die from the cold. His Highness and the crown prince stood together and pleaded verbally to heaven. "We have reached this situation. Is it because we, the father and the son, have committed crimes? If so, how could a fortress of soldiers and commoners be blamed? If heaven would condemn, condemn us, the father and the son. We plead with you to ensure the livelihoods of all of the commoners!" Their tears were shed, completely dampening their clothes, as they uttered these words. Their servants asked if they could enter, but they were not allowed. After quite some time had passed, the rain stopped. In the middle of the night, the Milky Way shone brilliantly. Also, the temperature gradually improved. All the people of the fortress were moved, crying intensely. Finally, no one among the troops defending the fortress had any feelings of disloyalty. This was because what His Highness had pleaded to heaven really touched them and was well received by the people. It was amazing to see how deeply awareness can penetrate people.

O n the twenty-fifth day of the twelfth lunar month, it turned extremely cold. The court intended to dispatch an envoy to the enemy camp. I then entered the discussion, saying, "On the previous day, the barbarians requested we dispatch someone to undertake peace negotiations, and we did not reply. Now, if we were to first send an envoy for no reason at all, then those barbarians would say that our soldiers began to freeze and grew hungry after the rain began falling, and this would have turned our situation into extreme distress, so we dispatched our envoy to request negotiations. We should not have revealed this weakness." All the courtiers said it was correct to send an envoy, except for Kim Sin'guk, who agreed with me. His Highness asked about an envoy, and even the Border Defense Command requested the dispatch of one.

His Highness said,

Our country has always been deceived and humiliated when we have negotiated [with the Manchu]. As for dispatching an envoy at this time, we could be humiliated again. But the opinions of various people support it, so I am compelled to do so. The Lunar New Year is approaching. I will send oxen and alcohol [to the

Manchu as gifts]. Also, fill small silver bowls to their brims with fruit and send them, reminding them of old times' sake. Carry out conversations with them and pay attention to their countenances.

On the twenty-sixth day of the twelfth lunar month, Kim Sin'guk and Yi Kyŏngjik took oxen, alcohol, and silver bowls to the enemy camp. The enemy said, "We catch our own oxen and drink alcohol every day in our military camps. These treasures pile up as high as mountains, so what are we going to do with these things you brought us? The king of your country and his officials have retreated to a stone cavern [the mountain fortress] and have been starving for a long time. Take these items back, and your people should use them." They did not accept the gifts, turned these officials around, and sent them back. It was the day our king was humiliated, and our officials were killed.

On the twenty-seventh day of the twelfth lunar month, we waited each day in the fortress for reinforcements to arrive. However, it remained silent, with no word or people. When night fell, everyone in the fortress climbed up to the top of the wall and looked in every direction.

Provincial Governor of Kangwŏn Cho Chŏngho, making an excuse that the provincial army had not all been mustered, withdrew his troops that had been heading toward Yanggŭn and waited for the soldiers left behind. He dispatched Chief Commander (*yŏngjang*) Kwŏn Chŏnggil to lead the troops, ascend Kŏmdan Mountain, and respond by torches. Magistrate of Wŏnju Yi Chunggil made an appeal that he would die for the country at any moment. His Highness appointed Yi to a higher rank and had those in the fortress celebrate. After a few days, Yi Chunggil was defeated by the enemy, and his troops fell and scattered. The appeal of Chunggil ended as a futile assurance, and nothing substantial came of it. After Yi left the fortress, he was captured, and the court stripped him of his rank.

O n the twenty-eighth day of the twelfth lunar month, several fortune-tellers (*sulsa*) entered the fortress. They all said, "Today is an auspicious day for either peace negotiations or fighting." Commander of War Kim Yu believed their words. He would ask for peace negotiations as well as call for fighting the enemy. I spoke to Field Commander (*ch'anhoeksa*) Pak Hwang, saying, "If you want to order an attack, then attack. If you want to order peace negotiations, then carry them out. But on the same day, how can you negotiate peace while attacking? This is akin to singing and crying at the same time; it is impossible."

At this moment, the commander of war personally led the generals and troops north toward the fortress to supervise the battle. Below the fortress, along a winding canyon, the enemy cavalry was scattered, hiding here and there. When the enemy heard the cannons, they feigned retreat, leaving a few soldiers with some horses and oxen. The livestock were all old and sick—what had been robbed earlier from our country. This was the barbarians' master plan for luring out our troops, but the soldiers and commoners who watched this from atop the fortress shouted in unison, "If we come down from the fortress and fight on the fields, then we can come and capture all of those people and the horses and oxen on the enemy lines. Those sad soldiers who march north can also attack." The supreme commander of war did not think much about this and did not investigate it. Instead, he pressed his troops and had them descend below the fortress and assault the enemy. However, his soldiers held back, not wanting to leave, because our military on the fortress knew the enemy quite well and could anticipate the strategy of the enemy. The military clerk (*ch'ebu pyŏngbang pijang*) Yu Ho fawned over the commander's intentions. He said, "If we behead the retreating generals and kill anyone who hesitates, how can they not go forward to fight?"

The commander agreed and gave a sword to Yu Ho to punish those who did not fight. If Yu Ho should encounter someone [a soldier unwilling to fight], he was to lash out violently without question. All the troops felt that they would surely die, either by remaining in the fortress or when going down the mountain to fight. So, they began descending from the fortress. This was when Special Commander Sin Sŏngnip said farewell to the others forever. Our soldiers descended the mountain fortress and took back the enemy camp housing the horses and oxen. The enemy pretended not to notice our troops. Not until our soldiers had all descended did the enemy's ambush suddenly spring. All those who had withdrawn returned. Within a moment, our troops were completely massacred.

At first, someone said that if one set the pinewood barricades on fire, our soldiers could advance without any obstacle. The commander immediately set fire to them. As for these pinewood barricades, after the enemy besieged the fortress, they cut down the trees from near and far and lined them up outside the fortress for about eighty *li*.[12] They tied the pinewood together with rope and hung iron plates on them. If someone tried to approach, it would make noise and alert the enemy. As for the inability to come and go from the fortress, it was because of these wooden blockades. Now that the north part of the pinewood barriers had been burned down, when the enemy attacked, our troops could depend on nothing impeding them. This was because there were no more wooden barriers.

In hand-to-hand combat, if you were provided with excessive gunpowder, then you could carelessly use it all up. If gunpowder was provided on a case-by-case basis, requests for more gunpowder [during hand-to-hand combat] could be heard here and there. When troops on both sides encountered each other and hand-to-hand combat ensued, there were no interludes requesting more gunpowder, only fighting with empty guns. Without gunpowder and bullets, the enemy could not be stopped. The mountain roads were very steep, so our troops could not ascend quickly while withdrawing to the fortress. In the end, our troops were annihilated. The supreme commander witnessed the defeat and the annihilation of our soldiers. He began to give orders to one company commander (*ch'ogwan*) to wave the flag and signal for retreat. However, the top and bottom parts of the fortress were separated by gates, which prevented the two halves from seeing each other. On top of that, all had suffered a complete massacre. In such a situation, how can one see a flag waving on top of the fortress? Yu Ho then told the commander again, "Our military hesitated and did not retreat because of the company commander. If you do not execute him, then the military situation will not improve." The commander immediately executed the company commander, but everyone regretted it.

Cho Yangch'ul, a person of extraordinary strength (*yŏksa*), made an enormous effort to shoot dead countless enemy soldiers. He survived nine arrows to his body while returning to the fortress.

The supreme commander said, "You fought but were defeated, and there is nobody else to blame." He pointed out that Commander of the North Fortress (*puksŏngjang*) Hong Tup'yo did not cooperate in the rescue and hence deserved harsh punishment. Left State Councilor Hong Sŏbong said, "The commander (*chujang*) erred, but the battalion commander was blamed. This is not correct." He defended Hong Tup'yo and tried to save him, but the supreme commander did not allow this. He ordered the guards to lay Hong Tup'yo down in front of the palace and await his punishment. Hong Tup'yo finally received eighty floggings by the central army, nearly beating him to death.

Crack troops, strong common soldiers, and brave warriors all gathered in front of the residence of the supreme commander, complaining, "There were no less than three hundred dead today; however, you, the supreme commander, disliked the true casualty report, so Yu Ho only reported a casualty number of forty. How could we tolerate this?" Special Royal Commander Sin Sŏngnip, Chi Hakhae, and Yi Wŏn'gil all died in this battle. Since then, the morale of the soldiers has fallen dramatically, and there was no longer any will to go out to fight. The court only thought about peace negotiations.

Capital Defense General (*yudo taejang*) Sim Kiwŏn wrote a report to the court, saying, "Third Minister of the Ministry of Taxation (*hojo ch'amŭi*) Nam Sŏn, the special royal commander (*ŏyŏng pyŏlchang*), and I took approximately three hundred and seventy cannon soldiers and assaulted the enemy stationed in the vicinity of Kyŏnggi Governor Sŏ Kyŏngu's house on the ridge of Agogae.[13] There were roughly four or five hundred enemy soldiers, and we killed many of them." As soon as the report came in, the court immediately appointed Sim Kiwŏn as special commander-in-chief (*chedo towŏnsu*), and Yi Chŏnggil was promoted in rank. At the time when the troops, led by the supreme commander, were defeated, this report was heard, and the people were pacified somewhat.

Based on the thoughts of the court, they intended to dismiss Kim Chajŏm and replace him with Sim Kiwŏn. Someone said, "Before the enemy is suppressed, if somebody makes a hasty judgment to replace the general who led the troops, things will become very difficult." Therefore, the court appointed Sim Kiwŏn as special commander-in-chief but did not dismiss Kim Chajŏm. Afterward, it was heard that Sim Kiwŏn's so-called defeat of the enemy was fabricated. Sim Kiwŏn and Nam Sŏn were carrying goods for the Ministry of Taxation (*hojo*) to Samgak Mountain when they were completely ransacked by the enemy.[14] The enemy's pursuit was rapid. Sim Kiwŏn withdrew to Kwangnŭng on foot and retreated further, deeper into Yanggŭn Miwŏn, to avoid the enemy's vicious assault.[15] The soldiers from each province knew the location of the commander. They all followed him. Therefore, not many were left to protect the king.

Earlier, after entering Namhan Mountain Fortress, Nam Sŏn and Section Chief of the Board of Ceremonies (*yejo chŏngnang*) Chŏn Kŭk'ang, Director (*chikchang*) Ch'oe Munhan, and Assistant Chief of the Ministry of Taxation (*hojo chwarang*) Im Sŏnbaek all volunteered to go to the capital as special branch officials (*punsa*), because it was said this would bring stability outside the fortress. Nam Sŏn and Im Sŏnbaek ran away to save their own lives. Chŏn Kŭk'ang and Ch'oe Munhan were both killed by the enemy. Among all of the provincial governors of the country and the military officials (*pyŏnsa*), there was not one person who came to help. Ch'ungch'ŏng Governor Chŏng Segyu shed tears and laid down his life. He led the troops from his province, encountered the enemy, and fought them. They came and encamped at the Kwangju Hŏmch'ŏn Mountain Fortress that overlooked the area. In the end, they were defeated by the enemy. They barely survived, and there was no final result. However, Chŏng Segyu's loyalty was greatly respected. Each time I held audience with His Highness, I would say,

Today, there is only one of Your Highness's loyal subjects and that person is Chŏng Segyu. After that there is Cho Chŏngho. Apart from these two people, all below the level of commander sit motionless. They only watch Your Highness's crises, and they exert no effort at all for Your Highness. They must all be punished according to the laws. As for the matters of our country, only after those affairs have been resolved will all of the people come to help and to save it. It is hard to define the crimes they have committed [of not saving the country beforehand] in the legal code. When inside the fortress, we must decide on the fate of these criminals. After leaving the fortress, Your Highness then can behead them. If Your Highness does not do that, then the laws of the country will not be on a firm foundation.

As for those criminals, among all of the people inside the fortress, there is no one who is not wringing their hands in sorrow. Isn't Your Highness extremely angry over this too?

His Highness did not reply.

Ch'ungch'ŏng military official Yi Ŭibae was an old and timid man. For a long time, he was stationed at Chuksan Mountain Fortress.[16] He hesitated and did not send his troops. He heard the scathing talk at the court. Belatedly, he approached the place where the left and right military divisions of Kyŏngsang Province engaged the enemy, but they were all defeated. Some said Yi Ŭibae ran away and survived. Others said he withdrew into a cave and ended his own life. Later, when his body was found, there was discussion to posthumously execute him (*pugwan*).

O n the twenty-ninth day of the twelfth lunar month, there was no real action.

O n the thirtieth day of the twelfth lunar month, the wind was very strong and the weather extremely dismal. On this day, the enemy advanced along three fronts, from Kwangnaru, Map'o, and Hŏllŭng.[17] From the moment the sun started shining in the morning sky, they began marching forward, and they ended their trek at dusk. The wind blew strongly. As soon as the enemy stopped marching, the strong wind ended too. It was unclear how many enemy troops there were. However, the large amounts of snow and cold daytime temperatures did not go away until the troops filled the mountains and plains, leaving not even a single white spot of snow on the ground. One can only imagine how many troops there were. The enemy force grew larger day by day. Our reinforcements were unable to reach us, and our situation deteriorated daily. Our troops had no intention of fighting.

In the vicinity of the temporary palace, southern magpies weaved a nest, and the people all looked up at it and called it an auspicious omen. As for the hope people were holding inside the fortress, there was only this omen. One can only imagine how desperate the situation became at this time.

After Councilor (*mun'gwan*) Yi Kwangch'un followed His Highness into the fortress, he submitted a petition that read, "Your servant's elderly mother is in Chŏnan. I will go to Hosŏ, gather food, and come back." His Highness forwarded this petition to the Border Defense Command. The enemy was besieging the fortress, so Yi was unable to leave. On this day, he came to the Border Defense Command and withdrew this petition. The Border Defense Command asked him for the reason. He replied, "In this petition, I referred to our enemy as 'thieves.'" He was terrified by this and had to retrieve his petition. There was no one that did not laugh at him.

On the first day of the *chŏngch'uk* year [1637], food was served.[18] Provincial Governor of Kwangju Hŏ Hwi prepared rice cakes in a metal bowl and presented them to His Highness. His Highness divided them up into several little bars and distributed them to all of the government officials. There was no one in the court who did not shed tears. His Highness sent Royal Messenger (*sŏnjŏn'gwan*) Wi Sanbo to the barbarians, with Kim Sin'guk and Yi Kyŏngjik, following him, and they journeyed to the enemy camp. The barbarians said, "The emperor departed yesterday. He investigated the conditions of the mountain fortress. We cannot know his affairs at this time. After the emperor returns to our camp, we will give you a response. If your envoy does not wish to come, then this is it. If you want to return, then come again tomorrow." The Border Defense Command heard this report and felt it was a very fortunate sign that they were asked to return again the next day.

When [Royal Messenger] Wi Sanbo first arrived at the enemy camp, a barbarian dragged him away by his hair. Other barbarians eventually stopped that barbarian from doing this. When Wi returned and reported this, he was so frightened he had nearly lost his mind. In fact, people like him are not very resolute. However, the court had to select such weak, spineless people. Each time they are dispatched to the enemy camp as envoys, it can be said that they are not the appropriate persons for the job.

In the afternoon, two large parasols (*yangsan*), two large flags, and one large cannon were set up outside the eastern side of the fortress. Without a doubt, the khan was present.

O n the second day of the first lunar month, Hong Sŏbong, Kim Sin'guk, and Yi Kyŏngjik reached the enemy camp. The barbarians composed on yellow paper a so-called imperial decree. As for this fiendishness, the envoys could not suffer to listen to it or bear to set their eyes on it.[19] Instead, they only wanted to die immediately and not know anything about it. The barbarians placed the yellow paper on the table. The first vice-premier and the others below him bowed four times, after which they held up the letter, emerged, and gave it to the envoys.

The letter contained the following:

The tolerant (*kuan*), kind (*wen*), benevolent (*ren*) sacred (*sheng*) emperor of the great Qing [M. *Genggiyem su huangdi*] orders this imperial decree to the king of Chosŏn.[20] Last year, when troops from our country struck Uriankhai, your country mustered forces and invited us to fight against you.[21] Later, you again cooperated with the Ming and harmed us. Even so, I still considered you a good neighbor and did not mind at all. However, after I captured the Liaodong Peninsula, again you recruited my people and dedicated them to the Ming. I hence grew enraged. In the *chŏngmyo* year [1627], I mobilized troops to subjugate you. By doing this, have we ever used our strength to intimidate you and dispatch our troops without a cause? How could you reason, as you authorized your frontier officials to take their own action by mentioning in your most recent letter, "now we make decisions with justice, persuade various districts to follow, encourage loyal people to each render their own strategy, and ensure brave people volunteer to serve in the army," and so on? Now, I personally lead my great army on an expedition. Why do you not make wise people each render their own strategy and brave people enlist to fight battles in person? I did not threaten you with our strength and greatness, nor did I attack your territory. Instead, as a small country, you violated our borders. You are the ones who dig up our mountain ginseng, and the ones who surround and hunt in our land. What is the reason for this? Some of my commoners fled. Did you bring them back and devote them to the Ming? When the two Ming generals Kong and Geng returned them, and my soldiers came to your border to pick them up, your soldiers fired cannons and intercepted them.[22] What was the reason? It is obvious that this conflict began with your country. My younger brother, my nephew, and various princes have written letters to you. How could you say that there has been no tradition of us communicating through letters? In the *chŏngmyo* year [1627], I came to conquer you. You fled to an island, only sent envoys, and sued for peace. At that time, as for dealing with the letters that came and went between us, were they not numerous princes who sent them? Who else could they have been from? Can my brother and my nephew not be compared to you? Moreover, the various princes from foreign lands sent you letters, but you refused to accept them. These princes are descendants of the emperors of the great Yuan dynasty.[23] Could they not be compared to you? At the time of the great Yuan, your country of Chosŏn never stopped presenting tribute.[24] How can you, the same country, grow so arrogant now? As for not accepting our letters that we dispatched, your obscureness and arrogance have reached extremes. Your country of Chosŏn submitted tribute to the three dynasties, the Liao, the Jin, and the Yuan, year after year, and you designated yourself subordinate to them generation after generation.[25] Since antiquity, have you ever not faced the north and served while you could live freely on your own?[26] I have already cordially received you as my younger brother. You are transgressing this oath more and more. You are making enemies on your own. You put the commoners in distress. You abandon the cities and palaces. You separate wives and children so that they will never meet again. Only you, by yourself, have fled into the mountain fortress. Even if you lived there for another one thousand years, how could this benefit you? You intend to wash away the humiliation of the *chŏngmyo* year, but actually destroy the contemporary comfort and happiness.[27] You provoke this disaster on your own and you leave this as a subject of derision for future generations. Humbled in this way, how will you ever cleanse your previous humiliation?[28] Now that you want to wash away the shame of the *chŏngmyo* year, how can you just shrug your shoulders and not emerge, like women staying in their bedroom chambers? Even though you hide yourself in this fortress and plan to live shamefully, how can I let you do so? The various princes of mine, plus all of my scholarly and military officials, suggest that I be called emperor. When you heard this, you said, "How can the king and the subjects (*sin*) of my country tolerate hearing these words?" What is the reason? As for calling me emperor or not, it is not up to you. If heaven has blessed it, then even an ordinary man (*p'ilbu*) can become an emperor. If heaven has condemned it, then even an emperor can become a lonely, ordinary man. Therefore, you are extremely presumptuous saying such words. Moreover, you betrayed your oath and constructed a fortress. You suddenly abandoned the courtesy of accepting envoys and instead had my envoy see your ministers. You schemed and intended to capture him. What is the reason? You treated the Ming as a father, but you conspire to harm us. What is the reason? Here I announce your many crimes. As for those remaining minor charges, it is difficult for me to name them one by one. Now, I have taken command of my main forces and have come here to exterminate all of your eight provinces. I would like to see how your father, the Ming dynasty, can come and save you. When the son is urgently in danger, how can the father not come to save him? Otherwise, you just bathe your commoners in water and fire. If so, how can the millions of people of your country not resent you? If you have any excuse or something to say, you can render a clear statement.

As soon as the barbarian letter reached the fortress, the court was panic-stricken and did not know how to respond. Everyone considered it a happy and fortunate event that they would soon be leaving the fortress. On this day, Mafuta said, "Besides the tenth prince, Ingguldai has also arrived and has said that fortunately he is indebted to the help of heaven, and now he can extract revenge on people like Yi Kwak and others." This is all because Yi Kwak and others did not take part in the congratulatory procession [of Hung Taiji becoming emperor].

Royal Assistant Commissioner (ŏyŏng chejo) Wanp'ung puwŏn Yi Sŏ died of an illness in the military camp. Five or six days earlier, a large meteorite fell from the sky outside the fortress. The people who witnessed the workings of heaven (ch'ŏn'gi) said the great general had, without a doubt, died in the enemy camp. Thus, we had lost an excellent commander. All the people of the entire fortress were overcome with grief. After that, they set up the altar for Onjo and enshrined (paehyang) him in it.[29]

On the third day of the first lunar month, the weather was extremely cold. When it turned a little warmer during the day, the wife of the warehouse clerk (*koji*) from the Office of Editorial Review (Kyosŏgwan) ran away from the barbarian camp and revealed, "On the last day in the twelfth month of the last lunar year, and on the first day of the first month of the new lunar year, the Mongols burned and plundered the capital. They captured commoners and pillaged the city. Much of the population in the capital was covered in the flames." Even hearing this was horrible.

Hong Sŏbong, Kim Sin'guk, and Yi Kyŏngjik carried our response letter to the enemy camp. It read:

> The king of Chosŏn respectfully submits this letter to the tolerant, kind, benevolent, sacred emperor of the great Qing. Our small country did anger your great country. We brought about this military disaster on our own. We have sojourned in this solitary fortress, and, from morning until night, the danger has been imminent. We wanted to dispatch special envoys to deliver our letter and convey our true sincerity to you, but fighting blocked us and there was no path to communicate with you. Yesterday, we heard that the emperor had arrived in our remote, out-of-the-way corner of the mountain district. Our doubts and beliefs met halfway, and our happiness and fear mingled. For a great country like yours, you have not forgotten the oath we took. You have clearly instructed us about the harm we caused you. We understand our crime. Certainly, for our small country, it is time to relieve that which weighs on our minds. How fortunate we are. How fortunate we are. As for our small country, in establishing good friendship with your great country following the *chŏngmyo* year [1627], it has already been nearly ten years of cordial relations of friendship and solemn etiquette. Not only does your great state know this, but heaven and earth can also witness it. It is completely my shame that I cannot carefully investigate most people's conduct, such as the commoners who collected wild ginseng along the frontier and the conduct

of Kong and Geng. Although it is not the intention of our small country, it is unavoidable that doubts will pile high and become a barrier. Thanks to the generous forgiveness of your great state, our small country can bask in eternal magnanimity. Our small country cannot truly absolve someone from blame regarding the events that occurred in the spring of last year. This is because the officials of our small country possess shallow knowledge and narrow insight. They only know how to protect their reputations. In the end, this made your envoy grow angry and leave in haste. As to the people who followed our troops to the Ming, they did so because they thought the main army would arrive soon, and they grew frightened. The officials from our small country were excessively concerned and warned the administrators along the frontier. When the officials composed the letter, there were a lot of false words in it. We did not realize we had angered your great country. However, I dare to say that it all resulted from our officials, and I know nothing about this. As for any talk of capturing and locking up your envoy, we have no knowledge of this matter. How could we presume that with the omniscience of your great country, even you cannot have doubts about this? Yes, the Ming is our father country. However, the soldiers of your great country have come several times to our land, and our small country has not resisted them with even one arrow shaft. We have always valued our oath of brotherhood. As for the rumor that we plotted to do harm to you, how could that happen? Surely, it is all because our small country's sincerities and beliefs are insufficient. Your powerful country has come to doubt us. Who is to blame? Also, according to General Mafuta, "We come with good intention." Our small country believes these words without any doubt. How could we presume it would eventually end up this way? At any rate, as for the affairs of the past, this small country already knows the crimes we committed. If there were crimes, then punish. If one acknowledges one's crimes, then forgive. This is how your great country understands the will of heaven and comprehends all things on earth.

If you consider the oath to heaven we took in the *chŏngmyo* year and sympathize with the lives of our small country, please allow our small country to amend our ways and plan anew. Then our small country will cleanse our hearts, and we will immediately begin obeying again, from now on from this very day. However, if your powerful country does not forgive us and pursues us by all means possible, then we will fall silent upon finding ourselves bested by this argument, our situation will grow dire, and we will only expect death. Stating all of the above from the bottom of our hearts, we submit this letter to you. With the utmost respect, we await your instructions and commands.

Mafuta replied, "Various princes, who are leading Mongol troops, are coming out of Ch'angsŏng. After we all convene, I will consult with them and reply to you." The officials below the rank of first vice-premier all returned with no results.

On the fourth day of the first lunar month, *Kip'yŏng* Yu Paekchŭng sent a petition to the court, where he criticized the crimes of *Haech'ang* Yun Pang and Commander of War Kim Yu, who devastated the country.[30] He appealed that they be executed. His Highness made a special proclamation, dismissing Yu Paekchŭng. Yu's position was replaced by Yi Mok, and Paekchŭng was reappointed as assistant defense officer (*hyŏpsusa*).

On the fifth day of the first lunar month, the guard soldier [in the elite ivory troops] of Southern Commanding Officer (*nambyŏngsa*) Sŏ Usin brought a special report (*changgye*) that stated: "The commanding officer (*pyŏngsa*) and Border Inspector (*sunch'alsa*) Min Sŏnghwi led thirteen thousand cavalry troops, and they have already reached the commander's residence of the newly appointed Sim Kiwŏn of Kwangnŭng. In a few days, they will advance and contact the enemy. In addition, the northern provincial commander (*pukpyŏngsa*) is leading four thousand cavalry troops and will arrive at the commander's residence." Military official (*kun'gwan*) Chŏlla Provincial Commander Kim Chullyong presented a report that stated: "The military officers are in command of more than ten thousand soldiers and have reached Kwanggyo Mountain where they are stationed.[31] Governor Yi Sibang is also leading troops and has already reached Chik Mountain."[32] Two soldiers from the ivory troops of Kwangju rushed out of the fortress and fled, but they were captured by a patrol and beheaded out in the open (*hyosi*) at the military camp.

On the sixth day of the first lunar month, fog descended thickly, and even the daytime grew dark. P'yŏngan Commander Yu Sim and Assistant Supreme Commander Sin Kyŏngwŏn submitted a report that stated: "More than five thousand barbarian soldiers on horseback have come out from Ch'angsŏng. We do not know if the magistrates of Ch'angsu and Sakchu are alive or dead. What is under siege is the location of the assistant supreme commander of Yŏngbyŏn." Hamgyŏng Provincial Governor Min Sŏnghwi submitted a report that read: "I have now come to Kimhwa. Southern Commanding Officer (*nambyŏngsa*) Sŏ Usin will arrive soon. We will join forces and advance." This report was written on the second day of this month.

Kangwŏn Provincial Governor Cho Chŏngho submitted a report that stated: "The soldiers of Kŏmdan have encountered the enemy and have been completely crushed. I have rallied the remaining troops and, via Kap'yŏng, Min Sŏnghwi and I will join forces at some point and advance."

On the seventh day of the first lunar month, Commander Kim Chajŏm submitted a report that stated: "Last month, on the twentieth day, I picked three thousand of the troops under my command after defeating the enemy of Tongsŏn and advanced with the troops of Hwanghae commander Yi Sŏktal.[33] We stationed ourselves at Sin'gye. At first, I ordered Kunsan Country Magistrate Yi Wiguk to lead five hundred soldiers to advance. He has already reached Kwangnŭng." This report was written on the second day of this month.

Chŏlla Provincial Governor Yi Sibang submitted a report that stated: "I advanced to Yangji. At first, I sent two thousand soldiers through Kwanggyo Mountain to join forces with the troops of an army officer (*pyŏngsa*). I recruited two hundred soldiers with the promise of rewards. I appointed three generals. Via the middle way (*chungno*), we took the opportunity and defeated the enemy.[34] I dispatched a letter to Messenger (*t'ongjesa*) Yun Suk, ordering him to lead three hundred soldiers under his command and arrive after a few days. From among the Buddhists (Kaksŏng), I appointed two Buddhist commanders (*sŭngjang*); each would lead one thousand monks throughout the province, and they arrived within a few days. In addition, because it was difficult for me to advance alone, I contacted the Kyŏngsang provincial magistrate Sim Yŏn. We will regroup soon and advance our troops together."

Chŏlla Provincial Commander Kim Chullyong's report said that because the enemy now depends on the rough terrain and their camps are everywhere, we must scout out the situation and advance accordingly. The person who brought this report said that, for three continuous days, he had to hide by day and come out by night, so that he could enter the fortress. He encountered one palace guard on the way, who said that the troops led by the provincial commander had already fought the enemy soldiers for three days and killed and captured many of their troops. Yi Huwŏn, the inspector general (*changnyŏng*), arrived. In front of various people who gathered around him, he said,

> After New Year's Day, they held a meeting at the Two Offices (Yangsa) [the Office of the Inspector General and the Office of the Censor General], and they decided the crown prince would be dispatched with a company of nine people from the Border Defense Command. At that time, the left state councilor (*chwaŭijŏng*) brought the frightful letter from the enemy camp. The minister of personnel (*ijo p'ansŏ*) insisted on peace negotiations, and that is what was to destroy our country. He deserved the death penalty, and this should be reported to the court. Among the great officials (*yangsa changgwan*) and various government officers, some intended to postpone this report until after matters had settled. Thus they tentatively put a stop to it.

However, several of the officers among them ended up with a plan for leaving the fortress [proposing peace negotiations]. They knew that they could not avoid facing public discussion.

On the eight day of the first lunar month, snow fell in the morning. The sky was cloudy and gloomy.[35]

On the ninth day of the first lunar month, the inside and outside of the fortress could no longer communicate with each other, and, from this day onward, the reports ended.[36]

On the tenth day of the first lunar month, two halos appeared around the sun.[37] His Highness sent for Minister of Rites (*yejo p'ansŏ*) Kim Sanghŏn and had him perform the rites for King Onjo. Special Royal Commander (*ŏyŏng pyŏlchang*) Kim Ŏllim, a person from Miryang, originally sucked pus from carbuncles (*yŏnong*) to form relationships with the capital elite (*sadaebu*).[38] He personally claimed that he was skilled in *ch'imsul* acupuncture.[39] In fact, he did not even know where the acupuncture points were. Previously, he had killed many people. He told the commander of war, "I can sneak out of the fortress at night and chop up some of the enemy until they're dead." The commander asked, "How many should accompany you to fight?" He replied, "I will only go with one person." The commander said, "What a small number that is!" He replied, "In my opinion, one person is actually more than enough." He must have had some deceptive ruse in mind.

In the morning on the following day, it was reported that Kim Ŏllim beheaded a barbarian and carried his head back in the fortress. The commander of war sat down, and received the left ear of the barbarian. He reported it to His Highness, who bestowed three *p'il* of cotton bolts on him.[40] The commander of war ordered the barbarian head hung at the military gate. However, when looked at closely, the head did not even have one drop of blood on it. Its flesh was frozen white as snow. All the people thought it was strange. Shortly after, one man, the guard officer (*changgwan*) from Wŏnju, pounced on the head, removed it, and held it in his hands. He prostrated himself and cried, "My brother! My brother! Ah, how could my brother die twice?" It transpired that the dead person was the former commander who had fought the enemy with troops from Kwandong on the day they were urged to fight. All the people watching around the guard cried. The commander of war sent Kim Ŏllim to the royal guard commander Wŏn Tup'yo, and he decapitated him in front of the soldiers.

On the eleventh day of the first lunar month, a halo formed around the rising sun, and white vapors (*kiun*) extended from east to west across the sky.[41] Minister of Rites (*yejo p'ansŏ*) Kim Sanghŏn petitioned His Highness, saying, "If a person is poor, then he should go back to his origins. At this time of emergency, Your Highness should conduct a ritual in front of the Sungŭn Palace portrait."[42] His Highness followed this suggestion and embarked for the portrait of Wŏnjong.[43] On this day, His Highness visited the portrait. He went to Kaewŏn Monastery where the portrait was enshrined and conducted a ritual.[44] His Highness left the palace at the break of dawn. All the government officials attended the ritual. Before the morning ended, His Highness returned after the ritual. From the moment we entered Namsan Mountain Fortress, the magpies and crows inside had all disappeared. However, on this day, many of them flew back in. Everyone said this was a good omen.

I told Chang Yu, "We have no other way but to ask for peace, but if we just beg for it, then it will certainly not turn out as we wish. We should clearly state to the enemy the gains and losses. If so, then that could be persuasive." Chang Yu strongly agreed with my opinion. Following my suggestion, he drafted a proposal and invited First Counselor of the Office of Special Counselors (*pujehak*) Yi Kyŏngsŏk for a discussion, stating every detail of this reasoning. His Highness read this appeal with Chief State Counselor (*yŏngŭijŏng*) Kim Yu. However, Ch'oe Myŏnggil also wrote an appeal in which he insisted that begging for peace negotiations should be the main idea. He petitioned for the acceptance of his appeal, so Chang Yu's petition was not adopted.

The enemy broke up into three main advances, and they reinforced their troops all along the riversides, setting up camps everywhere. We had doubted that the enemy reinforcements could arrive so soon. Our people became even more frightened. This evening, a halo appeared around the moon.

On the twelfth day, Left State Counselor Hong Sŏbong, Ch'oe Myŏnggil, Yun Hwi, and Hŏ Han were sent to the enemy camp. However, the sovereign letter (*kuksŏ*) was not accepted. They were instructed to return through the western gate the next day. They were also told that a new general had come, but Ingguldai seemed somewhat frustrated. From our two camps in the east and west, a rumor spread that most of the enemy troops had advanced. What Ingguldai had mentioned about the arrival of the new general seemed to be true. In addition, it was rumored that several thousand enemy cavalry troops were headed in the direction of Yip'irhyŏn. The fact that the enemy had become present in the vicinity of the fortress intimidated and puzzled our army. Hŏ Han had some words to share, endorsing an officer for promotion. His nephew, Yi Cho, who was working in the staff office (*chongsagwan*) for the commander at that time, was recommended to the commander of war and dispatched whenever the barbarians needed to be dealt with.

On the thirteenth day of the first lunar month, a southwesterly wind blew strongly. His Highness inspected the southern side of the fortress, then dispatched Hong Sŏbong, Ch'oe Myŏnggil, and Yun Hwi to the enemy camp. Ingguldai and Mafuta accepted the sovereign letter and blamed the envoys for violating the alliance oath without just cause. Ch'oe Myŏnggil pounded his chest and kowtowed to them, saying, "That is not the intention of His Highness, our king, but a crime of mine as his subordinate. I would stab my own body with a sword and pull out my intestines to prove that our fatherly king did not know any of this." Ingguldai and Mafuta promised that within three days they would report to Ch'oe about this, after the khan sent the orders.

The state letter (*kuksŏ*) read:

These days, high-ranking courtiers of our small country have honored this letter. They have visited the military gate, made inquiries, and come back reporting that in the future there will be an order from His Imperial Highness. Our small county's king and his subjects stretch out their necks and stand on their tiptoes, every day waiting for the words of His Imperial Highness. Now, already ten days have passed, and there is still no word expressing right or wrong. The situation has become very urgent. To obviate the recurring offense, we only hope that His Imperial Highness, the emperor, will investigate this with discernment. Previously, our small country enjoyed the benefits of the kindness of your powerful country, and it was a disgrace for your great country to have to forge a brotherhood with us, declaring to heaven and earth that even though the territory of our countries has a border, there was no gap between us in our affections. We thought our descendants would have endless good fortune for ten thousand years. Unexpectedly, when the sacrificial blood on the plate had not yet dried up [when the oath remained still fresh], there arose many doubts, so it collapsed into ominous misfortune. This again became laughable to the people living under heaven. However, if you search for its origin, it is all because our nature is vulnerable, and we easily make mistakes. All of the officials and subjects are fatuous and unobservant. This has resulted in the situation we have today. For this, except that we only blamed ourselves, what else could we say? But you, as our elder brother, when you see us do wrong, you grow angry and reprimand us. Although this is proper, if you are too reproachful, this is contrary to the loyalty of our brotherhood. How could heaven not consider this strange? Our small country is located in one corner of a remote sea. We still strive to follow the *Book of Songs* and the *Book of Classics*, and we are unfamiliar with war.[45] Through weakness, we obey strength. Through smallness, we serve greatness. This is all reasonable routine. How can we ever contend with a large country?

Only because we inherit the good fortune of the Ming from generation to generation, the original status regarding our tribute to the Ming has always been fixed. Earlier, when the crisis of Imjin arose and our small country was on the verge of destruction, Emperor Shenzong mobilized all the troops under heaven and saved our lives from untold miseries.[46] Therefore, the people of our small country have engraved this debt of gratitude into our hearts and bones. We would rather commit a crime against your large country than to betray the Ming. It is not for other reasons, but just because the Ming grace is so heavy that the hearts of our people are deeply moved. There is not only one way to bestow grace on others. If you can enliven all beings and overcome the threats to our ancestral shrines [the state] by dispatching your army to rescue us and furthering our survival by withdrawing your army, there would be different matters but the same grace.[47]

Last year, our small country was secretive and delusional and failed to handle the situation well. There have been many kind instructions from your large country, but we did not grasp them, so the troops of your large country have come. For a very long time, our king, officials, and fathers and sons have stayed in a solitary fortress, and our embarrassment has been extreme. Indeed, at this time, if your large country suddenly and completely forgives these mistakes and grants us a new chance to try again, we can preserve our ancestral shrines and the state altars and serve your large country forever. If so, the king and ministers of our small country will carry a debt of gratitude. We will carve it into our hearts and pass it onto our descendants, so forgiveness will never be forgotten. If the people under heaven hear this as truth, they will all admire the prestige of your large country.

Throughout the eastern lands, this establishes the immense grace of your large country. You grant expansive mercy upon all of the countries of the world. If this were not but a way to vent the anger of one's court, it would exhaust all of the military forces and injure our brotherly grace, and close the path to refresh our thoughts, thus putting an end to the hope of various small countries.[48] This structure will not work as a long-term strategy for your large country. By the extreme luminosity of His Imperial Highness, the emperor, how could such points not be taken into consideration?

It is to wither when it is autumn. It is to grow when it is spring.[49] Those are the ways of heaven and earth. To sympathize with the weak and the dead, this is the occupation of a dynastic ruler (*p'aewang*). Now, the emperor has stabilized all of the countries with his military strategy, whereas he established a new great title (*taeho*) and proclaimed it has four characters: *kuan* (tolerant), *wen* (kind), *ren* (benevolent), *sheng* (sacred) [K. *Kwanon insŏng*]. Thereby, he would emulate the way of heaven and earth, so as to restore the occupation of the dynastic ruler. He would have our small country's wish fulfilled, to correct mistakes that our small country has made in the past. As we consider ourselves protected by your powerful country, it seems that we will not be forsaken. So, we dare to make light of our dignity and state, as before mentioned, to petition for your orders to our royal offices.

At this time, the mounted cavalry of the enemy accumulated in the thousands outside the western and northern gates, probably coming as additional reinforcements. It seemed as though the number of those in our army who were being captured grew daily.

On the fourteenth day of the first lunar month, Kim Sin'guk and I initiated plans concerning the food supplies. Each day the allocation of food was reduced by three *hop* for the regular army and by five *hop* for government officials.[50] There was only enough food to last until the following month on the twenty-fourth day. The troops knew that there was no more food. If the enemy besieged the fortress for an extended time, then it would be hard to know what was preventable.[51] Kim Sin'guk and I went to the palace and reported the food status to His Highness. Shortly before this, the enemy had set fire to Kangnŭng and T'aerŭng.[52] This time, they set fire to Hŏllŭng. Smoke and flames pierced heaven. I could not bear to see this terrible sight.

On the fifteenth day of the first lunar month, the official reports to His Highness, which had ceased completely, resumed. New Supreme Field Commander Sim Kiwŏn, Provincial Governor Min Sŏnghwi, official (*nambyŏngsa*) Sŏ Usin, Provincial Governor of Kangwŏn Cho Chŏngho, Commander Im Myŏnghan, Field Commander (*ch'anhoeksa*) Nam Sŏn, and others wrote on the tenth day and on the eleventh day. Their letters read that they were stationed nearby in Yanggŭn Miwŏn, resting their troops for the time being. They were about to advance through Yongjin and so on. Two soldiers from among the troops of the provincial governor of Hamgyŏng delivered this report.

On the sixteenth day of the first lunar month, the wind blew strongly, and snow fell. Hong Sŏbong, Ch'oe Myŏnggil, and Yun Hwi went to the enemy camp to inquire why there was still no report back regarding the sovereign letter that had been sent before. Ingguldai and Mafuta made a number of threats, saying, "The two generals Kong and Keng command seventy thousand Ming troops.[53] They brought with them twenty-eight long-distance red barbarian cannons (*hongyipao*), and they will assault Kanghwa Island." The enemy's white flag had the two characters "invitation to surrender" (*ch'ohang*) written on it. They placed it at the foot of Mangwŏl Peak, and it flapped in the wind.[54]

On the seventeenth day of the first lunar month, Ingguldai and Mafuta looked for our envoy. Hong Sŏbong, Ch'oe Myŏnggil, and Yun Hwi went out and received the response letter. The content of it was frightful. It ordered us to immediately emerge from the fortress and surrender.

The great Qing dynasty *kuan wen ren sheng* emperor has issued an imperial letter to the king of Chosŏn, admonishing him. The letter they sent said,

"If you are too reproachful, this is contrary to the loyalty of our brotherhood. How could heaven not consider this strange?" I carefully considered the oath taken in the *chŏngmyo* year [1627]. Many times, I have repeatedly enlightened you when your country contemplated breaking the oath. You were not afraid of heaven. You did not want to save the commoners who were in distress, and you turned against the oath at first. My envoy Yingeerdai [Ingguldai] got hold of a letter from your subjects along the frontier. From that, we began to realize that your country was planning war. I used to tell the two Ch'unsinsa and Ch'usinsa envoys, and several merchants, "Your country is rude like this. We will invade your country soon.[55] You can return to inform your king and everyone under him to the commoners." The information we gave to them is clear, and we sent it to you. There was no treachery involved when I secretly mobilized my army. Moreover, I prepared a letter for these envoys to take back to you. After you violated the oath and troubled heaven, it was time that I consulted heaven and then dispatched the army to suppress you. If I disobey an oath, I would fear being punished by heaven. Because it is true that you betrayed the oath, calamity struck your country. How can you be like someone who is innocent and without any connections, yet do something so far-fetched like attaching only the character "heaven" (*tian*)?

You also wrote, "Our small country is located in one corner of a remote sea. We still strive to follow the *Book of Songs* and the *Book of Classics*, and we are unfamiliar with war." However, before, in the *kimi* year [1619] and without cause, you invaded our lands. I believe your country is familiar with military affairs.[56] Now, you have begun to provoke us again, and your troops grow seasoned. Do you still insist that you are unfamiliar with military affairs? Indeed, you have always been familiar with military matters. You have just not achieved your military goals. From now on, you will have more chances to train your army.

You also wrote, "Earlier, when the crisis of Imjin arose and our small country was on the verge of destruction, Emperor Shenzong mobilized all the troops under heaven and saved our lives from untold miseries." The world is expansive and holds many countries. As for saving your kingdom, the Ming is just one country, so how could troops from all the countries have come?[57] You and the Ming, always ridiculous and reckless, never cease falsities and absurdities. Now, you wearily maintain the mountain fortress, living on the verge of death. You still do not fathom your shame and still mention such nonsense. So how can you benefit from this?

You also wrote, "If this were not but a way to vent the anger of one's court, it would exhaust all of the military forces and injure our brotherly grace, and close the path to refresh our thoughts, thus putting an end to the hope of various small countries. This structure will not work as a long-term strategy for your large country. By the extreme luminosity of His Imperial Highness, the emperor, how could such points not be considered?" However, you violated our brotherly friendship and prepared for war. You trained your soldiers. You repaired the fortress. You improved the roads. You built wagons, and you readied your weapons. You are waiting for the day when I leave for expedition west [toward the Ming] so you can make the most of that chance to quietly use your soldiers and harm our country. By doing so, how could you patronize our country? You say it is not breaking the trust of all of the people. You say it is great brilliance. You say it is called a long-lasting plan. Do I call it sincerity? Do I call it a long-lasting plan?

You also wrote, "Now, the emperor has stabilized all of the countries with his military strategy, whereas he established a new great title (*taeho*) and proclaimed it has four characters: *kuan, wen, ren, sheng*. Thereby, he would emulate the way of heaven and earth, so as to restore the occupation of the dynastic ruler." However, all of my various princes and great ministers within and without have long called on me to take this imperial title (*chonho*). However, I have never given up restoring the occupation of the dynastic ruler. But it is not my intention to mobilize troops without reason to destroy your country and bring harm upon your commoners. The reason I mobilized troops was truly to distinguish between right and wrong. The way of heaven and earth delivers fortunes to the kind and misfortunes to the evil. There is fairness with no impartiality. I appreciate the way of heaven and earth. For those who follow full-heartedly, I give preferential treatment. For those who surrender according to the situation, I ensure their safety. For those who disobey commands, I strike them in the name of heaven. For those who gather a group and carry out evil acts, I put them to death. For those commoners who do not obey, I imprison them. By doing so, I will warn the stubborn and make the cunning speechless.

Now, you treat me as your enemy, so I have mobilized my army and come here to your lands. If your country merges into my territory entirely, how could I not protect you and love you like my child? As for your words and your actions, they are entirely dissimilar. When you communicate inside and outside of the court, the letters that circulated were always intercepted by our soldiers, and in your letters we have occasionally been called "slave-thieves" (*nojŏk*). This is because your king and officials have always called our soldiers thieves. As a result, whenever your officials open their mouths, they disparaged us as thieves. We know that one who conceals oneself and secretly carries things off is the definition of a thief. If indeed I am a thief, then why won't you catch me? Instead, why do you push me aside and just ignore me? This is actually how you reproved us by using your mouth and tongue.

There is a proverb about "a sheep in the coat of a tiger." I think you are that sheep. A Manchu custom says, "As for people, action that is agile is precious; words that are modest are precious." Therefore, as for our country, if we act without success, if we boast without shame, it will be taken as a warning. Let alone for your country, which cheats and is cunning, crafty, and presumptuous. These actions pervade you deeper by the day, and you do not feel shy about your shame. You are just preaching your irrational and careless words. Now, if you want to live, come out of the fortress quickly and surrender. If you want to fight, come out quickly and fight. When our two armies meet, heaven will surely know a way to end this.

O n the eighteenth day of the first lunar month, Hong Sŏbong, Ch'oe Myŏnggil, and Yun Hwi took the state letter to the enemy camp. Ingguldai offered the excuse that Mafuta had been traveling and could not receive it. He said, "Either tomorrow or the day after tomorrow, we will come to fight." Then the enemy advanced again and called on the troops protecting the fortress to emerge and surrender.

The content of the state letter was this:

The king of Chosŏn bows and submits this letter to the *kuan wen ren sheng* emperor of the great Qing. I prostrate myself humbly, accepting the brilliant meaning of the earnest remonstrance you sent down to us. Its reproach and sternness are the highest instructions. It comes to us like the autumn frost, biting cold, but it also ushers in the sprouts of spring. I prostrated myself and, as I read it, I grew uneasy. I was at a loss. Here again, I lie prostrate. For your great country, your majesty and virtue are far-reaching, so, with all of the foreign countries (*pŏnbang*) in chorus, heaven and the people are devoted to you. Your divine mission is fully new. For ten years, our small country, as a brotherly country with yours, has blamed others since the beginning of fate. We should seek the cause in our hearts instead of in someone else. We regret this like one biting his own navel [it is impossible to show enough regret]. As for our hopes now, they are only to correct our hearts and to change our thoughts, to cleanse the habits of previous years, to direct our entire country to receive orders from you, and to follow your commands like all of the other foreign countries have. We are granted a favor to compromise the crisis and a promise to correct our own mistakes. Therefore, there should be a written record and ritual concerning this. This is how we conduct such affairs, and these affairs should be conducted today. As for your order to descend from the fortress, this results from your true purpose to spread your benevolence (*inbok*) throughout our small country. But given the fact that the siege has not been lifted, and the anger of Your Imperial Highness is still immense, we may either die here or upon emerging from the fortress. For this reason, we look vacantly at the dragon banner (*yonggi*) of Your Imperial Highness and only wish to take our own lives. How sorrowful it is! Ancient people used to pay respects to the son of heaven on this fortress. This is because we cannot leave behind our manners (*ye*) at any time. But the military power is also frightening. However, our small country would like to speak out as mentioned above. These could be our last words, our acknowledgement to your warning; our full hearts follow your orders as our fate. Your Imperial Highness, the emperor, brings heaven, earth, and all beings into his heart. How can our small country not be preserved as part of it? Prostrating myself in front of you, I certainly believe that the virtue of the emperor is like heaven and will forgive us with mercy. I impudently speak my mind, and I humbly await your gracious words.

Minister of Personnel (*ijo p'ansŏ*) Ch'oe Myŏnggil composed this letter. Minister of Rites (*yejo p'ansŏ*) Kim Sanghŏn went to the Border Defense Command. As soon as Kim saw this letter, he tore it to pieces and wept intensely. His sounds reached every corner of the inner court, where His Highness resided. Kim Sanghŏn approached Ch'oe Myŏnggil and said, "As for the previous great minister (*sondaebu*)—your father, Ch'oe Kinam [1559–1619]—we had reputations as scholars and friends. How can Your Excellency do such a thing?" Ch'oe Myŏnggil smiled and said, "Your Excellency tore up the letter, but out of duty I will pick it up." He collected the letter that had been torn up and discarded, and pasted it back together. Minister of Military Affairs Yi Sŏnggu stood next to Ch'oe, extremely angered. "Earlier, Your Excellency rejected peace negotiations. That brought the affairs of our country to this point. Your Excellency, please go to the enemy." Kim Sanghŏn said, "Even though I want to die, I will not commit suicide. If I could be dispatched to the enemy camp and that would be the place where I die, I would treat it as an honor conferred by Your Excellency." Thus, he left his residence. Every time he encountered someone, he wept with tears that flowed like water. From this day onward, he declined food and fully expected to die.

On the nineteenth day of the first lunar month, the left state councilor became ill. Instead, Right State Councilor Ch'oe Myŏnggil and Yun Hwi were sent to the enemy camp and conveyed the state letter composed on the previous day. They only argued over one term in the letter, that they would not have to emerge from the fortress to surrender. At first, the enemy rejected this letter, but later accepted it and departed. The person below the right state councilor went again to collect the enemy's response, but he came back empty handed.

Assistant Councilor (*ch'amch'an*) Han Yŏjik asked Ch'oe Myŏnggil, "We have to go again to get their response letter, so what is the reason?" Ch'oe Myŏnggil replied, "We can't know the reason why." Han Yŏjik said, "Because you failed to write 'that character (*kwŏl*)' in the letter, I suspect that they will not respond. Composing this single character is truly the essence of the letter. Kim Sanghŏn has left his residence. Why not take this great opportunity to urgently write that character and deliver it to the enemy camp?" That character (*kwŏl*) referred to the state letter, in which we had to write the character depicting us as a *subject* (*sin*).[58]

Ch'oe Myŏnggil and others considered Han Yŏjik's words to be correct. The day had already grown dark. They wrote the character for "subject" and were about to send it, but someone said, "Violating the curfew to go now is absurd. If you send it tomorrow morning, it will not be late." Therefore, the letter was not sent. On the following morning, the envoy went out and Ingguldai said, "I have ordered the main army to each of your provinces. Your deputy commander has been captured. Kanghwa Island has already fallen. Now, you can learn about the general state of affairs."

Someone said, "In this extremely cold winter, how can one sail a boat on the land?[59] That Kanghwa Island has fallen must be a threat." District Magistrate of Ich'ŏn Cho Myŏngok died of illness. Apart from him, a few other court officials who had entered the fortress have already died. A male pheasant flew into the court from the south, and it was caught. Earlier, a deer was captured inside the fortress. They were submitted to His Highness.

On the twentieth day of the first lunar month, heavy snow fell, and the wind blew fiercely. Left State Council Ch'oe Myŏnggil and Yun Hwi went to the enemy camp to receive the khan's letter and returned with it.

The letter read:

The emperor of the great Qing Empire conveys a message to the king of Chosŏn, admonishing him. Because you have transgressed heaven and broken our oath, I am enraged and have come leading my troops to punish you. My aim is not to punish, even though I am angered. Now, you arduously maintain yourself in that lonely fortress. You saw the imperial letter I sternly reproached you with, and you then knew to repent your crimes. You have submitted a number of letters begging for pardon. I have spread my generosity widely and approve of you renewing your minds. It is not because I lack the force to attack and seize your country. It is not because I lack the power to lay siege to your fortress. Now that I am here and once I begin assaulting your fortress, I can surely overrun it. Then, because you need food and feed to supply your soldiers and horses, I can make you poor and distressed and thus capture your fortress that way as well. If I cannot conquer such a tiny fortress, then how could I ever take the You and Yan provinces in China later?

I command you to emerge from this fortress and to come meet me. First, I want to see that you act in good faith and loyalty. Second, I want to bestow kindness on you. Later, when I take your kingdom and return with my victorious soldiers, I will demonstrate benevolence and honesty throughout the world under heaven. If I lure you out with tricks, then I can still take your fortress. But now, I have just acquired a heavenly blessing and pacified the whole world. I am about to pardon your previous transgression and set an example for Namjo [the Ming]. If I take you through cunning trickery, given the expansiveness of the world under heaven, how can I use cunning trickery to deceive them all? That would be cutting off one's own retreat. This is common sense without the distinction of foolishness and wisdom.

If you hesitate and do not emerge from the fortress, then the area will be ravished and the fodder for your horses and rations for your troops will run out, all of the lives of you and your commoners will fall into extreme misery, and disaster and anguish will grow day by day. So, truly no time can be lost. Originally, for those of your subjects who first conspired to break our oath, I wanted to put them all to death. But now, if you emerge from the fortress and follow your fate, you can then first arrest a couple of the masterminds and dispatch them to us. I will hang their decapitated heads to warn people not to do the same in the future. If those are not the persons who ruined my great plan to invade west to the Ming and plunge your lives into water and fire, who else could they be? If you do not send me the ringleaders in advance after you immediately return, I will start to demand it. However, here is something I would never do: if you do not emerge then, even though you earnestly beg for it, I will never listen. I am deeply admonishing you here.

The previous night, the barbarians had come and pressed for a reply to the sovereign letter. If there was still no written response, they said that even replying by word alone would be acceptable. In the response letters, "subject" and "His Imperial Majesty" were referenced. The right state councilor was ill, so instead, Yi Tŏkhyŏng assumed the title, took the sovereign letter, and exited through the western gate. Because the enemy had already visited our camp, he simply returned. Ch'oe Myŏnggil fell behind, so he sent the interpreter Yi Sin'gŏm. Ch'oe wrote to the barbarians in secret, bribed Ingguldai and Mafuta, called himself subject, accepted the royal commands to express his gratitude, and so on, to the barbarians.

On the twenty-first day of the first lunar month, at dawn, someone at the level of the right state councilor or lower conveyed the sovereign letter from yesterday and returned. In the evening, he took our response and intended to approach the enemy camp. Because those courtiers who resisted the peace negotiations did not approve sending him to deliver the response, the enemy grew angry and handed back the state letter without saying a word.

Our response letter was such:

> Your subject (*sin*), the king of Chosŏn, humbly presents a letter to the great Qing *kuan wen ren sheng* emperor, Your Imperial Majesty. I, your subject, committed a crime against Your Imperial Highness. I sit wearily in this solitary fortress by myself, as I know that death will approach eventually. I am deeply considering the mistakes I have made in the past, and there is no way to atone for these on my own. Although I, because of selfishness, have submitted several petitions to seek self-renewal, I do not dare to incite the heavens, which are full of rage. Now, I have received the imperial edict (*sŏngji*) and feel entirely relieved for my previous fault. You loosen the dignity of the autumn frost and you spread the grace of a sunny spring. You will save the lives spanning several thousand *li* in the Eastern Land [Chosŏn] from water and fire. Why should this mere fortress survive? Only to preserve all the lives inside. Our king, ministers, fathers, and sons are in deep debt to your expansive gratitude, so we cry and know not how to repay you.
>
> Previously, when we received your order to leave the fortress, we feared and doubted it. Before you laid down your anger on us, we were afraid to state what we were thinking. Now, we have been earnestly enlightened to your complete sincerity and have repeatedly been given careful instructions. It is much like what ancient people called "taking one's heart and placing it into another person's breast."[60] I, your subject, have

been serving your great country for over ten years. It has been a long time that I have embraced your trust and justice. None of my ordinary words or actions disobey yours, let alone disobeying the imperial orders from you. Your letters are like the four seasons to me, so how can I not reply? I dare not fathom this.

Even when I have questions about your letters, because of my selfishness, I promulgate them for Your Imperial Majesty. The customs of the Eastern Land are destitute and narrowminded, and the etiquette is exacting and severe. In observing that the behavior of His Highness differs slightly from normalcy, our people were astounded and looked upon each other, feeling rather strange. However, if we do not rule our country through obeying our customs, governing finally ends with not being able to establish a country. After the *chŏngmyo* year, the councilors of the court held different opinions. However, we had to remain calm and not chastise others as we took all these into consideration. As for today, the government officials and the commoners of the entire fortress all realize that the current situation is dangerous. For pledging allegiance, they all agree in chorus, except for one stipulation. They all think that since the Koryŏ dynasty, this sort of issue [having a king remove himself from the fortress] has never happened. They would rather die to resolve this situation than to allow the king to come out of the fortress. If Your Imperial Highness keeps pressing me to leave this fortress, then later you will only acquire a fortress with corpses heaped up high. Now, all the people inside the fortress know that they will die eventually, but they still think this way. What of the other people throughout the country?

Since antiquity, the misfortune of subjugated countries has not been dependent only on the army of the enemy. Even though we receive the grace of Your Imperial Highness and then we place our realm on a firm foundation, through today's compassion, we observe this, but the people do not agree to support making you emperor. This is a great fear I have as your subject. The reason Your Imperial Majesty gave the command to approve the surrender (*kwi*) is entirely because you would preserve the shrines and temples of this small country. As a result, if there will be no approval from my fellow countrymen (*kugin*) and the country is destroyed, then it will not be because Your Imperial Highness has shown compassion. Moreover, the thunder-like powerful troops of Your Imperial Highness penetrate deeply into places a thousand *li* away.[61] This has all happened within less than two months. To rectify a country and comfort its people is a marvelous merit under heaven. This is also unprecedented in history. Why does it have to be called conquering the fortress only when I emerge? This causes no great damage to Your Imperial Highness's powerful military, but it concerns the life and death of this small country. It all rests here.

In addition, your powerful country sees this fortress, and it is not that you cannot attack or overcome it. Attacking or overcoming it is for rebuking the crime.[62] Now that I have pledged allegiance to you, then what is the usefulness of this fortress to you? I am prostrating myself in front of you. Your Imperial Highness's knowledge is exceptional, and you clearly discern everything in the world. As for the real circumstance and actual situation of our small country, you investigate every detail without exception. As for those subjects who rejected peace, there is a history of officials in our small country whose major duty is to debate and remonstrate. This is all that they have done in former days. This is really extremely absurd. Those who put the people of our small country into extreme distress are nobody else but these dissenters. Thus, in the autumn of last year, those officials who advocated hypocritical theories and false opinions were removed. Also, they were reprimanded and dismissed. Now, we have received the emperor's orders, so how could we dare disobey? However, given these subjects' original purpose, their knowledge and experiences are biased and secretive. They do not know where the mandate of heaven rests. In actuality, they just wish to stick to routines. Now, like the wind, Your Imperial Majesty blows the entire world through your righteousness, turning it into your subjects. These people should be part of your mercy and forgiveness. I am prostrating myself in front of Your Imperial Majesty. Your magnanimous generosity is akin to heaven. Now that you have already graciously forgiven my crimes as the king, for these small officials, who are like lice eggs or lice, they would be directly handed over for punishment in our small country. By allowing this, Your Imperial Highness's wide virtue stands out more. Therefore, here I express my foolish views. It is for Your Imperial Highness's judgment and decision. I, your subject, am given the trust of Your Imperial Majesty after you cease your anger. I unknowingly attach myself to you in all sincerity. I conclude every little thought here. There is no way to escape the disrespectful crimes I have committed. Thus, here I appeal to you at the risk of death.

This letter was also written by Ch'oe Myŏnggil. His Highness had ordered two people, Ch'oe Myŏnggil and the grand academic (*taejehak*) Yi Sik, to compose two response letters. Although Ch'oe Myŏnggil's letter was finally adopted, the meaning—the petition to surrender with flattery and obedience—in both letters did not differ in the slightest. Because Yi Sik's letter was not adopted, he constantly criticized Myŏnggil and tried to make himself appear superior. No one paid any attention to his words.

Because Commander-in-Chief Kim Chajŏm did not immediately come in and reinforce the troops, Vice-Minister of Personnel (*ijo ch'ap'an*) Chŏng On submitted a petition that read:

I prostrate myself in front of you. The day before yesterday, when the invitation for discussion of a countermove was received, there was no single strategy, nor a single plan of mine that could be a helpful supplement to the opinions of various people at the court. On the day when the court was full of people, I only want to turn toward His Royal Countenance and present my humble opinion. The royal face looked distressed and exhausted for any social interaction. He was short of breath and speech, unable to exert himself to the utmost. Frustrated and perplexed, he was in decline. He cried and then went out. Now, the will of heaven [the will of His Highness] has been revived and His Highness is furious. The various generals resolve to die, and the soldiers do not wish to live. The enlisted army grows more numerous by the day. The reported deaths of the enemy grow more numerous by the day as well. A time of crushing bamboo will come at any moment, a turning point from precarious danger to peace.[63] It is time to recover our territory.

Yesterday, the comings and goings of the barbarian messenger were not his real intention. It was to provoke us and mock us. If we believed his sweet words and fell for his trickery, then those who used to hold the intention to die shall certainly want to live. Those who do not wish to live shall wish not to die. The royal shrine [where royal ancestors and the gods of earth and grain (*chongsa*) are worshipped] will perish. Nevertheless, let us put these aside for a moment. Let us first talk about the imminent suffering of His Highness and some recent hearsay about the severing of fingers (*tanji*).[64] These are the strangest things I have ever felt.

What our commander has been doing is leaving behind those barbarian enemy soldiers to our fatherly king (*kunbu*), thereby making His Highness desperate and cornered in a desolate fortress, where he has retreated peacefully. Insofar there has been no voice from the king to go and rescue us from disaster. Throughout the whole world, through both ancient and modern times, has there been anyone like him to conduct his duty like this? I humbly prostrate myself and petition Your Highness to have steady aspiration, unoccupied by those evil ideas. Immediately dispatch a junior officer from the State Tribunal (Kŭmorang) to retrieve the head of the commander-in-chief and hang it on a pole in the military camp. After that, not even a single wheel of a war wagon will return.[65] Here, I am humbly awaiting your decision to go further or to stop.

He wrote another petition, regarding the self-styled "subject" in the state letter [the one drafted by Ch'oe Myŏnggil, in which he called himself "the subject" and the Qing emperor "His Imperial Majesty"], and it was presented to the court. It read:

Prostrating myself in front of you, I humbly submit this petition. As I hear, the clamorous words outside the court rumored that when the envoy went to the enemy camp yesterday, they referred to Ch'oe Myŏnggil as subject, and he implored for mercy. Is this rumor true? If this is true, then this is certainly Myŏnggil's words. It remains unknown to me. Had Myŏnggil received authorization from the king or, if not, was it that he secretly decided all of this on his own? In this way, I learned about it. Unconsciously, my heart and gallbladder both dropped. I cried and could not utter a sound. The former and latter state letters were both composed entirely by Myŏnggil's hand, full of servile and vulgar words. It is thus a written surrender. Even so, if the character for subject (*sin*) was not written, the status could remain undecided. Now, if we use the designation of subject, then the division between ruler and subject is decided. If the division between ruler and subject is already decided, then we must only follow orders from the emperor. If we follow through with this and there is an order to come out of the fortress, then Your Highness must leave the fortress. If there is an order to go north, then Your Highness must go north. If there is an order to change clothes and pour wine, then Your Highness must change clothes and pour wine. If these orders are not obeyed, then based on the loyalty between ruler and subject, it will be called a crime that could be further punished. If that is the case, then the country will have been destroyed. Under that circumstance, whence does Your Highness reside?

It is the intention of Ch'oe Myŏnggil that the use of the single character "subject" in the state letter could lift the siege of the fortress and secure our fatherly king. Assuming this is the case, his intension could still be understood as the loyalty of women, eunuchs (*sa*), and persons of low birth. However, there is no measurable logic at all. Since ancient times until now, for all of the countries under heaven, were there any that could last forever and never decline? Rather than one getting on one's knees to live, why not hold fast to correctness and die for our state? Moreover, if father and son, ruler and minister, stand with their backs to the fortress and fight as one, would it not be to protect the fortress and keep it intact as well? Alas! The relationship between our country and the middle kingdom [China] is not like that between Koryŏ-Yi and the Jurchen Jin–Yuan. How could one forget the grace between father and son? How can the righteousness between the ruler and his minsters be breached? Heaven does not have two suns, while Myŏnggil wants to create two suns. The people do not have two sovereigns, while Myŏnggil wants to make them have two sovereigns. Even though anything else could be tolerated, how could this be endured? I am exhausted and have little strength. Even though I cannot use my hands to strike him, I have no desire to stand in the same court with him. Prostrating myself in front of you, I hope Your Highness will rebuke Myŏnggil's words and correct his treasonous criminality. If Your Highness should not do so, you should immediately dismiss and reprimand me, and thereby put my words to no use.

O n the twenty-second day of the first lunar month, at the time the Border Defense Command was summoned to the court, Hong Ikhan was appointed the head of the anti-peace negotiations group. His Highness the crown prince ordered, "We must leave the fortress, prepare a horse and a servant." However, they could not carry out his orders and gave up.

Vice-Minister of Personnel Chŏng On supported the anti-peace affair. He submitted a note that said,

I am prostrating myself humbly in front of you. The meaning of this trifling note I submit to you is to prevent Myŏnggil's wish to use the character for "subject" (*sin*). In one single night, he quickly came up with his plan. Because of the risk of death, I did not have the time to uncover it and so could not prevent him from carrying it out. This is my great crime. When the sovereign is humiliated, then it is natural for the subjects to die. As for my hesitation to take this action, I just bear it, as I cannot resolve it by myself. This is all fortunate because I am glad His Highness certainly does not plan to leave the fortress. How could I, as his subject, so rashly die?

However, I have also heard that those barbarians demand the officials who rejected peace, calling the return of these officials to enemy hands extremely urgent. Even though I am not their leader, I am the person who petitioned to decapitate the enemy envoy and burn their correspondence. As for those who have proposed fighting, I am indeed one of them. If my death can be even a little beneficial to the plan of survival or downfall of our state, how could I cherish my body and not die for my fatherly king? Prostrating myself humbly before you, I petition Your Highness to command the court to assign me to deal with the enemy's demands. Here, I await your decision to move forward, and stop. [The End.]

O n the twenty-third day of the first lunar month, His Highness was not at rest. The Royal Clinic (Naeguk, also Naeŭiwŏn) dispensed some medicine. They could only carry ten *chŏp* of Chŏnggisan, and that was all.[66] They administered two *chŏp* of Chŏnggisan. After giving him these dosages, he immediately recovered.

Recently, with the excuse that the anti-peace officials were not sent to the barbarians, the enemy did not permit negotiations for the stalled peace talks. Provincial Chief Military Officer Messenger (*ch'ebu chunggun t'ongjesa*) Sin Kyŏngin, Prince Nam Yang, and Hong Chindo stayed up throughout the night and went back and forth between the camps of Ku Koeng and Sin Kyŏngjin. They discussed some matters in secret. Hundreds of guards (*changgwan*) and training officers (*hullyŏn ch'ogwan*) from Suwŏn, Chuksan, and other places hoarded together in front of the palace and demanded that the anti-peace officials be delivered to the enemy. First, they went to the provincial clerk (*ch'ebu*), slapped their swords, shouted loudly in chorus, and marched in unison. Commander of War Kim Yu was afraid. The clerk paid no attention to what was right or wrong and just said, "We will try our best to meet your demands. Quickly withdraw from here!" At that time, District Magistrate of Suwŏn Ku Inhu was staying in the military camp of Ku Koeng. The district magistrate of Chuksan was Ku In'gi. The military magistrate in Ku In'gi's district is also part of Ku Koeng. Sin Kyŏngjin was now the military training general (*hullyŏn taejang*). The military insurrection that occurred today was not the intent of these troops. An official below the level of the right state councilor carried the state letter and took it to the enemy camp. He was possibly delayed and then dispatched by the anti-peace negotiations official Hong Ikhan.

The letter read:

The king of Chosŏn respectfully submits this letter to the *kuan wen ren sheng* emperor of the great Qing. I, your subject, weak and exhausted, humbly dispatch this letter to you. My sincerity is superficial. It is not certain whether I would receive your permission. I am ashamed, terrified, worried, and frightened. If there is no approval, please bear in mind that the distinction between ruler and subject cannot be randomly established. Not all of the matters regarding the state can be controlled by me alone. Even though I am harshly condemned, I face it with no avoidance. I am prostrating myself in front of you. Your Imperial Majesty, please investigate this affair.

Our small country is a weak foreign state and is distant from the lands of China (Chungdo). For those that are powerful and strong, we are subjects to them and become obedient to them. An example of this was Koryŏ to the Khitan Liao and Jurchen Jin dynasties. Now, Your Imperial Highness receives heaven's blessing, and you flood the world with good fortune. Our small country borders with yours. We have been serving you for a long time. It is certain that we should pledge allegiance to you first and set an example for other countries. The reason why we didn't respond until now is as follows: We have served the Ming for generations. Our status was fixed, and we could not suddenly change this as their subject. This was because of our emotions as well as proper Confucian ritual (*li*). As a result, we appeared absurd and committed many acts of disrespect. Since the spring of last year, the affection with which your great country treats our small country never fades. Our small country has interacted with your great country in a myriad of ways. Your great army arrives to punish us, and this is what we deserve. Ruler and subjects, high and low, anxiously live out the days and only wait to die. It was not expected that your sacred virtue could be like heaven in that you conferred compassion, as only preserving the shrines and altars of the state was considered. On the seventeenth day of this lunar month, Your Imperial Highness said, "If your country merges into my territory entirely, how could I not protect you and love you like my child (*chŏkcha*)?" On the twentieth day of this lunar month, Your Imperial Highness issued an imperial decree that said, "I have spread my generosity widely and approve of you renewing your minds." Once these gracious words spread wide, all living things met spring. This is truly to raise the dead and give life to the people once more. As for our people from our small country, our sons and grandsons, they will all praise the achievements and virtue of Your Imperial Majesty—let alone for myself—who is bestowed with the grace of rebirth.

Now, the reason why I call myself by the term "subject" and present myself to you with this expression is to hope that our country can be your tributary state and so that all our generations will serve the great imperial court of the Qing. This derives also from human emotions. Heavenly principle (*ch'ŏlli*) can never violate this. As for a so-called subject, the division between ruler and subject cannot be carelessly established. Since I already entrust my body to Your Imperial Highness, then Your Highness's orders should be enacted quickly and not delayed. As for not daring to leave the fortress, my circumstances are as honestly stated before. Merely this one transgression makes my crime deserve death.

It is written in a biography (*chŏn*), "What the people desire is what heaven allows." Your Imperial Highness is my heaven. How could this fact not be recognized? Although Your Imperial Highness forgives our crimes and approves of me, and I serve your Imperial Highness through rites (*ye*). My coming out of the fortress is a minor affair. Would Your Imperial

Highness rather permit something big and not permit something small? Therefore, what I wish for is to wait for the day the celestial troops withdraw and then intimately pay respects for your grace within the fortress.[67] I will establish an altar and bow toward your direction, so as to see off your horse and carriage. Promptly, I will dispatch a high-ranking minister (*taesin*) and appoint him as emissary, expressing gratitude for imperial grace (*saŭnsa*), to demonstrate the sincerity and gratitude of our small country. From this time on, we will decide upon the etiquette to serve the great (*sadae*), and it will become a constant routine, never severed. I serve Your Imperial Highness with my sincerity and loyalty. Your Imperial Highness also treats this small country with proper etiquette and righteousness. The relationship between ruler and subject is fulfilled completely. This way, it bequeaths good fortune to the people and sets a perfect example for future generations. Hence, for our small country, raising troops today will indeed lead to endless peace for our descendants.[68]

As for the matter of the various officials who opposed peace negotiations, we have already written about it previously and explained it fully. In general, this group of people dared to use absurd and deceptive words, destroying the grand design of our two countries. This not only angered Your Imperial Highness, but it also caused regret and indignation among the ruler and the ministers of our small country. How could there be any scruple against executing them using an axe and hatchet? However, last year in early spring, when the celestial troops reached the capital, the [anti-peace negotiations] group leader, Censorate Officer (*such'an taegan*) Hong Ikhan, scolded the officer of P'yŏngyang and replaced him as the vanguard. If he has not been captured, then he must be on the road, withdrawing troops home, so it will not be difficult to tie him up and send him to you. As for the other anti-negotiation officers who have been expelled from the fortress, the road is impassable, so it is not easy to locate their whereabouts. This is a reasonable result. With the magnanimity and generosity of Your Imperial Highness, I know you will certainly tolerate and forgive them. If you would pursue this by all means, then on the day your troops withdraw, we will find them and wait to execute them. I cautiously risk my own life by submitting this to you.

Kim Sanghŏn submitted a petition regarding the anti-peace negotiations matter. He stood outside the royal court. His Highness replied, "Your request seems excessive. Please be at ease and withdraw from here." Since Kim Sanghŏn tore up the sovereign letter on the eighteenth day, he began refusing food. He would not allow even one morsel of rice to pass through his lips for six days. His life was on the verge of ending. When he heard that the anti-peace officials would be dispatched to the enemy camp, he arose and began eating from that day onward. He said, "If I do not eat anything and die first, then certainly everyone will think I might have done so to avoid being sent to the enemy."

Former Censor-General (*taesagan*) Yun Hwang also came to the palace to petition being sent to the enemy camp. His son held up a written petition to be offered to the king. He asked to be sent to the enemy camp in place of his father. His Highness answered, "I have no thoughts about this. Do not fear at all." Fifth Counselor (*kyori*) Yun Chip and Censorate Officer (*such'an*) O Talche submitted a joint petition, requesting to be turned in as members of the anti-peace negotiations group. His Highness did not respond. There was an action to look into the anti-peace officials, possibly based on the opinions of Commander of War Yi Sŏnggu and Ch'oe Myŏnggil.

At midnight, the enemy quietly erected a tall ladder at the location where Yi Sibaek was guarding the west area of the fortress. Before they could pass over it, only one footstep away from the fortress, an officer of the Defense Command (*suŏsa*) discovered it first. Not to frighten the masses, he kicked awake the sleeping guard on the fortress wall and said, "The patrol of the royal messenger (*sŏnjŏn'gwan*) is coming." The plan for the patrol was to take place in the first *kyŏng* of the evening, patrolled by the troop-rallying officer (*tokchŏn ŏsa*).[69] The second *kyŏng* of the night was to be patrolled by the military clerk officer (*ch'ebu kun'gwan*), the third *kyŏng* of the night by the royal messenger, and the fourth and fifth *kyŏng*s by the gate defense officer (*sumunjang kun'gwan*). After all of the sleeping troops awoke, the officer [who had discovered the ladder] whispered that the enemy was entering the fortress, so the soldiers would not scatter because of such a great surprise. In the midst of this great rush, they did not have time to shoot any of their arrows at the enemy. The soldiers first tried to throw large rocks. After that, they used metal ingots and then fired arms at the enemy. The enemy fell in large numbers and finally retreated. The night was black, so at first it was unclear how many of the enemy had been killed. The next day at first light, we could see the enemy dragging their dead companions away. The blood glowed red in the snow and ice. It was understood that there were many killed.

At first, considering that the soldiers would be wearing no armor, Defense Commander Yi Sibaek, as superior commander, took the lead and never put on his armor or helmet, despite the urgency of life or death. For this reason, His Highness sent palace officials to urge him to wear his protection, but he did not receive the order in time. Therefore, he was hit by two arrows. There was much concern about him in the court, but he fortunately recovered. The troops that Sibaek led were Kyŏnggi provincial sentry troops (*ch'ogwan*) that had not been well trained. They lived through good times and hardships as one, and these soldiers became unexpectedly strong. Each time the enemy arrived for the sovereign letter, they would advance and retreat through the western part of the fortress. This was because the mountain fortress was full of dangers. Only through the western part of the fortress was it easier to move the troops. They wanted to take the advantage offered by the terrain. In the fifth *kyŏng* of the night, the enemy assaulted the east side of Namhan Mountain at Mangwŏn Fortress, but Sin Kyŏngjin repulsed them.[70] More enemy troops died here than those in the battles on the western side of the fortress. During the fighting, when there was pressing danger, three people dug holes to hide in for survival. After the battle, these holes remained. All the troops ridiculed them by calling them Yun Hole (*hyŏl*), Chŏng Hole, and Ch'oe Hole.

On the twenty-fourth day of the first lunar month, at dawn, the enemy assaulted the southern area of the fortress, where Ku Koeng defended. At dusk, they assaulted Kok Fortress.[71] Ku Koeng and his troops struck them all down, and it was a big victory. Our troops went secretly out of Kok Fortress and fired cannons. Again, there were many enemy soldiers killed, and they were defeated once more.

A few days ago, seven or eight enemy soldiers ascended Mangwŏn Peak, where they put in place large cannons. Sin Kyŏngjin ordered the experienced military trainees (*hun'guk*) to set up and fire our own heavenly cannon (*chŏnjap'o*) in response. One of them hit the enemy commander and a few of his soldiers. The remaining enemy troops withdrew. All day today, the enemy assembled another large cannon. They positioned it toward the royal residence and fired volley after volley. From where I could see, the cannonballs were as large as rice bowls. They fell onto a house where the officer in charge of the village granary (*sach'ang*) resided. There was a tower in the house and a cave below the tower. The cannonball penetrated three layers of his house and struck deep into the ground, more than a foot. Moreover, the enemy climbed over the southern side of the fortress and set up another cannon. These cannonballs crossed over the fortress toward the north, around ten *li* outside the city, and fell on an enemy camp. There appeared to be enemy people struck and killed, so they immediately withdrew from that location. When they tried to fire the cannon on Mangwŏn Peak, their gunpowder ignited, and many enemy troops were killed. When our soldiers campaigned south outside the fortress, another fire broke out, but not one of our men was killed. This was because of heavenly grace. However, military officer Yi Sŏngik was injured in the fire and, unfortunately, he succumbed to disease. After sunset, the enemy appeared outside the western gate, requesting our envoy. An officer below the rank of right state councilor took the sovereign letter and departed. Because the enemy did not receive the sovereign letter yesterday, they came again. The Three Offices (Samsa) insisted that selecting and sending a different person other than Hong Ikhan was inappropriate. His Highness approved of this.

O n the twenty-fifth day of the first lunar month, the enemy came to the western gate and requested our envoy. The envoy [Left State Councilor Yi Hongju] was ill, so Yi Tŏkhyŏng took his place. Yi Hongju went to the enemy camp, along with Yi Sŏnggu and Ch'oe Myŏnggil. The enemy returned the sovereign letter sent yesterday and said, "His Imperial Highness will leave tomorrow. If you do not emerge from the fortress immediately, it will be difficult to conclude peace negotiations. Hereafter, you ought not to come again." They also said that reinforcements from our various provinces had already been defeated. All day long, they fired cannons freely, hitting people from our country. Among the killed were the royal stable records officer (*sabok sŏri*) and military officer Yun Chŏnji, who was under Sin Kyŏngjin's command.

In the third *kyŏng* of the night, the enemy assaulted Mangwŏn Fortress again, but our soldiers were well prepared. Therefore, the enemy withdrew. The eastern part of the fortress was hit badly by cannon fire, and the battlements of the fortress were destroyed.

Four or five hundred empty bushel baskets used for grain were carried there, filled with earth, and used to reinforce the fortress. Then they were filled with water to freeze and turn into ice. Even if the fortress was hit by cannonballs, the ice-filled baskets would not allow them to penetrate the earth, and they would not cause much damage. Sin Kyŏngjin saw a military officer struck by an enemy cannonball and die right in front of his eyes. The fortress was damaged, but there was no sign of fear in him. Sin Kyŏngjin showed all of the traits (*p'ung*) of a real general.

On the twenty-sixth day of the first lunar month, the soldiers under the command of Sin Kyŏngjin and Ku Koeng came to the palace again and demanded that the anti-peace negotiations officials be handed over to them. They referred to Kim Sanghŏn, Chŏng Un, Yun Hwang, and others. The soldiers marched up to the royal secretary and made a terrible unending clamor. Royal Secretary (*sŭngji*) Yi Haewŏn appeared before them and said, "We are experiencing such a crisis, how can you come to this place so close to where His Highness resides and dare to do such a thing as this?" The soldiers were extremely angry, with eyes flashing wildly. They advanced before him, saying, "You, Royal Secretary Yi, seem like a resourceful man. If we could accompany you to the enemy camp, then we could defeat them. Let's go quickly!" A colleague advised Yi to stay away from this, and then Yi stopped. From this time onward, the situation seemed to become even more rebellious. People's hearts grew more shaken and frightened. The people said, "Of all the soldiers who are guarding the fortress, only the soldiers of the two generals of Sin and Ku came and gathered outside the palace. Other military officers did not come and demand the anti-peace negotiations officials. We all know the reason." Through persuasion, the officer from Ch'ongyung at the northern part of the fortress was ordered to come. Magistrate of Ch'ongyung Wŏn Tup'yo did not know this at all. Not one of the troops under the control of Yi Sibaek of the western part of the fortress came.

When evening arrived, Hong Sŏbong, Ch'oe Myŏnggil, and Kim Sin'guk went to the enemy camp. The two barbarians Ingguldai and Mafuta ordered the display of those captured on Kanghwa Island, the burial mound guards for the royal concubine (*changnŭng surŭnggwan*), the royal family member Prince Chinwŏn (Chongsil Chinwŏn'gun), and the eunuch (*naegwan*) Na Ŏp. They said, "Previously, on the twenty-second day, our soldiers crossed over to Kanghwa Island and besieged the royal fortress. The grand prince brothers (*taegunhyŏngje pun*), the party of the royal noble consort (*sugŭi*), and the crown princess consort (*pin'gung*) have already arrived in T'ongjin.[72] They held up the personal calligraphy set of the grand prince and conveyed the letters (*changgye*) of former Chief State Councilor Yun Pang. That night, the high-ranking ministers held an audience with His Highness, and they discussed leaving the fortress.

On the twenty-seventh day of the first lunar month, heavy fog descended. Yi Hongju, Ch'oe Myŏnggil, and Kim Sin'guk carried the sovereign letter to the enemy camp. His Highness had already agreed to leave the fortress. The sovereign letter was written as follows:

The king of Chosŏn respectfully submits this letter to great *kuan wen ren sheng* emperor of the Qing. I, your subject, on the twentieth day of this lunar month, venerably accepted your imperial edict, "Now, you arduously maintain yourself in that lonely fortress. You saw the imperial letter I sternly reproached you with, and you then knew to repent your crimes. I have spread my generosity widely and approve of you renewing your minds. I command you to emerge from this fortress and to come meet me. First, I want to see that you act in good faith and loyalty. Second, I want to bestow kindness on you. Later, when I take your kingdom and return with my victorious soldiers, I will demonstrate benevolence and honesty throughout the world under heaven. But now, I have just acquired a heavenly blessing and pacified the whole world. I am about to pardon your previous transgression and set an example for Namjo [the Ming]. If I take you through cunning trickery, given the expansiveness of the world under heaven, how can I use cunning trickery to deceive them all? That would be cutting off one's own retreat."

Since receiving this imperial edict (*sŏngji*) with honor, I have been admiring Your Imperial Highness's expansive virtue that covers all of heaven and earth. My eagerness to realign my allegiance to you grows more and more. When I look back on myself, my crimes have piled up like a mountain. I have failed to recognize the loyalty and grace of Your Imperial Highness, which had been clearly written in your imperial edict. Even though supreme heaven (*hwangch'ŏn*) has come, I bore fear and wandered around for several days. In vain, I accumulated my guilt from not observing the decrees. Now, I hear that Your Imperial Highness is about to make your triumphant return. If I could not come out early on my own and not look up at the imperial countenance, there would be no path for spreading even a little of my sincerity. Later, in my yearning for this, how would I regret this? Now, I am your subject, so I humbly consign our people and all living things (*saengnyŏng*), the thousands of *li* around us, and three hundred years of the royal temples and shrines (*chongmyo sajik*) to Your Imperial Majesty. I am so proud of my sentiments and principles (*chŏngni*) for doing this. If a setback arises, then it would be like taking a sword and ending my life. I prostrate myself in front of you here, and wish for your heavenly blessing to descend and examine my utmost sincerity and to clearly pass down your esteemed orders. This then will pave a path for me to pledge allegiance with comfort. I respectfully appeal here at the risk of death.

I went to the palace with Senior Minster of Personnel (*ijo ch'amŭi*) Yi Kyŏngyŏ. We reported to the king that we were ready to die to defend the fortress. His Highness appeared angry and ready to announce his decision to step outside the fortress. That was exactly when someone suddenly said that Minister of Rites (*yejo p'ansŏ*) Kim Sanghŏn had hanged himself and was near death. Immediately, I ran to his residence to find out. He was barely alive. The color of his face was pale like a man already dead. I could not witness his death. I untied what he had used to try to hang himself with. A short time later, he tried to hang himself again with the belt from his waist, but he was immediately saved. I went out and ran into Sanghŏn's nephew, Vice-Minister (*ch'amp'an*) Kim Kwanghyŏn and his son, the former section chief of personnel (*chŏn chŏngnang*). They had changed their clothes and were beating their breasts, as if they were performing services at a funeral for someone who had already died.

I told the two, "The death of your esteemed uncle is to establish the bonds of virtue and faithfulness (*kangsang*). How can you only watch and let him take his life?" While weeping, Kim Kwanghyŏn responded, "As for my uncle, my father's elder brother, you know him very well. Apparently, he decided to sentence himself to death. Even though we want to save him, how could we dissuade him from suicide?" I replied, "Even though the determination of your esteemed uncle is all that you say it is, if you and others could have just removed all the ropes and straps from his room, and if both his left and right arms could have been restrained, then how could he have possibly had the freedom to kill himself?" Soon after, Minister of Personnel (*ijo ch'amŭ*) Yi Kyŏngyŏ also arrived. I told him, "I happen to have an urgent matter to deal with, so I cannot stay here. Please stay and help out." Yi Kyŏngyŏ stayed and tried his best to assist in saving Kim Sanghŏn. Kwanghyŏn and Kwangch'an held Sanghŏn by the arms, making it impossible for him to commit suicide. From the following day on, there were proposals again about sending Kim Sanghŏn to the enemy camp, so eventually Sanghŏn did not die. After that, someone said that Sanghŏn had only pretended to die.

Vice-Minister of Personnel Chŏng On contemplated committing suicide without any hesitation. Earlier, a person from his home village asked him to compose an inscription and, on that very same day, he produced it. He asked his secondary son (*sŏjado*) to convey the inscription to that person. Simultaneously, he also composed several poems, including one titled "Robe and Belt Praise."[73] The poem read:

> How can a life in the world become so perilous?
> Three periods of ten days in a month are full of moon halos
>   (*wŏrhun*).[74]
> Losing my single body is not regrettable,
> But how could our state with a thousand palanquins come to
>   an end?
> Outside, we lost all of the soldiers guarding our king,
> Whereas in the court there are numerous criminals who
>   betray our country.
> What can an old man like me do about it?
> Under my waist do I wear a sword with a shining blade?

His other poem read:

> The sound of cannon fire from all around is like thunder striking,
> Which breaks down the desolate fortress and the morale of
>   soldiers, so turbulent.
> Only I still talk cheerfully, but listening,
> I elect to name my thatched house "calm" and "peaceful."

He also wrote his own eulogy (*ch'an*), and it read: "Disgrace to our king is more than plenty. Why is my death coming so late? I should discard fish and take a bear.[75] Now it is time. Accompanying the royal palanquin to surrender, I feel very disgraceful. Let's die a hero's death and treat death just like one is coming home." With the sword he was wearing, Chŏng On pierced his abdomen. Blood soaked his clothes and his bedding, dripping down on him, but he did not die. When I went to see him, he smiled at me and said, "Sometimes, when I read the *Classics*, I do not understand their meaning. I did not die today, so it can be said that I faked my death. There is an old saying, 'To lie face down on a sword means death.' If you lie face down on a sword, your five internal organs will rupture. If you lie on you back, then it is possible your five internal organs will not be damaged. From now on, I am beginning to understand the righteousness of lying face down on a sword." These kind of men have no fear at all. People like Kim Sanghŏn and Chŏng On were men of unwavering integrity. They can win glory over the sunlight.

A person named Sŏ Hŭnnam, who lived in the mountain fortress, carried the king's letters (*yuji*) on the twelfth day of this month to each province. Today, he returned and reported, "Chŏlla Army Officer (*pyŏngsa*) Kim Chullyong struck the enemy at Kwanggyo Mountain in Kwangju. They fought several hand-to-hand battles, and many enemy soldiers were killed or captured. A well-known enemy general also died. With their supplies depleted, our military collapsed." He also went to Ssangbu in Suwŏn. There, the enemy had plundered the land. He said that on the sixth day of this month, former prime minister (*chaesang*) Chŏng Ch'angyŏn died and was given a grass burial (*ch'obin*).[76] The majority of the enemy camp is now located in Ch'ŏnan. However, there are not many soldiers dispatched to the camp. He continued, "The Chŏlla provincial governor (*kamsa*) withdrew to Kongju, where he is rallying his scattered forces. The provincial governor of Ch'ungch'ŏng was nearly killed, but he survived and returned to his headquarters." Also, on Sŏ Hŭnnam's way to Ch'ŏngju, he passed by Sangju. He said the enemy still had not reached it yet. He also said,

> When I arrived in Wŏnju, the provincial governor of Kangwŏn fled toward Ch'unch'ŏn and is residing there now. Regional Naval Commander (*t'ongjesa*) Yun Suk passed through the vicinity of Wŏnju. There were no surprise attacks by taking this detour. The overseer of the station inn (*chayŏ ch'albang*) Sim Ch'ong commanded many surrendered Japanese (*hangwae*) and several of our gunners, and they encountered a dozen enemy guerrilla units but killed all of them. The enemy encamped in places like Yich'ŏn and Yŏju. Two generals were then in Yanggŭn Miwŏn, and they were blocked by the enemy from retreating.

Hŭnnam went toward the enemy, pretending to be a man who could not leave the fortress because of illness. He removed his trousers, put on all of his worn-out clothes, and crept out. There was one person wearing a crown adorned with beads, draped by a yellow cloth, sitting up before a yellow curtain and an iron plate (*ch'ŏlp'an*). Beneath the iron plate, charcoal was burning, warming him. He must have been the Qing emperor. He took pity on Hŭnnam and gave him a meal. Without using his hands, he opened his mouth and ate. He urinated in his chair. The enemy was not suspicious. After a while, he walked on his knees until receding far enough away from them, and then he stood up, ran away, crossed the wooden barricade, and returned inside the fortress. The Qing emperor suspected that he was an assassin, so the next day the emperor ordered the relocation of the camp to Samjŏnp'o.

Hŭnnam did not have a steady occupation. Sometimes he worked as a shaman and other times he worked as an ironsmith (*ch'wich'ŏl*). Now, he was doing things like this. No one could look down on him. As a result of his efforts, he was given the position of a civil official above rank three (*t'ongjŏng taebu*) as a reward.

The enemy constructed an enormous person out of wood, and it had a similar size to "the stone general" (*changgunsŏk*).[77] They loaded it into a cart, covered it, hollowed out its wooden abdomen, hid a person inside it, and built a mechanism so it could cross into the fortress. They fabricated two of these units and wheeled them next to the fortress, showing that they would cross over into it. They dug a trench outside the pine barricade, and it appeared they were unable to move it through to the fortress. Although the official envoy arrived, and we intended to come out of the fortress, we needed to prepare for climbing over it because of their newly dug trench. Moreover, the cannon fire did not cease all day long.

On the twenty-eighth day of the first lunar month, Kim Yu, Hong Sŏbong, and Yi Hongju came to the palace and held an audience with the king.[78] Chief State Councilor and Minister of Rites Kim Sanghŏn, Second Minister of Personnel (*ijo ch'amp'an*) Chŏng On, former censor-general Yun Hwang and his son, and O Talche, Yun Chip, Kim Suik, Kim Ikhŭi, Chŏng Noegyŏng, Yi Haengu, and Hong T'ak—a total of eleven people were requested to be sent to the enemy camp. The enemy only allowed the anti-peace negotiation officer Hong Ikhan, and no one else, to come. He had not approved the peace negotiations. Because of this situation, Hong Ikhan was chosen. Kim Yu, finding it difficult to make his choice about whom to send and whom to leave behind, simply sent in a petition. Also, regarding Kim Yu's discussion about leaving the fortress, he always had similar thoughts to those of Ch'oe Myŏnggil. Recently, Kim Sanghŏn's words had been uncongenial to Kim Yu's. This was all because Kim Yu boasted such claim with regard to leaving the fortress. His Highness asked the left state councilor and the right state councilor whether such requests could be met. They said they would follow what the chief state councilor decided. His Highness permitted sending eleven people instead of Hong Ikhan and declined the other request.

Kim Yu went straight to the government office. The left state councilor and the right state councilor stayed in their offices at the royal secretariat. I said to both councilors,

> In ordinary times, Your Excellences, what could you assume yourselves to be? What could people expect you to be? Now, how could you think about the work you undertook today? Later, how could you expect people to evaluate you in the annals of history? For thousands of years under heaven, is there any event similar to this? Given the lifetime affection between the left state councilor and Kim Sanghŏn, although it is not like brotherly love, as for the request of the chief state councilor, you did not think it wrong, but instead you gave him your consent. Even if you judge using personnel sentiment, how can you have such a heart to do so?

The right state councilor looked up to heaven and sighed longingly. The left state councilor appeared immediately anxious and said to Kim Yu, "As for the eleven people we ordered to go, that is a lot. Please ask again, and it might be proper to send only a few people." Kim Yu said, "I have now heard your words. You seem to know who should be sent and who should not. If you can advise explicitly regarding the persons we could send, I will follow what you suggest." I told Special Councilor Yi Kyŏngsŏk, "I wish I would be sent to the enemy and face their questioning. Unfortunately, my position is not to debate, so my words do not hold weight. You, honorable gentlemen, are the leaders of the Military Training Administration (Oktang). So how can you remain silent?" Kyŏngsŏk responded, "If Censor-General Pak Hwang comes, I will try my best with him." I told the censor-general about this in detail. He answered quickly and said, "At first, we could report this argument to the chief councilor. If he would not approve, then it is not too late to decide who should be sent." He still went to see Kim Yu and said, "Today, we have to send somebody to the enemy camp. Only a few people need to be sent, which can fulfill our responsibility. There is no need to send more than ten people. O Talche and Yun Chip wrote appeals from the start, fighting to oppose reconciliation, but this was not their personal crime.[79] Now, if these two men were sent, I could not bear to do it. But if being sent to the camp is unavoidable for these two, why don't we send them anyway?" Kim Yu retorted, "Originally, when we discussed this at the court, if I pointed out sending someone, as the minister said, why should I suggest more? Now, as the minister mentioned, let's just send those two." Pak Hwang said, "If we dispatch O and Yun, then they will blame me for this, considering the feelings of their children. Since these are state affairs, rather than sending many, sending a few is definitely better." In the end, only the two men O and Yun were sent according to Pak Hwang's advice. Yun Mun'gŏ [Yun Chip's son] never got involved with the anti-peace negotiations. Because he requested to go in place of his father, he was included among the names of those to be sent. People thought he was being treated unfairly, so Pak Hwang set him free.

Hong Sŏbong, Ch'oe Myŏnggil, and Kim Sin'guk visited the enemy camp and discussed the procedure for entering the fortress. The enemy said, "From antiquity until now, this matter has had regulations. The grade-one procedure is too cruel to be adopted. Following the grade-two procedure would be proper." The so-called grade-one procedure included "the person who surrenders holding a piece of jade in his mouth as an act of submission and carrying an empty coffin as an act of courtesy" (K. *hambyŏk yŏch'ŭn*, C. *xianbi yuchen*).[80] With this, the surrendering king should lead five hundred of his officials and subordinates, remove the defending troops along with their dignity, and come out of the fortress on the last day of the lunar month. However, it never stressed that blue clothes should be worn.[81] Presumptuously, Ch'oe Myŏnggil came in and said, "The enemy agreed on the grade-two procedure. However, it is not permitted to dress in red royal robes. They should be changed to blue clothes." Therefore, the blue clothes that His Highness and the crown prince would wear were sewn overnight. In addition, Ch'oe addressed the enemy, asking them to cease their cannon fire. At sunset today, they ended it. Those who were killed by the cannons in the entire event included six persons and one horse.

That night, a letter from Ingguldai and Mafuta was handed to the court.[82] This letter read:

> *Kuan wen ren sheng* emperor to the king of Chosŏn, as for the imperial edict sent on the twentieth day, considering the royal temples and shrines and all living things, I gave you a clear imperial edict and set your mind at ease. As for asking you to open the road and surrender to our mandate (*kwimyŏng*), shall I eat my own words? I always spread sincerity. Not only is it that I must carry out my words, but I also will help you carry out your future reformation (*yusin*). Now, you are released from your past crimes. I herein establish the regulations for you, which can become trust and righteousness between you and me as my eternal subject. Thus, if you repent and start anew, not be ungrateful, and surrender yourself fully to our mandate— making long-term plans for your offspring—then you must submit the imperial reference (*komyŏng*) and the imperial seal conferred by the Ming dynasty, apologize humbly, sever your relationship with the Ming, and cease using their reign year titles (*yŏnho*). In all of the diplomatic correspondence, accept my new calendar (*chŏngsak*). Your eldest son and the second son should be dispatched as hostages. As for all of the ministers, those with children should have their children taken as hostages and those without children should have their younger brothers taken as hostages. As contingency, if something unexpected

arises, I will establish a hostage prince (*chilcha*) as inheritor to the throne. If I campaign against the Ming, I will send down an imperial order and dispatch an envoy. I will procure foot soldiers, cavalry, and naval units from you. It might be several tens of thousands, and I might set a timeframe and a place to rendezvous. You must act without fail. Now, I am on my way back and will attack and seize the island of Kado. You should dispatch fifty vessels. In addition, naval troops, firearms, cannons, and bows and arrows should all be prepared by you. When my great army withdraws, you should reward the troops with rites. Also, when it is time for the new year (*chŏngjo*), winter solstice (*tongji*), the birthday of the empress, the birthday of the emperor, and on occasions for celebration or condolence (*kyŏngjo*), you must present tribute. Order your ministers and eunuchs to be respectful by coming forward to accept the imperial decree. As for the formality of the order, I will send a letter about it to you later. In addition, when a matter arises, if I dispatch an envoy and convey an imperial decree to you, either you must meet him in person, or your ministers must pay a formal visit to him. The imperial acceptance and farewell ritual used when meeting my envoy must not breach the same protocols as those with the Ming.

After the mass of military prisoners of war crossed the Yalu River, there might have been some who escaped and returned. Seize them and send them back to us. If you want to ransom some, you have to listen to my decision at my convenience. If one of our soldiers died fighting and was taken by your troops, you cannot keep him by making the excuse that you cannot bear binding up his corpse. All the families of ministers inside and outside the court should marry ours to make our good relationship solid. I do not approve of you building a new fortress or repairing the old one. Jurchen people who fled to your country should all be repatriated. As for trade with the Japanese, it is allowed to continue as in the past. You should instruct the envoys to visit the imperial court. I will also dispatch an envoy there. Do not resume trade with the Jurchen who escaped and are living along your eastern frontier. If you see any of them, capture them, and send them to us. As for your dead body, I bring you back to life again. I preserve your moribund temples and shrines. I locate your lost wives and children. You should think about how your country can be reconstructed. Regarding your posterity, your sons and grandsons should not violate good faith, then your country and homes will be settled forever. I, because your country is cunning and relapsing, so promulgate this imperial order.

There was a list of yearly tribute items: one hundred *nyang* gold; one thousand *nyang* silver; two hundred bows decorated with water buffalo horns; two hundred cinnabar trees; twenty one-handed sabers; one hundred tiger skins; one hundred deer skins; one thousand packets of tea; four hundred otter skins; two hundred Eurasian red squirrel skins; ten pecks of black pepper; twenty-six fine, small belt swords; one thousand rolls of fine large paper; one thousand rolls of fine small paper; four claw-dragon print floor mats; forty bunches of a variety of flower seats; two hundred bolts of white ramie cloth; two thousand bolts of various thin silk tabby; four hundred bolts of hemp cotton; ten thousand bolts of various colors of cotton cloth; one thousand bolts of linen; and ten thousand bags of rice.[83]

In-text diarist note: At first, the daughter of Prince Hoeŭn became the Khan's sixth imperial consort.[84] Later, she was remarried to his favored minister (*ch'ungsin*) from the Pipai Bo clan.[85] A concubine being offered to a favored minister is a barbarian custom. In the autumn of the *kyŏngjin* year [1640], Prince Hoeŭn became an envoy for the king, An Ŭnghyŏng became a district magistrate (*pusa*), and Yun Tŭkyŏl became a secretary (*sŏjanggwan*). Through his daughter, Prince Hoeŭn was able to reduce the tribute levy to nine thousand bags of rice. Therefore, because of this merit, all of the envoys had their official government ranks promoted. Prince Hoeŭn was bestowed male and female slaves (*nobi*) and paddy fields as rewards.

The evening of this day, O Talche and Yun Chip were about to be sent to the enemy camp. Their appearances were rather normal and they were just presentable enough. The king requested their presence and wept. He granted them a drink of alcohol as a farewell gesture and said, "As for your parents, wives, and children, I will look after them with complete sympathy. Do not worry about them." He then bade them farewell. After providing their families with rice for several years, there were no additional favors granted to them. O and Yun wept and bowed, thanking him, saying, "How could our deaths be more pitiful? Our deaths will actually be Your Highness's offense against the celestial court. We will be truly disgraced by this." With tears in their eyes, they offered their gratitude and walked out. When entering the fortress, O Talche and his elder brother Talsŭng did not have any horses. They had been walking on foot until today. Now, Talsŭng wept and spoke to the Border Defense Command, saying, "My younger brother does not have a horse and must walk on foot. Now, I cannot stand that he is being sent to the enemy camp on foot. I hope to procure someone's horse and let him ride it." Of the people who heard this, there was no one who did not weep. He did not depart because it was already dusk.

On the twenty-ninth day of the first lunar month, a state letter (*kuksŏ*) was written that read:

The king of Chosŏn respectfully submits a letter to His Imperial Highness, the *kuan wen ren sheng* emperor. There has already been baseless discussion in our small country [over war or peace], which is destroying the affairs of the state. After the autumn of last year, I picked a few of the most extreme men who held baseless debates and dismissed them. As for the person who took the lead in remonstrating [for war], I demoted him to deputy magistrate of P'yŏngyang (P'yŏngyang *sŏyun*). When your heavenly troops arrived at our frontier, I ordered him to leave promptly on that day. He may have been captured by your imperial soldiers, or he may have taken the back roads (*mundo*) and returned to his post. There is no way of knowing. As for those inside the fortress now, their crimes might be the same; however, if we compare them to those who have previously been expelled, there is a great difference. Nevertheless, when I prostrated myself and saw the earlier imperial edict issued on the day before yesterday, its meaning expressed sincere affection for our small country. If I keep this trouble from the beginning to the end, then I am afraid Your Imperial Highness has not yet examined the affairs of our country, and you suspect me of holding back secrets. If so, my sincerity to obey your will shall never be vindicated. For this reason, I investigated two people [O Talche and Yun Chip] and sent them to the entrance of the military camp, waiting for your sentence. I risk my own life informing you of this.

In the morning, the two men, O Talche and Yun Chip, departed for the enemy camp. The court did not order anyone to accompany them. However, Ch'oe Myŏnggil took it upon himself to escort the two without authorization. He told O and Yun, "If you follow my words when facing them, then there will not be any trouble at all." What he said was all about flattery and admission to the crime. O and Yun went along with this and just smiled to each other and said several yeses, to be compliant. When they were close to the enemy camp, Myŏnggil untied their straps, tied their hands behind their backs, and presented the two personally. As for the rat-like cunningness of Myŏnggil, it is worthless to mention.

The Khan bestowed Myŏnggil with a sable coat and offered him alcohol, rewarding his obedience. Below the main hall, the Khan asked O and Yun, "How could you destroy the oath between our two countries?" O Talche said, "Our country has been a tributary state (*sinsa*) with the Great Ming for three hundred years. We only know the Great Ming, and we do not know the Qing state. How would we not reject the peace negotiations?" Yun Chip added, "Our country has been a subject of the Ming for three hundred years. Our loyalty to the Ming is as the subject to the ruler, and our love to the Ming is as the son to the father. The Qing state arrogated the title 'emperor' and dispatched envoys to us. As an officer whose duty is to remonstrate, how could I not reject you? I have nothing else to say. Please kill me quickly." He said nothing more after this. They were calm and straightforward, without saying any words of flattery or submission. The two, O and Yun, were true men with moral integrity. Even if a mountain could be moved, moving their integrity was difficult. They illuminated the great righteousness that has existed since antiquity and embarrassed the traitors of the past thousands of years. They could win over the rays of the sun. As for the integrity of O and Yun, one is really neither better nor worse than the other. People who approached them sometimes spoke of the strength of Yun and the weakness of O, and sometimes the strength of O and the weakness of Yun. The common world of superficiality brings about sighs. Ch'oe Myŏnggil returned and sighed, saying, "If O Talche and Yun Chip had acted like I instructed them, they would not have been harmed. When we went out, I instructed them constantly. However, by the time we appeared in front of the khan, they replied in an opposite manner. They must certainly have been afraid and so ended up this way." Myŏnggil carried out his wicked plan through a hundred different ways, and it grew more and more extreme. Of all those who heard of it, everyone sneered at him.

Vice-Minister of Personnel Chŏng On submitted a petition:

I prostrate myself here, ready for suicide. It is because I cannot bear witnessing the affairs of today. Even though my life is nearing its end and I may only take breaths for a few more days, I really have to blame this on Myŏnggil. Although Your Highness claims himself subject and comes out of the fortress to surrender, accepting the distinction between the emperor and his subjects, as for a subject to his emperor, obedience does not only mean politeness. For matters that are arguable, it is right that you argue about them. If the Qing demand us to submit the imperial seal [of the Ming], Your Highness should argue about it. It has been almost three hundred years since our ancestors first received and applied this seal. We should send it back to the Ming dynasty. We definitely should not present it to the Qing. If the Qing request us to assist them by attacking the celestial troops, Your Highness should argue, countering: "The kindness of the Ming to us is like father to son, and the Qing knows this. Inciting the son to attack the father is related to a matter of ethics. Not only does the attacker commit a crime, but what the instigator does is also wrong." Taking this chance, their brutality and cunningness must be excused. I prostrate myself here and petition Your Highness to argue about these points, so as to make no offense to the people under heaven. That is a great fortune for our descendants. I am in my last minutes and cannot guard Your Highness nor cry at the left side of the road.[86] My crime is enormous. I hope Your Highness will come to change my occupation, and all my other work, so I can close my eyes in death.

On this day, the two generals, Sin Kyŏngjin and Ku Koeng, together with Ch'ŏe Myŏnggil and Yi Sibaek, convened in one location. I sat politely and told Ch'ŏe Myŏnggil, "Now, if you do not specifically decide on the procedure for leaving the fortress, then someday, even if there is a demand from the enemy that is difficult to obey, it will be hard to argue against it. You have to decide on the procedure today." He replied, "Today, we just keep silent. After leaving the fortress, we then make a statement about it. It will not be too late." While laughing, I replied,

Today, if we do not debate this, then when can it be better discussed? They pressure us to submit the imperial seal of the imperial dynasty (*hwangjo*) [of the Ming]. For the treasure of three hundred years that has been successively passed down to us from all of the sages, how can it be bearable to submit it to the enemy? Moreover, they will assault Kado Island and have ordered us to defile the Ming dynasty; how can that demand be followed? You need to tell the enemy, as for our dynasty's relationship with the heavenly dynasty, in righteousness we are the king and the minister, in affection we are the father and the son. The imperial seal bestowed on us cannot be submitted to you. To our parental country, we cannot attack. As for such a thing, if it is not rated difficult, what your country asked is abhorrent. Later, if someday we are instructed to betray your country, just like today when we are instructed to betray the heavenly dynasty, this cannot be followed. You should say something like this. Even though they are dogs and goats, how can it be rational if they do not listen to that? Also, gold is not originally produced by our country, and it definitely cannot be part of the tribute. This is also arguable.

In the end, Myŏnggil did not listen. He feared that unexpected issues would otherwise crop up, thus causing the negotiations to fail.

Sin Kyŏngjin said to me, "Sir, you used to remonstrate in front of His Highness. Today, there would not be a more suitable person than you to stand in front of the Khan. Why don't you speak to them?" I said, "I care nothing about myself. If you send me to the enemy camp, I will fight to the death. Why does Your Excellency not send me?" Kyŏngjin grew reserved. It is all because I previously reported his mistakes many times to His Highness.

Kim Yu told His Highness, "The crown prince will proceed north. Now, seeing the three moral advisors to the king (*samgong*), who are all old and diseased, it would be difficult for them to accompany the crown prince. I petition to select someone with physical strength who can be appointed as the new prime minister." His Highness agreed to this. The position of the right state councilor was just vacated, and Minister of Military Affairs Yi Sŏnggu was appointed to fill the post. After Sŏnggu, Right State Councilor Kim Yu repeated, "The person who accompanies the crown prince may not be a prime minister. Sending someone from the second rank (*chŏngip'um*) will be fine. Yi Sŏnggu was very talented and wise. If he remains here, it would be better because he can be consulted about the affairs of the country." His Highness approved this. He dispatched *ch'unsŏng* Nam Iung as the envoy instead.[87] It is all because Sŏnggu used to be vice-supreme commander of war, and he handled things with determination, no matter whether they were great or small. Earlier, Yu Paekchŭng submitted an appeal to behead Kim Yu, but it went unreported for three days. This was because in times of disorder, there were no daily gazettes (*chobo*) and nobody from the top to bottom ranks who could connect with Kim Yu.[88] There was no one who would say anything, so only Kim Yu spoke. That was how he could be promoted as such. Moreover, although His Highness was to leave the fortress, not a single soldier from the army troops protecting the mountain fortress was allowed to guard him. It seemed that the supreme commander of war could not be removed. Once His Highness left the fortress, there was one concern that the enemy would attack and contend for the mountain fortress. The security of the fortress was something that could not be guaranteed. In addition, it was said that Kanghwa Island had already fallen to the enemy, so it was impossible to know if family members were dead or alive. For this reason, he became eager to leave the fortress. Yi Hongju was given the title supreme commander of war [as a ruse], and took command of the soldiers (*changsa*) inside the fortress. None of these troops was at ease. We understood the hardships they had experienced on previous days.

When they left the fortress, the five hundred accompanying men were all from the office of the supreme commander (*ch'ebu*). Servants asked for permission from Kim Yu so that they could be let out. The majority of them were minor government functionaries (*isok*) and servants working for the Three Medical Offices. However, the high officer in the Three Medical Offices did not accompany them. By orders of His Highness, Yi Hongju left the fortress on the second day of the second lunar month. Without superior officers, the soldiers who were protecting the fortress scattered of their own will. Since the enemy had not pulled down all of their camps, they killed and robbed many people from our country. Out of those who had experienced many hardships and survived thousands of deaths, there was only a small number of people clinging to life. It is sad how things developed to such a point!

On the thirtieth day of the first lunar month, there was no sunshine. His Highness and the crown prince dressed in blue military uniforms (*namyungbok*).[89] They left the fortress through the western gate. Earlier, the Khan was encamped at Samjŏnp'o. He built up an altar south of Samjŏnp'o that had nine stories. He spread a yellow curtain behind him and unfolded a yellow parasol (*ilsan*). He displayed his mighty army and weapons. His military camp was orderly and solemn. Their helmets and banners shone brightly in the sunlight. The khan's seasoned troops, amounting to tens of thousands, were very tall and their bodies well built, all similar to each other. They wore cotton clothing (*myŏnsugap*) five layers thick and stood in line from left to right.

His Highness bowed three times in front of the troops and kowtowed with his head [touching the ground with the forehead] nine times. His Highness was guided to walk down the stairway and, facing west, he sat on the right side of various princes while the khan sat on the upper floor of the altar facing south. Wine and side dishes were served, and military music played. When it ended, the khan presented a gift to His Highness—two sable fur coats—and gave gifts to each of the ministers, including six high officers and royal secretaries—one sable fur coat each. His Highness donned a sable fur and expressed his appreciation under the altar. There, all the ministers also expressed their gratitude in successive order.

By that time, the crown princess consort (*pin'gung*), the grand princes (*taegun*), a middle-ranking concubine of the king (*sugŭi*), and the wives of two grand princes had already arrived at the enemy's frontline from Kanghwa Island.[90] That evening, His Highness was required to leave for the capital. The middle-rank concubine accompanying the third royal son, Grand Prince Inp'yŏng, and his wife were also allowed to enter the fortress. The crown prince, the crown princess consort, and the second royal son, Grand Prince Pongnim, and his wife were to leave for Mukden, so they were left in the camp to pitch tents and rest in the middle of the field on the enemy's frontline.[91]

Ch'unsŏng Nam Iŭng was promoted to a high-ranking courtier (*chaesin*). Censor-General Pak Hwang and Third Minister (*ch'amŭi*) Kim Namjung were elevated in rank to fourth mentors (*pubin'gaek*). Yi Myŏngung of the Crown Prince Tutorial Office (Sigangwŏn podŏk), Yi Sihae of the Tutorial Office (P'ilsŏn), and the librarian (*sasŏ*) Yi Chin were tasked to accompany them, moving north. Librarian (*munhak*) Chŏng Noegyŏng volunteered to go with them. At this time, Pak No was released and returned. He was appointed fourth mentor (*pubin'gaek*) and accompanied them north because he possessed some authority among the enemy. Kim Namjung took this chance to return and was excluded.

Assistant Supreme Commander (*puwŏnsu*) Sun Kyŏngwŏn used to fight against the enemy, but he was defeated and captured together with Pak No at the foot of Namhan Mountain. On this day, he was also released and so returned. He was given back the official seal of the assistant supreme commander that had been taken from him. When His Highness came out of the fortress, those inside wept, filling it completely with noise while seeing him off. Heaven and earth were shaken violently by those sounds.

On the first day of the second lunar month, Ŭm P'yosin, the royal messenger (*sŏnjŏn'gwan*), arrived. He said the army was disarmed and tomorrow all should come down from the fortress.

On the second day of the second lunar month, the people of the fortress all awoke and had breakfast early in the morning before they came down from the fortress. The enemy troops were everywhere in large numbers. The places that had been so familiar were now unrecognizable, and they could not distinguish east from west. Our people, who were captured, exceeded half the population of the fortress and all of the rest would not take the risk to leave the fortress or to make a sound. They were either weeping secretly and looking at each other with tears in their eyes or raising their heads and clasping their hands together, prostrating themselves on the left side of the road, which made it appear as though they were pleading. Once the enemy saw this, they struck them with iron whips. This cruel circumstance was too horrible to witness. There was a woman dressed up, face powered and proudly riding a horse. They said she was a *kisaeng* from Kwansŏ taken by the enemy.[92] In addition, within the enemy camp, there was someone lying face upward and arrogantly smoking a tobacco pipe hanging from his mouth, not showing any sadness or even the slightest concern. Feeling angry about it, I wondered where his heart was. The wives, concubines, and unmarried women of the capital elite did not dare to expose their faces to people, and they tried to cover their heads with their clothes. Almost all of them did that. When they arrived at the main camp of the enemy at Samjŏndo, the crown prince happened to be staying there. However, since the enemy camp's enforcements were very strict, there was no path through which to pay their respects to the crown prince. With the affection as his subjects, the immensity of this situation could not be spoken.

The water in the river shoal grew very deep. On the one hand, one could cross the river through the shoal, and the water flooded up to the leather saddle of his horse. On the other hand, one could take a ferryboat and each strove to be the first to cross. The chaos continued from morning until night. The enemy loaded cannons, attached devices onto wagons, and departed. These devices were as long as the ridge beams spanning two houses. The system of the wagon was very prompt and simple, and it was driven by one ox, whereas wagons were followed by more wagons on the main road. From the foot of the mountain fortress until west of Map'o, from the Han River until east of Hyŏnsŏk, enemy troops filled the fields.

The enemy soldiers coming farther south had not yet returned, but on this day, the khan departed. His Highness came out to the eastern suburbs (tonggyo) and saw him off. Starting from Chŏn'gwan, the khan went directly toward Yangju and passed Iktam Ridge, heading west.[93] The remaining troops were disbanded little by little each day, until this ended on the thirteenth day. The troop levels there could be observed. The Mongol forces in Kangwŏn Province went north. Originally, when Mongols arrived, they brought their elders, wives, and children with them. To their eyes, our country was nothing. From Chŏn'gwan until Hanyang, there were no enemy camps anymore. Dead Chosŏn people had piled up on the sides of the roads. To sadden our hearts and terrify our eyes, there really were such sights!

I entered the fortress of the capital. The houses of all of the commoners were destroyed. From the Hyanggyo village entrance until the left and right sides of the calligraphy shop (*p'ilsa*), the entrance building (*haengnang*), Taegwangt'ong Bridge, and Sogwangt'ong Bridge, all the houses had been destroyed by fire.[94] All the government officials had gone inside the palace, and the royal secretariat relocated in front of Ch'abi Gate.[95] Various government officials went inside with the royal secretariat, with no distinction of their ranks. All of the royal librarian officials of the capital bureau (*kaksa sŏri*) went to see if their fathers, mothers, wives, and children were alive or dead. The only ones left were someone called Ko In'gye, who was an official from the royal secretariat, one person who was an official of the Ministry of Taxation (Hojo), and an official from the Ministry of Military Affairs (Pyŏngjo). When I emerged from the mountain fortress, there were people who had been pillaged by the enemy. Former third minister (*ch'amŭi*) of the six ministries Yi Sanggŭp grew sick when he stayed in the mountain fortress, so he fell behind and came out alone. The enemy stole all of his clothes, and so he froze to death that night.

On the third day of the second lunar month, the two barbarians Ingguldai and Mafuta brought the interpreter Chŏng [Myŏngsu], and they came in front of the royal palace. Left State Councilor Kim Yu told them, "From now on, our two countries become father and son. What words will we not obey? Later, if you attack Kado, or if you strike the southern dynasty [the Ming], we will follow your commands." Hong Sŏbong said, "Gold is not a product of our country, so I hope you would please inform His Imperial Highness, the emperor, to remove this from the tribute list. This is the wish of our entire country." The interpreter Chŏng Myŏngsu said, "For your Eastern Country, you did not mention this clause on that day when we discussed the surrender terms. As for now, how could I dare ask General Ingguldai about this? How could General Ingguldai dare declare this in front of the khan? Your Excellency, didn't you think of propriety?" Hong Sŏbong replied, "That is so true."

Kim Yu's concubine and daughter were seized by the enemy. When His Highness entertained Ingguldai, Kim Yu informed His Highness about this and asked His Highness to inquire about them. His Highness abided by his request and asked Ingguldai. Ingguldai did not reply. After the entertainment, Kim Yu said to Ingguldai and the others, "If they can be ransomed (*sokhwan*), I am willing to pay a thousand gold." The reason that the price of captured people was absurdly high was all because of Kim Yu's single word. Kim Yu said to Ingguldai again, "As for my women's ransom, His Highness made a request, and I hope Your Excellency can help me deal with it." Ingguldai did not reply again. As soon as Ingguldai went out, those two left the court. Kim Yu embraced Chŏng Myŏngsu and whispered in his ear, "Now, together with you (*pansa*), we serve in the same family. If you have a request, I will not disobey. For my request, how can you bear to refuse? Please make every effort you can regarding the ransom of my women." Chŏng Myŏngsu did not say a word. When Kim Yu embraced Chŏng Myŏngsu, Myŏngsu hated it and he left hastily in an ill temper. It was because originally, according to barbarian custom, embracing each other is considered a familial or friendly act.

In the evening, the crown prince arrived at the palace. Five or six barbarians accompanied him. Before long, the barbarians left urgently. The interpreter Chŏng Myŏngsu rode his horse and entered the palace, just as if riding on a road. Myŏngsu urged the crown prince to immediately return after going into the palace. How could the grief of our ministers be expressed?

O n the fourth day of the second lunar month, nothing occurred.

T he fifth day of the second lunar month, I attended the discussion of the Ministry of War as the third minister of the military (*pyŏngjo ch'amji*). The ministry included Minister Sin Kyŏngjin and Minister of the Military Chŏng Kigwang. In anger, the ministers rebuked the councilors, saying, "Like rats you've brought about this situation to our country." Chŏng Kigwang forcefully agreed with his words. The wife and children of Assistant Second Chief (*chwarang*) of the Six Ministries Nam Nosŏng were captured by the enemy, so he paid a visit to the enemy camp at Map'o. That evening, before Nam could enter the meeting at the enemy camp, he was whipped by Kigwang and dragged around. This was the reason why Kigwang was shunned by scholars for a long time. It was that he stuck to the generals and was violent like them. Since returning to the capital, Ku Koeng pushed up his sleeves and bared his arms, saying loudly, "Yun Hwan used to proclaim that if the enemy comes to our country, he would lead his eight sons out to defeat them. However, where are his eight sons now? He insisted on rejecting the peace negotiations, but things came to this end. If we don't cut off the head of Yun Hwang, then how can our country be our own kingdom?" All the military people, no matter whether they were high or low rank, were still angry, and they treated the scholars as servants and slaves. These soldiers all looked awe-inspiring, and people did not know whether they would live through the day or night. All of the military people told themselves that success, preserving Namhan Mountain Fortress, was due to the effort of the military. Today, when I descended the fortress, it looked as if there had been a resurgence of the country (*chunghŭng*), the grounds were full of military arrogance.

O n the sixth day of the second lunar month, after an early breakfast, I escorted His Highness to the ninth prince (K. *kuwangja*, C. *jiuwangzi*) of Hung Taiji, who was located at Sŏgang Mountain Fortress. The crown prince was residing nearby. After first visiting the tent of the crown prince, His Highness later visited the ninth prince. The ninth prince was the ninth youngest brother of the khan.[96] The ninth prince came out following the main path to greet His Highness, and they bowed to each other while mounted on their steeds. Side by side, they held the reins of their horses as equals. The two reached the tent that was divided into left and right for sitting, facing each other, and all their respective ministers were sitting behind them in rows. After the ninth prince greeted us, food and wine were brought out and offered. Court music played. The ninth prince divided his extra food among his generals. Just like him, His Highness also divided his food up among those around him. All the ministers were originally served food. Because they had endured starvation and thirst, they ate hungrily. The only people who did not eat were three, including the *tongyangwi* Sin Iksŏng and the *hallim* Yi Chihang.[97] When His Highness returned to the palace, he had the crown prince lag behind. I grabbed the reins of my horse, cried, and said my goodbyes. The crown prince told me tearfully, "You ought to go look for your mother. I will depart westward on the beginning of the eighth day. You shall see me off in the western suburbs." I listened to these words and burst into tears. If you walk along the western river, you will see the enemy lines. As for people of our country, some were massacred while others were struck by arrows and still lived. Some saw His Highness pass by and chased after him, but they were caught and dragged away. Some faced His Highness, put their hands together and prayed. Feeling miserable, I witnessed all of this.

On the seventh day of the second lunar month, nothing much happened.

On the eighth day of the second lunar month, His Highness dispatched the crown prince. At the break of dawn, they passed toward Ch'angnŭng. Somebody incorrectly reported that the ninth prince was traveling on the low road to Ch'angnŭng, so His Highness took a detour with his escort of ten more *li* to welcome the ninth prince. Then some other person said that the ninth prince was traveling from Hongjewŏn. Before His Highness made it there, they happened upon the ninth prince en route. Therefore, they encamped there for a while and held a short conversation, bidding their farewells. After they returned to the tent of the crown prince, His Highness, the crown princess consort, and the wife of the grand prince entered the tent and talked, while the crown prince remained outside the tent.

All the ministers outside the tent where the crown prince was staying bowed and wept hysterically. The crown prince asked me, "Your old and sick mother of ninety years of age, where is she now?" I replied, "I have not heard where she has gone or whether she is dead or alive." The crown prince said, "You set aside your parents and followed your fatherly king, His Highness. When we stayed in Namhan Mountain Fortress, you sacrificed many more times than others, so you are forever in my heart." I was so moved and choked up with tears. The crown prince calmed my heart and said, "As for the affairs of heaven, who knows what will happen?"

Before this year, a person called Han Poryong, the post station attendant (*yŏkkwan*) of Ŭiju, came here as a barbarian interpreter.[98] He told the capital elites, "Although I base myself in barbarian lands, how could I lack sincerity when speaking to my home country?" He told us in great detail about the situation of the barbarians. I asked him, "How many barbarian soldiers invaded this time?" Poryong said, "They claimed to be two hundred thousand, but indeed it was just one hundred forty thousand." I asked him, "If so, how many enemy soldiers died in our country?" Poryong said, "Fewer than thirty thousand." I asked, "Did any enemy generals die?" Poryong said, "The khan's younger sister's husband, who held the title of army officer (*pangŏsa*) as we have in our country, died fighting on Kwanggyo Mountain." I asked, "So there were no troops in Mukden at that time?" He replied, "How could they empty their country of troops and all come here? There were sixty or seventy thousand left behind there." Just then, a different interpreter arrived. From that moment onward, Poryong did not utter another word. Then the crown prince and his brother, the second royal son [Grand Prince Pongnim], departed. Six attendants of the crown princesses and the four attendants of the wife of the grand prince followed. Various officials (*paekkwan*) began wailing at the same time. His Highness also shed tears. From ancient times until now, the spectacle of this day had never been witnessed.

As soon as the morning sky grew light, the enemy began marching in rows of three along the main roads. As several hundred people of our country marched in front, one or two barbarians followed, and all day long they did not stop for a break. The day after next, the population of Mukden grew to six hundred thousand, but it is said that among this number, Mongol captives were not included in the count. One can see what a great number of people were there.

His Highness did not bear to see these horrible situations. When His Highness arrived, he did not enter through the main road. He came east over the mountains, on the Sŏ Mountain Songch'ŏn road, and returned to the palace through Sin Gate (*Sin'gun*). This time, on the road in the brush market (*p'ilsi*), an elderly woman clawed and shouted aloud at the dirt, uttering,

We built up Kanghwa Island for many years and thought our soldiers and civilians could rely on its strength. What made us reach this point today? The prosecuting official [Kim Kyŏngjing] is the person who assumed the important responsibilities of the country, but he drank each day on duty. He caused all the living to die. Whose fault is this? All our children and my husband died by the sword of the enemy. Only I remain. Ah, heaven! Ah, heaven, is this not such a regrettable thing?

All the people who heard her grew miserable. The evening of this day, I inquired with His Highness about searching for my elderly mother and he gave me leave. Therefore, I did not directly see the affairs from this day onward. But I will not in the least omit to write about the matters that I heard of in detail, such as the affairs of the magistrates and army officers of the eight provinces, the beginning and ending of the Kanghwa Island incident, the confrontational affairs of future enemy negotiations, and others. I will never miss one single detail and will record all.

RECORD OF LOYALISTS EVERYWHERE

When Southern Commanding Army Officer (*nambyŏngsa*) Sŏ Usin and his troops first arrived as reinforcements, he took the main road and immediately marched toward Namhan Mountain Fortress. Provincial Governor Min Sŏnghwi advanced where the supreme field commander (*wŏnsu*) was stationed. Usin said, "Marching over a rugged road tires out the troops and exhausts the horses, making it difficult to replenish them. It would be better to head straight to Namhan Mountain Fortress." The provincial governor ignored his advice, but Usin argued for it through correspondence (*kongmun*). Until Usin reached Miwŏn, he sent petition after petition to the new general-in-command, Sim Kiwŏn, advising him to quickly advance, but his requests were never approved. He was then flogged as punishment. After emerging from the fortress, he should have been sentenced to death, but instead he was demoted and banished to the river frontier. Soon after, because Kim Siyang submitted again a memorial to His Highness, asking him to arrest and detain Usin, he was ready to be punished according to military protocol. Owing to his argument with the commanding officer through correspondence about advancing the troops quickly, which by then had just arrived at Namhan Fortress, Kim Siyang petitioned to have Usin beheaded, so as to compensate for those killed at Anbyŏng.

When Usin retreated with the troops and returned to Pondo [Hamgyŏng Province], the Mongol army was marching from Yŏngsŏ through the northern and southern provinces. Even though the peace treaty had been concluded, they slew people and plundered wealth. There was no difference between that and when they had first invaded. This is when Usin encountered Mongol troops above Ch'ŏllŏng Pass and killed many of them. The Mongols, feigning defeat, withdrew. They first stationed themselves at Anbyŏng, where they ambushed soldiers in the valley. The general of Namdo grew arrogant and negligent from this trifle victory. He unstrung his bow, returned his arrows to his quiver, and did not consider returning to battle again. Without any thought, he marched onward. The troops that he had led were attacked by these Mongol forces, and almost all of them were wiped out. Magistrate of Tŏgwŏn Pae Myŏngsun, Provincial Army Aid (*uhu*) Han Chinyŏng, and Lesser Prefectural Magistrate (*hyŏn'gam*) of Hongwŏn Song Chim all perished. The recklessness of this general was inconceivable. This was exactly what Kim Soyang's appeal referred to.

The reason Min Sŏnghwi went to Miwŏn was because he knew the supreme field commander had no intention of fighting. Every time he submitted a petition to advance and fight, Sŏnghwi was turned down by the supreme field commander and always received written documents rejecting his proposal. This is why he avoided being charged with a crime or punished. He immediately returned to the army headquarters (*ponyŏng*). On hearing that Mongol troops were riding their horses freely throughout the area and causing turmoil, he galloped his own steed alone and tried to find the enemy general, in an attempt to rebuke them for failing to keep the pledge of peace. He was treated in an extremely generous fashion. From Hamhŭng onward, the enemy did not incite any further disturbances. This was because of the accomplishment of Songhwi.

As for the military action of Chŏlla Commander Kim Chullyong, he selected nimble and brave troops and assembled them into a square, where all of the soldiers positioned on the four sides faced outward while their provisions were placed inside the square. He adopted this strategy whenever they encountered the enemy, and he led the battle. When they came upon Kwanggo Mountain, they stationed themselves there. It only takes a breath to get from there to Namhan Mountain Fortress. The next day, the enemy appeared and launched an attack, but our forces killed countless numbers of enemy troops. They also killed a well-known enemy general. That general was the brother-in-law of the khan. Then they ran out of arrows, exhausted all their supplies, and withdrew to set up camp at Suwŏn, where they searched for provisions to advance forward. However, the soldiers gave up, scattered, and finally could not prevail. This was why Chullyong was dismissed.

Provincial Governor of Py'ŏngan Hong Myŏnggu ordered Army Officer (*pyŏngsa*) Yu Im to assume command of the troops. They both took charge of their soldiers, marching them forward. Because Yu Im did not immediately accept this, Myŏnggu threatened that he would face military punishment. Yu Im had no other choice but to obey the command. From this moment on, the two generals no longer cooperated and disrespected each other at every turn. When they arrived at Kimhwa, countless enemy soldiers sprung out to attack. Yu Im camped on a high mountain top, while Hong Myŏnggu set up camp below. Hong wanted to combine the two camps, but Yu failed to comply with this order. The enemy attacked the provincial governor's camp first. Yu Im and Yi Irwŏn only watched and did not come to their aid. Hong knew that he would unavoidably die but remained calm and would not retreat whatsoever. He did not stop shooting his arrows at the enemy until he was killed. Yu Im and Yi Irwŏn were both famed military officials. Also, the arquebus troops under the command of the royal guard were numerous. They tried their best to fight, killing countless enemy soldiers. The enemy retreated after exhausting all of their efforts. In the *pyŏngja* year [1637], the defeat of the enemy, unlike this battle, was not equal to the battle of Kim Chullyong at Kwanggyo Mountain. Yu Im's victories were the greatest. The enemy treated this as medium defeat.

Assistant Supreme Commander (*puwŏnsu*) Sin Kyŏngwŏn defended Ch'ŏrong Fortress.[1] When he sighted the enemy, he sent several hundred troops to engage them in battle, killing and capturing a few enemy soldiers. Our troops were greedy for small rewards, thus they did not return immediately. After a while, the main force of the enemy suddenly appeared, and our soldiers ended up behind enemy lines, unable to enter the mountain fortress. Some of them were killed by the enemy and some scattered. The enemy besieged the impregnable fortress for many days, but because the fortress was rugged and could not be taken, they pretended like they were raising the siege and retreated. Kyŏngwŏn promoted Kwaksan County Magistrate Chŏng Pin and advanced to reconnoiter the situation. Chŏng Pin was hit by an enemy arrow and took rest in a commoner's house. He returned and reported that the enemy was no longer present. Kyŏngwŏn, not doubting this report, led troops out to load horses with containers of provisions for the frontline. The enemy ambushed them at the approach to Hyang Mountain, having seized refugees from our country so they could learn the details of Kyŏngwŏn's timeline to advance. When Kyŏngwŏn's troops passed by, they mobilized their forces and violently attacked them. All of our military troops scattered and fled, but Kyŏngwŏn was captured alive and held in the military camp of Prince Mingdal (K. Myŏngdal). Prince Mingdal was one among the ten princes. While spending his time with this barbarian prince, Kyŏngwŏn became very close to him. After leaving the fortress, the barbarian prince feared that Kyŏngwŏn would receive the death penalty and begged Kyŏngwŏn to come in front of him. The prince organized a small ritual where he first bowed to Namhan Mountain. Kyŏngwŏn was soon released. Despite that, the Censorate insisted the situation with Kyŏngwŏn was incorrect and His Highness called it distressing, but in the end dismissed the Censorate's suggestions. Before long, the court designated him general of Ch'ongyung (*Ch'ongyung taejang*).

When Governor of Kangwŏn Province Cho Chŏngho first heard about this upheaval, he took command of his troops and brought them to serve as reinforcements, doing this before the officers from all of the other provinces. Still, his soldiers scattered before succeeding in their duties. However, compared to those who never dispatched their troops to reinforce us, his actions were totally different from what they had done. A military man (*muin*) called Im Mongdŭk came from Wŏnju and entered the besieged fortress. His Highness asked him about the situation in Kangwŏn Province. Mongdŭk, wanting to boast about himself, falsely slandered the provincial governor, saying, "The provincial governor doesn't do anything during the day. He just sits inside the governor's office (*kamyŏng*). I rebuked him loudly, so he finally began dispatching troops there." The magistrate from Wŏnju, Yi Chunggil, resented Cho Chŏngho, who had been promoted to a higher rank. Thus, he arrested Chŏngho and locked him up in prison. By all means, he unreasonably slandered Chŏngho. His Highness heard about this and ordered Chŏngho exiled, but he was released from exile the following year. Mongdŭk was appointed to be chief of ten thousand households (*manho*) because of this.[2]

Supreme Field Commander Kim Chajŏm advanced his troops to Tongsŏn, where they killed and captured many enemy soldiers.[3] But after the khan took command of the main invasion force to engage in combat, he did not dare think about striking the enemy again. After Yi Paewŏn, the provincial governor from Hwanghae, was charged with protecting the province (*pondo*), he, together with Provincial Commander (*pyŏngsa*) Yi Sŏktal, led five thousand troops from Haesŏ [Hwanghae Province] along with several thousand arquebus soldiers from the royal guard and marched to T'o Mountain to serve as reinforcements. However, they failed to dispatch scouts and departed early. At sunrise, five or six thousand enemy troops suddenly ambushed them. Almost all of Haesŏ's forces were killed. The supreme field commander escaped alone by riding off on his horse and ascending into a village behind Chu Mountain. Staff Officer (*chongsa*) Chŏng T'aehwa quickly rushed toward the county office. Prefecture Magistrate of Kangum Pyŏn Sagi entered a nearby home of a commoner. At that time, when they were unable to take any action and were waiting to be captured, the arquebus troops of the royal guard (*ŏyŏngch'ŏng*) unleashed a volley of bullets in unison. The enemy advanced and repeatedly attacked, but time after time, they were beaten off. Of the original five thousand–plus troops, no more than several thousand survived. At dusk, the enemy troops withdrew. The next day, hand-to-hand combat broke out again. Finally, the enemy could not continue fighting and ended up withdrawing. This was not a victory for the commanders. It was the royal guard that had made the effort. However, the court praised Chŏng T'aehwa and Pyŏn Sagi for their courage and resourcefulness, and, years later, they were promoted. Chaeryŏng Country Magistrate Ch'oe Taeksŏn, who insisted on not promoting them, was killed because of this. Kim Chajŏm led the troops of the royal guard. He marched to Miwŏn and camped there for twenty days with new Supreme Field Commander Sim Kiwŏn, the provincial governor, and the army officers (*pyŏngsa*) from each of the provinces. They heard of His Highness and the others emerging from Namhan Mountain Fortress and that is when they started to advance. Because of this, Sim Kiwŏn was exiled to Naju and shortly afterward he was relocated to Namhan Mountain Fortress, which was not long before he was released. Kim Chajŏm was exiled to Chindo and then was immediately relocated to Chungdo. In the autumn of the *kimyo* year [1639], he was released and sent back to his hometown. In the Two Offices, their cases [the demotion of Sim Kiwŏn and Kim Chajŏm] stirred controversy and debate for several months. They did not reach an agreement about this. Later, these two people were both designated ministers of war (*pyŏngjo p'ansŏ*).

Provincial Governor of Chŏlla Yi Sibang posted countless numbers of troops to the cavalry commander (*pyŏngsa*). He enlisted several associate commanders for the remaining troops to supplement them and had them march forward. The troops would sweep up any enemy guerilla fighters or launch attacks at night. Yi dispatched the chief military officer and Yŏngam Country Magistrate Ŏm Hwang to set up a garrison at Yangsŏng and serve as vanguard. He claimed that he waited by himself for the monastic soldiers (*sŭnggun*) to arrive, so he could then join forces with Provincial Governor of Kyŏngsang Sim Yŏn to fight together.[4] When he learned that the troops of Kim Chullyong, the army officer at Kwanggyo Mountain, had totally crumbled, he pulled back to Kongju on the pretense of rallying the scattered forces. Since the provincial governor had retreated, all the soldiers had withdrawn. Because of this, Yi Sibang was exiled to Chŏng Mountain, where he lived for a year. He was then pardoned and promoted to magistrate (*moksa*) of Cheju Island.

Following the correspondence, Yi Sibang sent messenger (*t'ongjesa*) Yun Suk to abandon the main garrison (*ponjin*). Yi had Provincial Army Aid (*uhu*) Hwang Ik head the naval forces. Yi led several hundred troops under his command and marched to the mountain valley districts in the vicinity of Wŏnju, cleverly avoiding the enemy. In the end, they did not encounter even one enemy soldier. Afterward, while being exiled to Yŏnghae, he died of disease. Each of the generals of the naval or land forces should have their own jurisdictions. If they had been at the main garrison, led the naval forces of the three provinces, and promptly come up to Kanghwa Island, how would they have been defeated there?

Provincial Governor of Kyŏngsang Sim Yŏn commanded his own provincial troops. There was not much worth seeing. From Ch'ungju Mokkye, he came to the distant mountain fortress, but in the end did not advance. On the second day of the first lunar month, he began to march toward Yŏju Yŏngnŭng [the royal tomb of King Sejong]. Hearing about the defeat at Ssangnyŏng, he quickly passed over the mountains and ran into Kim Sik, the general from Choryŏng (*ch'angǔi taejang*). The people Kim Sik led amounted to only a few hundred, which included country scholars (*sain*), personal slaves (*nobok*), and others. He also let advisors (*ch'ammo*) and military officers (*kun'gwan*) lead their own troops. With merely six or seven of the capital elite, Sik stealthily marched somewhere between Choryŏng to Chungnyŏng. When he arrived to greet the provincial governor, somebody sparked a rumor that the enemy was near. Those below the rank of provincial governor each whipped their horses and fled. Afterward, having learned about the false rumors, they appeared embarrassed, and their faces turned bright red.

Later, Sim Yŏn was sent into exile at Imp'i.[5] Not long after that, he was promoted to magistrate (*moksa*) of Cheju. Afterward, his rank was greatly elevated as he was appointed to a prominent post. Sim Yŏn was designated chief advisor officer. When he assumed his post, he appointed an ex-staff officer named To Kyŏngyu as his associate officer (*chongsagwan*) and left all the military affairs to him. The provincial military commander of the left and the provincial military commander of the right led the troops of the nearby township, advancing them to the foot of a hill. However, the majority of the troops coming from afar barely made it, and their supplies all remained in the rear. Thus, the left and right commanders withheld their directives and did not advance any further. To Kyŏngyu beheaded Pak Ch'unggyŏm, the provincial military commander of the right's military clerk official (*pyŏngbang kun'gwan*). Day by day, he pushed urgently to advance the troops.

Thus, the left and right commanders had to advance reluctantly. However, in the extreme cold, these soldiers had to forsake all of their clothing. The unlined clothes they wore were extremely thin and were cut even shorter. Every day, as they were forced to march, they grew so frozen and hungry that their morale plummeted. As a consequence, it was said that their defeat at Ssangnyŏng was all because of Kyŏngyu. After the enemy withdrew, Kyŏngyu returned south, but on his way he was struck by a bullet and died. The family members of Kyŏngyu reported to the government office that his death was caused by Pak Chunggyŏm's two sons. These two people were arrested and imprisoned for several years. Finally, the charges were dropped, and they were released.

Provincial Military Commander of the Left Hŏ Wŏn and Provincial Military Commander of the Right Min Yŏng led troops of over four thousand men in total. Hŏ Wŏn was old and so frightened he began sobbing. When he faced others, tears streamed down his face, thus everyone knew that he would surely be defeated. They advanced toward Kwangju Ssangnyŏng. Min encamped on the right side of a hill while Hŏ set up camp on the left. The elite hunting troops (*p'osu chŏngbyŏng*) were not stationed on the outside but rather placed inside for defense.

On the third day of the first lunar month, the enemy rushed into combat with the provincial military commander of the right, penetrating the wooden barricades. The troops did not fight but scattered instead. After the left army was defeated, the enemy fought Min's troops to a stalemate. Later, a few of Min's troops were killed, as their gunpowder caught fire and exploded, causing a huge disarray among the men. Taking advantage of this, the enemy attacked them brutally. The two forces of the left and right armies were immediately defeated. Both commanders of the left and the right were also struck down in the battle. After they died, Provincial Governor Sim Yŏn, in his emergent correspondence, reported that Hŏ fled to escape death. Hence, a memorial ceremony and a ritual sacrifice were held to canonize (*chŭngjik*) Min Yŏng but not Hŏ Wŏn. Hŏ's son submitted a petition to the court, and, after complaints of injustice, ritual sacrifice was later offered for Hŏ.

Chŏng Hongmyŏng, the general of the righteous army of Chŏlla and the former advisory officer, reached Kongju. There, he learned that the enemy had withdrawn, so he escorted His Highness on his return to the capital.[6]

W hen I departed from my original residence (*kŏbin*), Kim Kyŏngjing was leaving to enter Kanghwa Island.[1] He had his mother and wife ride in palanquins, covered each of their female servants with felt rain hats (*chŏnmo*), and he and his servants mounted their horses. There were fifty horses, including all the horses carrying baggage. This number of horses and grooms nearly equaled that which could be found in the vicinity of the capital. Because the horse that one female servant was riding limped and fell behind, he blamed the escort as being unsafe. For this reason, he took a local official who was accompanying them to the side of the road and beat him.

At first, Kyŏngjing, along with Magistrate Yi Min, begged Staff Officer Hong Myŏngil to let them enter Kanghwa Island. High Minister (*wŏnim taesin*) Yun Pang, Kim Sangyong, Vice Minister Yŏ Ijing, Board of Ceremonies (*chŏngnang*) Ch'oe Siu, Shrine Official (*sajiknyŏng*) Min Kyŏn, *ch'ambong* Chi Pongsu, Yu Chŏng, Shrine Attendant (*chongmyoryŏng*) Min Kwanghun, Director (*chikchang*) Yi Ŭijun, and Official (*pongsa*) Yŏ Ihong all conducted rites for the royal ancestors and the gods of earth and grain (*chongsa*).

Royal Secretary (*sŭngji*) Han Hongil gave his services to Her Highness—the crown princess consort (*pin'gung*)—and the eldest son of the crown prince (*wŏnson*). Two junior concubines (*sugŭi*), Grand Prince Pongnim [future King Hyojong], Grand Prince Inp'yŏng, his wife, the servants of the royal palace, sons-in-law of the king (*puma*), the princesses, and the king's daughters by a royal consort (*ongju*) all followed. First Minister (*p'anbusa*) Chŏng Kwangjŏk, Councilor (*sajae*) Pak Tongsŏn, former minister (*p'ansŏ*) Yi Sanggil, Kang Sŏkki, Official (*tongji*) Chŏng Hyosŏng, Military Training Commander (*tojŏng*) Sim Hyŏn, all being old, infirm officials, went to Kanghwa out of obedience to His Highness. Director of Military Affairs (*musin chisa*) Pyŏn Hŭp, former third minister (*ch'amŭi*) Hong Myŏnghyŏng, Sim Chiwŏn, former junior third minister (*chŏng*) Yi Sijik, Official of Ancestral Rites (*pongsangjŏng*) Cho Hwijin, Inspector-General (*changnyŏng*) Chŏng Paekhyŏng, Tutorial Official (*p'ilsŏn*) Yun Chŏn, former fifth councilor (*kyori*) Yun Myŏngŭn, Censorate Officer (*such'an*) Yi Ilsang, Assistant Section Chief at the Ministry of Works (*kongjo chwarang*) Yi Haengjin, Pak Chingbu, temporary lecturer (*chinggang*) Pyŏn Pogil, Inspector of the State Tribunal (*tosa*) Ki Manhyŏn, Assistant Section Chief of the Ministry of Taxation (*hojo chwarang*) Im Sŏnbaek, Copyist of the Diplomatic Correspondence Office (*sŭngmun chŏngja*) Chŏng T'aeje, Im Pu, Third Proctor from the National Confucian Academy (*hanggyu*) Yun Yang, former prefecture magistrate (*hyŏn'gam*) Sim Tonggu, Royal House Administrator (*ch'ŏmjŏng*) Yi Sagyu, Royal Chief Archivist (*sabok chubu*) Song Siyŏng, Assistant Proctor (*pyŏlchwa*) Kwŏn Sunjang, and Ritual Archivist (*pongsang chubu*) Ko Chinmin all followed. Those who did not assemble in time, or those who scattered to other places, followed them onto Kanghwa Island afterward.

Minister of Rites (*yejo p'ansŏ*) Cho Ik did not receive the orders and thus fell behind. He ended up going to Namyang. At first, he organized some righteous troops there and then moved onto

Kanghwa Island. Former Chancellor of the National Academy (*taesasŏng*) Yi Myŏnghan, and Third Minister (*ch'amŭi*) Yi Sohan were in the middle of mourning for their parents. Feeling such deep regret about having to give up their mourning rituals, they fled to Kanghwa Island.

At this time, Her Highness arrived at Kapkok for the ferry between Kimp'o and Kanghwa Island, but the boat was not there, and so she was unable to cross.[2] She remained on the river bank for two days and nights, growing extremely cold. The prosecuting official (*kŏmch'alsa*) held the authority for ferrying people across. All of the boats had ferried to the other side of the river and could not return. From inside the palanquin, Her Highness kindly raised her jade-like voice and said loudly, "Kyŏngjing! Kyŏngjing! How could you let this happen to me?" Special Mayor (*yusu*) Chang Sin learned about this and spoke to Kyŏngjing. They barely had time to assist Her Highness across to the other side of the river. For the other people, refugees amounting to thousands and tens of thousands of commoners, they were found everywhere near the ferry. Despite their eager pleas for help, they were unable to cross the river. Then the enemy cavalry arrived quickly, and, in the blink of an eye, trampled them violently. Some were injured and robbed. Others plunged into the water.

Kyŏngjing transported grain from Kimp'o by boat ostensibly to assist the capital elites on the island. However, no one ate it except Kyŏngjing's friends and relatives. Grain was invaluable, and [material] treasure was worthless at that time. Kyŏngjing only planned on profiting from this. Also, he intended to transport grain to Haeju and Kyŏlsŏng for storage. Because of the fall of the island to the enemy, his plan was foiled. Kyŏngjing thought that Kanghwa Island was an impregnable city and that even if the enemy could fly, they would be unable to cross over to it. From morning until evening, he feasted, and he drank every day. The mountain fortress had been under siege for months. There was no correspondence inside or outside the fortress. But Kyŏngjing did not even think about our fatherly king. If the high ministers raised some issue, he would say, "Should high ministers, who have come here as refugees, tell me what to do?" If the grand prince (*tae-gun*) expressed his opinion, he would respond, "How can the prince interfere at this critical juncture?" The prince and the high ministers could not even open their mouths.

Special Commander (*pyŏlcha*) Kwŏn Sunjang and the scholar (*saengwŏn*) Kim Ikkyŏm submitted a letter to Kim Kyŏngjing, Yi Min'gu, and Chang Sin: "This is now a case of enduring unspeakable hardship. Now is not the time to consume alcohol." Kyŏngjing grew enraged. He did not deserve all the blame. All the remaining people were beaten down by the hardships of Kanghwa Island and so they spent no effort toward preparing its defenses. They dismissed all of the company commanders (*ch'ogwan*) back to their homes, thus no scouting was conducted outside the island, and all of the people who knew about these failures felt disappointed and hopeless. Rumors circulated that Ch'ungch'ŏng Governor Chŏng Segyu was killed in the enemy camp, and news arrived from the court (*chojŏng*) that Yi Min'gu was appointed in his place. Min'gu thought that Kanghwa Island was a secure location, but that Hosŏ was certainly a dangerous place. He intended to quickly escape by any means possible. The local branch office (*punsa*) urged him to leave as soon as possible, but he retorted that he needed some alcohol to fend off the cold, because the bitter wind was blowing wildly. That he was in need of warm wine was an excuse to kill time. Also, he asked to bring his wife and children. Former chief state councilor Yun Pang was Min'gu's uncle-in-law (*ch'ŏsamch'on*). Min'gu's wife tried to get assistance from Yun Pang, but Min'gu essentially prevented her.

Prior to this, the capital governor of Kyŏnggi was walled up in the besieged mountain fortress and could not attend to the matters in Kyŏnggi. The court requested that Min'gu be designated the governor (*kibaek*). His Highness said, "This person can be entrusted to take care of my young orphan. Try to find another candidate." A high-ranking minister suggested, "Even if Min'gu is appointed to this position, when he might be needed in the future, he can still accept the responsibility." Therefore, His Highness approved this. Because the enemy siege was severe, the royal edict could not go out. There was no single person from the naval forces of the three provinces [Ch'ungch'ŏng, Chŏlla, and Kyŏngsang] who was willing to come save the kingdom from this great crisis.[3] Only Naval Commander (*susa*) Kang Chinhŭn arrived on Kanghwa Island one starry night. The prosecuting official (*kŏmch'alsa*) arranged for the boat that Kang Chinhŭn had commanded to Yŏnmi Pavilion and various other locations off the island. Boats from the island were moored at Kwangjin Harbor.

In the *chŏngch'uk* year [1637], on the twenty-first day of the first lunar month, Local Magistrate of T'ongjin Kim Chŏk reported to the prosecuting official (*kŏmch'alsa*). The official said, "The enemy has loaded play carts (*tongch'a*) onto little boats, and they are leaving for Kanghwa."[4] Kyŏngjing responded, "The river is still frozen, so how could they do this by boat?" He thought this rumor was meant to undermine army morale and wanted to cut off Kim's head. The reports of the guard (*p'asu*) from Kapkok were exactly what Kim Chŏk had described. Only then did Kyŏngjing grow horrified. He appointed Naval Officer (*haesungwi*) Yun Sinji to defend the Taech'ŏng Ferry, former officer (*ch'anggun*) Yu Chŏngnyang to defend Purwŏn, Yu Sŏngjŭng to defend Changnyŏng, and Yi Hyŏng to defend Kari Mountain, whereas Kim Kyŏngjing stationed his camp below Chinhaeryu and defended Kapkok on his own. There were only a few hundred soldiers, and the situation had become extremely urgent. When the military equipment and gunpowder were distributed, they were immediately depleted. Things were prepared in such a haste, so how could one expect a good outcome?

At first, Grand Prince Pongnim accompanied Kim Kyŏngjing to review the military camp. Finding only a few soldiers present, he returned inside of the fortress. He wanted to establish a strategy to take charge of the military affairs and arrange the defenses, but all of the people had fled and scattered, and no one remained. Failing all else, he intended to defend the fortress.

Special Mayor (*yusu*) Chang Sin was appointed commander of the fleet (*chusa taejang*). He quickly dispatched a naval vessel from Kwangjin up the river in the direction of Kapkok. It was the time when the moon was in the last quarter, thus the tide was very low. They poled the boats all night long. On the morning of the twenty-second day, they had nearly reached only five *li* away from the lower part of Kapkok.

Kang Chinhŭn took charge of seven boats and stationed them at Kapkok, where he engaged in an intense battle against the enemy, sinking several of their vessels. Chinhŭn's boats were struck by heavy cannon fire, and dozens of soldiers were killed. Even though Chinhŭn was hit by a few arrows, he seized a number of bows, arrows, and weapons from the enemy. Chinhŭn only commanded a few boats, but Chang Sin, gauging the urgency of the enemy's power, had no intention to advance. Chinhŭn beat a drum and waved a flag to boost Chang Sin, but he did not advance even in the slightest. On his boat, Chinhŭn moved forward, shouting angrily at him, "You owe a great debt to our country. How can you bear this? I must behead you!" In the end, Chang Sin did not move and, following the current, began moving back down stream.

At that time, Chŏngp'o Chief of Ten Thousand Households (*manho*) Chŏng Yŏn and Tŏkp'o Associate Commander (*ch'ŏmsa*) Cho Chongsŏn were serving as troops on the front line. When the enemy first crossed the river, Chŏng Yŏn sank one of the enemy vessels and wanted to move forward and fight. Chang Sin struck a gong to signal retreat, so Chŏng Yŏn and others withdrew and then returned. At first, the enemy had suspected an ambush, thus they hesitated and did not send out any boats. Then one enemy vessel approached, engaged in battle, and landed on the riverbank. Seven enemy soldiers gained a foothold ashore. Without firing any arrows, they each grasped their swords, moved along the riverbank without any horses, traveled north, and scampered up the top of a hill to look around. There were no ambushes anywhere. Knowing it was impossible to defend themselves, they encamped at a high elevation and raised a white flag, signaling to the enemy [their own forces] to cross from the other side of the river. Only then did the enemy ships begin filling the waterway and cross.

Kanghwa Island Chief Military Officer (*chunggun*) Hwang Sŏnsin took command of over one hundred troops from the company commander (*ch'ogwan*) and fought intensely just below Chinhaeru. Sŏnsin himself shot and killed three enemy soldiers. Other troops shot and killed six of them. Hwang Sŏnsin made a valiant effort but was killed in action. All of his troops fled, scattering. When this happened, the company commanders of Kanghwa were in Chang Sin's boat. Because the leader, Chang Sin, was not with them, not even one person would step ashore. Kim Kyŏngjing knew now that nothing could be done. He rushed to the harbor, abandoned his horse, and waded into the water where he boarded a boat to flee. At that time, Kyŏngjing's and Chang Sin's mothers were both inside the fortress, but the two men took the boats to escape. Both of their mothers eventually died in the fortress.

A prime minister led several people to defend the fortress. He said that whoever goes out of the fortress must first carry military orders. Her Highness, the crown princess consort, ordered all five eunuchs (*naegwan*)—Kim In, Sŏ Huhaeng, Im Yumun, Kwŏn Chun, and Yu Hosŏn—to escort the eldest son of the crown prince (*wŏnson*) to shore. Song Kukt'aek, Min Kwanghun, Yŏ Ihong, Min Kyŏn, Yu Chŏng, Yi Ŭijun, and Battalion Commander (*pujang*) Min Usang met to discuss this, saying, "The eldest son of the crown prince has already departed. Why should we still defend our fortress for no reason?" Therefore, they were escorted out of the fortress. Kim In embraced the eldest son of the crown prince and traveled west, but his horse grew exhausted, and the enemy was approaching. Song Kukt'aek traded the horse he was riding with Kim In, and thus they could reach the shore. Coincidently, a boat was moored there, just as though it was waiting for them. They boarded it and sailed out to sea. Several days later, they reached Kyodang. This indeed was heaven's will.

There was word that the two enemy generals, General Kong (K. Kyŏng) and General Geng (K. Kyŏng), wanted to search for people on the islands. They moved from Kyodong toward Chumun Island and then from Chumun Island toward Tangjin Island. When this happened, the local inhabitants of Chumun Island all assembled at the harbor and asked, "Is this the boat from Kyodong?" The person in the boat asked them why, scolding them. An islander replied, "It's because last night, many inhabitants of this island dreamed that a boat riding on a five-colored cloud came to our island from Kyodong. That is why we asked." Everyone on the boat was surprised by this strange event. Director of Military Affairs (*chisa*) Pak Tongsŏn and Third Minister (*ch'amŭi*) Sim Chiwŏn were also in the boat. They heard this themselves and later reported it. Song Kukt'aek had his rank upgraded (*kaja*), and others were also promoted. A high minister submitted a memorial and stated that the people in the boats were all government officials and had thrown away their ancestral tablets (*chongmyoju*). Except for Kukt'aek, the others were all reprimanded and deprived of their promotions.

The enemy troops assaulted from all directions. Former right state councilor Kim Sangyong knew that the situation was precarious. He removed the clothes he was wearing and presented them to his servant, saying, "If you leave here safely, offer these clothes to my sons. Someday, in place of my body, they could have these clothes entombed." He immediately stepped outside the southern gate and sat atop a chest of gunpowder. All the people around him were told to leave. However, Kim Ikkyŏm and Kwŏn

Sunjang asked, "Your Excellency, are you carrying out something good on your own?" They would not leave. Sangyong lit a fire and blew himself up, burning himself to death. Ikkyŏm and Sunjang also died along with him.

Yun Pang, as assistant commissioner for the royal ancestral shrine (*chongmyo chejo*), remained behind, at the place where the ancestral tablets (*myoju*) were preserved. When the enemy reached them, he shouted, "You must kill me!" The enemy did not respond and threw the ancestral tablets into a dirty ditch. Yun Pang collected them, wrapped them in a straw mat, and trotted off on his horse, declaring, "When I cross the sea, I will cast myself into the water and die." The enemy threatened him, forcing him ashore. Yun Pang worried about the enemy capturing the ancestral tablets. He divided them up, wrapped them in slaves' clothes, and loaded them up on a horse. He had a slave girl ride a horse with them. After this incident, the Three Offices undertook an investigation and insisted on punishing him. He was penalized and removed from his post and detained in exile. He was later released and returned, but he died shortly after.

Chief Rector (*tojŏng*) of the Military Training Administration Sim Hyŏn was determined to die with his wife. He composed a letter to the throne, tucked it into his chest, and they took their lives together. It read, "I, your humble servant, face east and bow a hundred times. I submit this letter to His Highness in Namhan Mountain Fortress. Along with my wife of the Song clan, I have committed suicide to repay my obligation to the country."

Chief Archivist (*chubu*) Song Siyŏng used to live with Yi Sijik in a single house. At that time, Siyŏng was the first to commit suicide. When Sijik tied up his neck and asked his servant to pull tightly, his servant could not bear to follow his demand. Sijik handed his servant a suicide note, and his headband to leave behind for his children, then hung himself on his own. His suicide note read,

The powerful turbulence of the water of the Yalu turned it into a moat protecting Korea from invasion, but now that defensive barrier is gone, and the northern military rapidly ferried across, like they could fly.[5] While the drunken generals just know to cry over their losses, they betrayed their country to live out their lives. While the defenses have collapsed and all the people have just become fish and meat to our enemy, your mountain fortress at Namhan will fall in a day or two. It is not righteousness to live out a worthless existence, so I am willing to take my own life and die a martyr. Whether to be looked down upon or be paid respects to, I feel no regrets. Oh, my son. Do not feel saddened by my loss. Just take my remains and bury them. Serve your elderly mother well, hide your residence in our hometown village, become a hermit there, and never leave. Those are merely my last wishes, and I am here to narrate them.

The capital elite who committed suicide were Yi Sanggil, Chŏng Hyosŏng, Hong Myŏnghyŏng, Yun Chŏn, and Chŏng Paekhyŏng. They were all honored and publicly memorialized. Among them, a couple of people were said to have been killed by the enemy, but no one witnessed this directly. How can rumors cover up their mere kindness?

Sŏng, the son of the late high-ranking courtier Min Inbaek, first killed his wife and children and then committed suicide. Another son of Sŏng was far away, so he survived. Yi Sagyu died by the sword of the enemy. The people who died like this could not all be recorded.

The women who committed suicide were the wives of Kim Yu, Yi Sŏnggyu, Kim Kyŏngjing, Chŏng Paekch'ang, Yŏ Ijŏng, Kim Pan, Yi Sohan, Han Hŭngil, Hong Myŏngil, Yi Sangil, Yi Sanggyu, and Chŏng Sŏnhŭng. Moreover, they included the concubine of *sŏp'yŏng puwŏn'gun* Han Chun'gyŏm and her son, the concubines of Yŏllŭng *puwŏn'gun* Yi Homin and Chŏng Hyosŏng, and others.[6] There were countless numbers of women who died to maintain their chastity. It is regretful that all of them cannot be known. Kim Chinp'yo forced his concubine to take her own life. The wife of Kim Yu and the wife of Kyŏngjing, observing the death of their daughters-in-law, followed and committed suicide.

Yi Kasang, who had recently passed his exam, was exceptional at literary composition. From early on, he earned a name for himself, and his family disposition was extraordinary compared to others. His mother was sick for a long time, and for six or seven years he remained by her side, attending her and never leaving her for a moment. He served his mother with medicine and food and never allowed servants to do so. All of the people who knew about this conduct admired him. However, when the enemy reached the island, he could only hide his mother before he was seized by the enemy. After the enemy withdrew, instead of him doing so, his wife put his mother on her back and fled. Unexpectedly, his wife was the first to run away, leaving his mother to die in the place where he was first seized by the enemy. In the face of danger, he escaped from enemy capture and returned home, maneuvering back and forth through the enemy camp in search of his mother's corpse. It was said that he was captured and escaped six times. One day, he entered a remote Buddhist monastery in the middle of the island. He was going to return to the enemy camp, but an elite friend of his, who had come to the monastery as a refugee, grabbed him by his shirt to prevent him from leaving. However, in response, Yi exclaimed, "I also know I will live if I remain here, while I will certainly perish if I leave. It is hardly possible that my sick mother is still alive. How can I sit here alone by myself?" He composed a letter and told the monk of the monastery to convey a message to his father and brother that he was prepared to die. He insisted on returning to the enemy camp and was finally killed. Dying from this act of fidelity is the same as dying a martyr's death. I risk charges to record his story here.

After Kwŏn Sunjang killed himself with explosives, his wife, who was the daughter of Yi Kuwŏn, first hanged her three daughters and then followed them by hanging herself. Sunjang's sister, a twelve-year-old virgin, also hanged herself. These were all women who made the correct decision.

Yi Hyŏng and Yun Sinji were at the army officer's residence while their fathers were inside the fortress. Because the enemy clogged the roads, Yi Hyŏng and Yun Sinji each climbed into boats and fled. After the incident calmed down, they were both impeached. Yu Sŏngjŭng and others did not stop the enemy and were the first to flee.

The person who captured Kanghwa was the ninth prince (K. Kuwangja). When he withdrew, the people detained inside the fortress were released. Those people captured outside the fortress were taken and carried away. Han Hŭngil and Yŏ Ijing took off the clothes they were wearing, changed into fresh ones, and said, "When one meets a person from a foreign land for the first time, one must be exceptionally neat." They were the first to exit the fortress. They bowed to the enemy and said, "The father-in-law of the crown prince Kang Sŏkki is also present." They were referring to Kang Sŏkki and hiding his whereabouts. Under the pretense that he was ill and was thus unable to walk, Kang did not emerge. Finally, the enemy, giving up on Kang Sŏkki, departed. It was said that Kang Sŏkki had first planned to commit suicide, and Her Highness the crown princess consort was going to follow him in death. The two grand princes [Pongnim and Inpy'ŏng] dissuaded them, and they did not carry out their plans.

For those elites near and far, many of their highborn wives were seized by the enemy. However, what the wife of Yi Min'gu and his two daughters-in-law did was indecent, and others spit at and cursed them. Saying that his wife had perished at Kasan Mountain, Min'gu insisted that she died to preserve her chastity. He composed a biography for her, praising her beauty and requested calligraphy by *tongyangwi* Sin Iksŏng.[7] Everyone scoffed at this. When it was time to prosecute the crime of dereliction of duty for all of the Kanghwa generals, they included Chang Sin, Kim Kyŏngjing, Yi Min'gu, and other criminal generals who failed to maintain military discipline. The Censorate Office (Taegan) petitioned for days to order Chang Sin to drink poison (*sasa*), but His Highness would not approve and ordered him to kill himself.[8] His residence was outside the west gate, where he took his own life by hanging himself. Because the State Tribunal (Kŭmbu Tosa) did not witness his death directly, they dismissed it. It was widely rumored and suspected that Chang Sim might be alive or had fled. Royal Secretary (*sŭngji*) Hong Hŏn requested holding an audience before His Highness to inspect Chang's coffin, but His Highness would not approve. As for Kim Kyŏngjing, the Censorate Office (Taegan) first insisted that he be executed, but he was exiled to Kangje. With the petition of former minister (*p'ansŏ*) Kim Siyang, Vice-Minister (*ch'amp'an*) Yu Paekchŭng, and others, discussion about his prosecution reemerged. Kim Kyŏngjing was arrested again and forced to consume poison. Kang Chinhŭn made no effort to fight, which allowed the enemy to cross the river. At first, he was exiled to a remote location, but the Censorate Office ordered him arrested again and had his head severed and strung up for display (*hyosi*).

The military officials of the Ch'ungch'ŏng naval base (*suyŏng*) and their lower-level officers appeared successively before the royal palace, weeping bitterly. They submitted a letter to the Border Defense Command, pleading for Chinhŭn and hoping to redress his injustice, but in the end, Chinhŭn could not avoid death. In the State Tribunal (Kŭmbu), Kyŏngjing and Chinhŭn heard the royal command for them to consume poison had passed. Kyŏngjing melted into tears, forgetting all decorum, but Chinhŭn just smiled and asked Kyŏngjing, "Can you avoid this by weeping?" Chinhŭn just ate and drank as though everything was normal. Moreover, he presented a formal dress sword to the man about to execute him, adding, "This is an exquisite sword. End my life with this sword quickly and then take it with you." There was no other person on Kanghwa who had fought as valiantly as Chinhŭn had, but in the end, he was killed. Even in the face of death, he was honorable. Truly, it was the personal integrity of a brave man. Everyone lamented his death. The soldiers of the naval base, young and old, all held memorial services for him, shedding tears, as though they had lost their own relative.

RECORDS OF SEVERAL PEOPLE WHO
REJECTED PEACE NEGOTIATIONS
AND DIED OF RIGHTEOUSNESS

Yun Hwang, Yu Ch'ŏl, and Yi Ilsang had all rejected peace negotiations. Yun and Yu were detained in a designated area (*chungdo puch'ŏ*), and Yi was exiled far away. Fifth Tutor (*sŏlsŏ*) Yu Kye, who was in Namhan Mountain Fortress, petitioned for the beheading of Kim Yu. His words were very sharp and straightforward. Earlier, Cho Kyŏng had attacked Hong Sŏbong. The three moral advisors to the king (*samgong*) agreed with him and decided on Sŏbong's crimes. Yu Kye was detained in a designated area, and Cho Kyŏng was thrown out of the city walls (*munoe ch'ilsong*). After that, Cho Kyŏng was released by the report of the Censorate (Taegan).

Hong Ikhan was deputy governor (*sŏbun*) of P'yŏngyang at that time. When the enemy withdrew, our country appointed and dispatched a special officer, Chŭngsan Local Functionary (*hyŏllyŏn*) Pyŏn Taejung, to send Hong Ikhan to the enemy camp under his escort. Pyŏn Taejung tied up Ikhan, insulted him severely, and prevented him from consuming any food. Ikhan begged to be untied, but Pyŏn would not listen. This was the twelfth day of the second lunar month.

On the eighteenth day, Ikhan arrived in Yongman [Ŭiju, on the border] and, on the twentieth, he reached Tongyuanpu (K. T'ongwŏnbo).[1] Barbarians approached and inquired about the reason for coming such a great distance. They fed him and treated him fairly. Even though these people are more like pigs and dogs than humans, they were far superior to the general public (*taejung*) of our country. On the twenty-fifth day, he arrived in Mukden. The khan ordered the Ministry of Rites (Libu) to provide him with lodging and prepare a feast. It seemed that there was no intention to harm him.

On the seventh day of the third lunar month, Hong Ikhan underwent examination. Ikhan, not bending the slightest, resisted their questioning. He provided a written report of his testimony. It read,

A certain Hong, the captured envoy from Chosŏn, will, point by point, explain the purpose of rejecting the peace negotiations here. Verbally, we did not communicate very well with each other. Dare I say that I wrote in ink words to express myself more clearly. Within the four seas, everyone can become brothers, but throughout the world, there is no child with two fathers. Originally, Chosŏn treated each other with courtesy and ritual. Officials who remonstrate with the king have become customary for the state. Last spring, while assuming my duties of remonstration, I heard that the Jin dynasty had broken the oath and begun using the term "emperor." Indeed, if the oath had been broken, then it would be defying brotherly relations. If the term "emperor" were used, then this would be having two sons of heaven. Within a family, how can brotherly relations be defied? Under the same heaven, how can there be two emperors? Moreover, the Jin dynasty just recently enacted a pledge with Chosŏn and betrayed it first. But the Great Ming used to bestow the expansive grace that binds us deeply together. If we forget this deeply binding great grace but maintain the pledge we could first betray, this would not even be close to rational. It would not be proper at all. Therefore, I became the first to offer this proposal [rejecting peace negotiations] because it was my duty to obey the way of ritual and righteousness. There was no other reason, just my righteousness as an official subject to the king. It was my loyal and filial duty. Superior to me were the king and my parents, whom I could not protect or comfort. Now, the crown prince and the prince (*taegun*) are both prisoners. I do not know whether my elderly mother is alive or dead. This was all because once I pleaded irresponsibly; this delivered disaster and harm to my family and kingdom. Quoting the way of loyalty and filiality, my deeds should be looked down upon. As I gauge my own crimes, I deserve to die with no pardon. Even though I am put to death ten thousand times, I am truly willing to accept it. My blood will smear the drums, my spirit will fly high, and I will return to my home country (*koguk*). I feel so elated about it. Except for this, I have no additional words and would like to die quickly.

The khan grew enraged. He found other excuses to dispatch his servants everywhere, so as to make it difficult for them to communicate with each other. But after this, he directed a servant to our country. It was not clear what happened to Hong later. Some say he was killed on the tenth day. When he died, it was said that his expression did not alter in the slightest, as though he was proud of himself. All the barbarians admired him, and there were many who cried.

Hong Ikhan's wife and two sons were killed by the enemy. His elderly mother and one daughter survived. All of this appears in his diary before the third day of the third lunar month. On the double third festival (*tapch'ŏngil*), Hong Ikhan composed the following poem.[2]

On the sunny slope, the new grass spreads out covering,
A lonely bird perches in a solitary cage, turning sad.
I followed the Chinese custom of hiking on a spring day,
In my dream, where I drank a full cup of wine from the
    Brocade City
When wind overturned the night stone and Yinshan shook,
Snow fell into spring and the moon began to cave.
The quest of hunger and thirst can only make you live,
A hundred years from today, my tears will still fall on cheeks.[3]

O Talche sent four poems back home. One poem was about
missing his mother, and it read:

The wind blows dust north and south, but the duckweed
    remains [the water has not been disturbed].[4]
Who is the one that knows we have been so separated because
    of my travels?
On the day of their departure, two sons pay respect together
    to their mother,
In the season of return, only one son will greet her in the
    front yard.
When I cut the clothes you were holding, determined to leave,
    I disappointed you and your Mencian teaching.[5]
I cried and felt so sorry about your motherly care.
Now, the fortress is blocked, the road is distant, and the
    evening grows darker.
When, in my life, can I return to you peacefully?

His poem about missing the king read:

As a lonely official, I am full of righteousness, never feeling
    ashamed.
The grace of my sagely king is so profound that my sacrifice
    for death is very light.

This life of mine holds no regretful sorrow,
Except that of my mother leaning against the door and
    waiting for me in vain to return.

His poem about missing his older brother read:

Namhan was the time you died,
In distant lands, I am a prisoner, not yet someone who can
    return.
Since coming westward, I have shed tears, thinking about my
    older brother.
When I look eastward, I feel distant pity for that person who
    always recalled his younger brother.
Your spirit chases the flying geese, while I feel such sorrow
    about your lonely shadow.
I awoke from a dream when the pond grass reminded me of
    the remaining spring.
In a scenario where I could wear refined clothes to visit home,
How could I ever greet and comfort our mother then?

His poem for his wife read:

Marital kindness and affection run so deep,
Although it has not been two years since we first met.
Now we are thousands of *li* apart,
A marriage that lasts forever cannot be promised.
The great distance impedes the delivery of my letter,
The high mountains also delay my dreams of you.
As my life cannot be foretold,
You must take care of our unborn child.

All of these poems hold heartbreaking words and reveal bitter minds. Hearing them, there is no one who was not sad. Some said that maybe O Talche was killed with Yun Chip. Some say perhaps he was locked away in some distant place. After several years, there has been no news. It appears he was killed.

Yun Chip's older brother Kye was also a man of talent. In the *pyŏngja* year [1637], he was ordered to leave for the area of Suryŏng as a drafter of royal decrees (*ŭnggyo*). He went to Namyang as district magistrate. When war broke out, he organized righteous army troops to diligently serve the king. People heard this rumor and volunteered to be recruits, so more and more people who were going to take part gathered. He was about to find success when the enemy troops heard about the soldiers mobilizing and suddenly attacked the government seat (*pujung*). In the courtyard, Yun Kye planted two military banners. He sat up straight and would not move. He was detained by the enemy. In a loud voice, he shouted at them, "You can cut off my head, but you cannot make me kneel!" He also said, rebuking them, "You barbarian bastards! Why don't you kill me quickly?" The enemy grew enraged, violently knocked him down with their swords, and trampled over him. There was not an uninjured place on his body. With their swords, they gored and cut off both sides of his body, and they cut out his tongue and flailed his skin. Yun Kye's old slave and one servant covered him and stopped them. It was said all of them died in that one spot. All of the people who heard about this shook with fear and were full of sorrow. Yun Kye's grandfather died in the *imjin* year [1592] at Sangju. The three of them, the grandfather and grandsons, all died for the affairs of the country. This is truly honorable.

MISCELLANEOUS NOTES CONCERNING
WHAT HAPPENED AFTER THE UPHEAVAL

I n the winter of the *pyŏngja* year [1636], King Kwanghaegun, the deposed ruler (*p'yeju*), moved from Kanghwa Island to Kyodong and was exiled to a house surrounded by a thorn hedge (*wiri anch'i*).[1] When he was traveling from Namhan Mountain Fortress, Sin Kyŏngjin, Ku Koeng, Sin Kyŏngwŏn, Sin Kyŏngin, Hong Chindo, and others submitted a joint letter to Kyŏnggi Naval Commander Sin Kyŏngjin [not the same Sin as above], requesting him to take the appropriate steps of action. This letter was about secretly killing Kwanghaegun, but Kyŏngjin would not listen. In the second lunar month, Kwanghaegun was moved from Kyodong to Cheju Island. Fifth-Level Military Official (*ch'ŏmji muin*) Hwang Ik made a request to be appointed the special commander there, to build his achievement and fame, but he did not succeed. This was also Sin Kyŏngjin [the former Sin above] and the others' intention to incite trouble. The deposed ruler passed away on Cheju Island on the second day of the seventh lunar month in the *sinsa* year [1641].

Kip'yŏnggun Yu Paekchŭng sent a memorial to the throne,

Yun Pang and Kim Yu harmed our country. My memorial of the first lunar month provides a rough outline of their actions. After the first lunar month, I here list every detail of the crimes of Yun Pang and Kim Yu. Before the autumn and summer of last year, Kim Yu argued firmly for resisting peace negotiations. He said the deployment of the term "Qing" was unjust, and he argued against dispatching an envoy. Your Highness said, "If the enemy deeply penetrates our country, the commander of war will be unable to avoid punishment." From that time onward, he accompanied the peace negotiations. He tied up and dispatched Yun Chip. It was Kim Yu who insisted that Yun Hwang and others were criminals. With the mountain fortress under siege, being our general and prime minister, he had Your Highness emerge from the fortress. So far, Kim Yu has not even claimed any responsibility for this. For the crimes committed by those below the supreme field commander, they should all certainly claim their responsibilities. At first, a Qing person invited the crown prince (*tonggung*) out of the fortress. Kim Yu urged the crown prince to emerge and was willing to accompany him. When the crown prince arrived at the north camp, Kim Yu offered the excuse that he [Kim] was elderly and infirm, so he departed. I do not believe the duty and loyalty of a minister can be like this! A scoundrel enticed the troops protecting the fortress. A crowd congregated outside the royal palace to demand the dispatch of an envoy who was resisting peace negotiations. The sentiment of the military was that if one move was made, then everyone would attempt to be the first to put Kim Yu to the sword. Kim Yu knew it was difficult to prevent this. He had Yi Hongju assume the responsibility of envoy. Would Your Highness think that Kim Yu was loyal? Or that Kim Yu only thought of himself?

Kyŏngjing, the son of Kim Yu, held a high government position. After he died, his name was inscribed on the national roll.

In a loud voice, Kye Koeng said, "Is the status of the crown prince not as high as the one of Kyŏngjing? The queen (*chungjŏn*) passed away and now the first anniversary of her death has gone by, but Kyŏngjing's mother will receive a noble title."[2] Kim Yu immediately silenced this. Last year, when Ingguldai arrived, the Border Defense Command presented a plan for terminating peace negotiations. The royal secretariat copied it down and passed it on to the prime minister, according to Your Highness's will. This was revealed to a person of the Qing. If we had then dispatched people who resisted peace negotiations, it would have been suitable timing for the court. How could this be the crime of a someone from the Young faction (*yŏnsoin*)? Cho Kyŏng and Yu Kye were the two people who offended the ministers. Therefore, these two should decide their sentences. This is something I have never heard of before.

Apart from the above, Kim Yu never hesitates to accept bribes in ordinary times. He seeks the personal and looks down upon the law. Without scruples, he forgets about the king and turns his back on the country. However, when rewards were distributed the other day, he was compensated with a horse. Has Your Highness forgotten that previously Your Highness said that if the enemy should penetrate the country deeply, then Kim Yu will be unable to avoid punishment? On the twenty-ninth day of Nabwŏl [the final month of the year], Kim Yu was in command when war broke out. Many generals died and the troops grew extremely demoralized. However, Kim Yu, attributing this crime to Sin Kyŏngin and Hwang Chŭp, flogged them. This is akin to Huan Wen being defeated at Fangtou and yet punishing Yuan Zhen.[3]

For a long time, Yun Pang held the place of prime minister. He oversaw many matters and is guilty of crimes for which even his death is insufficient punishment. But at the beginning, as he was bestowed the power of managing the country by caring for the ancestral shrines (*myosa*), was not his duty heavy enough?⁴ Kim Kyŏngjing's appointment as an inspector was at Kim Yu's recommendation. That was a strategy to avoid disaster befalling their family. When Kyŏngjing escaped to Kanghwa, he first ferried over his family, servants, and transportation. For this reason, the ancestral shrines and Her Highness, the crown princess consort, could not cross the river and had to remain at the ferry landing for three days. For this, the eunuch Kim In wept bitterly. Kyŏngjing not only committed a crime against Your Highness, he also committed a crime against Kim In. Moreover, he ordered the military banners to only transport the people who were close to him, which resulted in all of the soldiers and commoners filling the shore, all of whom were finally seized by the enemy. This kind of situation did not happen just once or twice. It was truly a deplorable matter.

If the person who served as the minister had, in the name of his crimes, hung up the head of the decapitated criminal Kyŏngjing, then why would Chang Sin and others have fled, Kanghwa fallen, and Kim Sangyong committed suicide? Because Yun Pang failed to manage affairs and surrendered everything like a crazy child, there was nothing else that could have been done. How can Yun Pang alone avoid such heavy crimes? The issue was that he did not fight and only fled. Is there anyone from inside or outside the court who commits a crime like Kyŏngjing? Is there any person like Kyŏngjing who abandoned his mother as one would abandon broken shoes? The Two Offices [the Office of the Inspector General and the Office of the Censor General] could only listen to Kim Yu and cover up his major crimes. For this careless irresponsibility, I cannot look at him directly. Kyŏngjing treated Yi Min'gu as his superior. For anything that happened, he asked Min'gu for his opinions. Therefore, Min'gu's nickname on Kanghwa Island became "Kyŏngjing's nanny." As for the crimes of Min'gu, there was no difference from those of Kyŏngjing.

When the general of Chindu lost his defensive positions, he quickly escorted the shrine (*myosa*) and petitioned Her Highness to board a vessel and flee. In contrast, Yun Pang covered his face and crept away like a rat, hiding in a commoner's residence. A eunuch discovered him. He defiled the shrine (*myosa*), scattered it, and lost it. Finally, he approached the enemy camp and kowtowed. This is an incident that happened when Your Highness was still residing in the mountain fortress. The crime of Yun Pang is such. However, he was only punished because he lost the ancestral tablets (*myoju*), which ended up with him losing his office. When will the public expect a fair sentence to be made? Moreover, Chang Sin protested against this decision, arguing that Kim's original crime deserved to be one grade more extreme, meaning he should have to take his own life. Since antiquity, where does death by suicide as a military punishment come from? Really, this kind of death sentence is no different from a sentence of no death.

The response from the Office of the Inspector General (Hŏnbu) stated, "Do not aggravate the crimes and cease these petitions for selfish ends. This would make those who have died object deeply." Your Highness probably understood it to be regretful that Chang Sin died alone while Kyŏngjing did not die, based on the lack of proper punishment. If so, then who would be fearful and only wait for the opinion of the Two Offices? The response of the joint petition (*hapkye*) was unable to enforce the law for the only son of an elderly statesman. Thus it would appear that Kyŏngjing was innocent. If the petition was continuous without end, I am afraid it would be approved. Thus, I ordered it ceased. But this was prevented by Censor-General (*taesagan*) Kim Namjung. The next day, he expunged my order, ending the petition. He did whatever he wanted. By this means, is Kim Yu's influence heavy or light? In comparing the son of an elderly statesman with the tablets for the royal ancestors and the gods of earth and grain, which is heavy, and which is light?

Is that because Your Highness will consider the tablets and Her Highness not as important as Kyŏngjing? Fearful of Kim Yu's authority, Your Highness could not execute the law but borrowed the help of the Two Offices. If Your Highness is afraid, will the Two Offices not be afraid?

Sim Chŭp informed a Qing person about the imposter prince (*kawangja*) and the imposter minister (*kadaesin*). The state affairs were twisted around because of him and, in the end, he ruined the country. At that time, it is extremely deplorable that his head was not cut off. He was saved. I have been dismissed because of my petition about the crimes of Yun Pang and Kim Yu. Now, less than a half year later, I again speak such foolish words to Your Highness. Do my words benefit only myself? Will they benefit my country? I petition Your Highness to consider this deeply.

His Highness held on to Yu Paekchŭng's petition and did not send it.

In Namhan Mountain Fortress, the royal attending (*hojong*) officers who benefitted from the accomplishments of their ancestors (*ŭmgwan*), scholars, and all the troops protecting the fortress were tested in the civilian and military examinations. For the scholar exam, they were provided with the essay questions (*nonje*), and for the military exam requirements, they passed anyone who struck more than one out of fifteen shots with a bow or an arquebus. Of those taking the civilian exam, Chŏng Chihwa and ten others passed. For the military exam, seven thousand people passed. The public and private slaves (*kongsach'ŏn*) from outside the capital and government cannoneers (*p'osu togam*) all took part. The court had difficulty [telling the slaves from the cannoneers], so they moved one thousand people into one bureau (*kuk*) and recorded their origins based on that one bureau (*kuk*) [even if they were not born there].⁵ If they came from a humble social rank, they would be punished by losing their occupations and being deprived of food and clothing. The lowborn people of the capital rioted, and everything grew expensive as a result. All the people who thought about this worried.

In the eleventh lunar month of the *chŏngch'uk* year [1637], the khan of the Jin dispatched a barbarian envoy (*hosa*) in the name of conferring the title of king. The envoy was given the title of imperial envoy (*ch'ŏnsa*), and the letter he carried with him was referred to as an imperial decree (*che*). The khan bestowed upon himself the title "the Qing emperor who has accepted the mandate of heaven" (K. *ch'ŏngguk pongch'ŏn sŭngun hwangje*, C. *qingguo fengtian chengyun huangdi*). The letter was such:

Heaven and earth arrange the cold and the warm. Likewise, the emperor maintains a just path of reward and punishment. However, because there is always disobedience and obedience, I have to differentiate my kindness and penalties. Given that your Chosŏn is a neighboring country to us, we have had many contacts. More than brotherhood, I considered our relationship as solid as gold and stone (*kŭmsŏk*), whereas your king treated our relationship as the constellations Shen and Shang by refusing my diplomats and warning your subjects about me along the frontier.⁶ What you actually did is equal to being our enemy, thus I displayed my military force. Although I declared that I would expose your crimes and strike you, I was hoping you would change your minds and attempt to obey. Now that your king has regretted his earlier transgressions, how could I only take your past crimes into consideration? From now on, this position will be accepted, as I consider this a new restoration, and I have already set the outer vassal relationship (*pŏnbong*) with you. In this, I will melt down and throw away the royal seals of your country that have been passed down from ruler to ruler. You will respect these new orders, and you must use the seal with the same characters as the king of Chosŏn. Therefore, I have dispatched special envoys to deliver you the seal and the letter. In still investing you with the title "king of Chosŏn," I reward you for your respect and loyalty with a golden seal and jeweled booklet of your royal appointment. Serving as my outer border vassal state is unchangeable and permanent like the Yellow River and Mount Tai. Once your roles and obligations are established, if you secure permanent norms of proper conduct, then heaven and earth will not change, like a cap and a shoe cannot be interchanged. If your king cleanses his mind and thoughts, you and future generations will serve out your tribute obligations as a constant, ensuring an auspicious beginning and a perfect end, and then I can preserve your good fortune forever. With respect and full effort, do not betray the orders of the emperor.

Moreover, he issued another imperial decree:

I never discard righteousness. The reward of jade and silk bestowed to those who are loyal and honest is time-honored. Because of your obedience, I here bestow them upon you. Now, I have especially dispatched Yingerdai [Ingguldai] and Mafuda Daiyun [Mafuta], to invest you with the title of the king of your country and offer you the royal seal, sable furs (*ch'ogu*), and cavalry horses. Your king respectfully accepted our most sincere sentiment that we have bestowed upon you. Accordingly, we have presented one black fox fur, one silver fox fur, one hundred red mink furs, one fine horse, and one bejeweled saddle (*yŏngnongan*) to the king of Chosŏn. The twenty-sixth day of the tenth lunar month of the Chongde era.

As for the so-called Yingerdai, that was the name of Guldai; the so-called Mafuda held the name of Futa. These were their occupational names. On top of a seal were four characters in

Chinese seal script, and below were two words in Mongol. One item did not have a seal.[7] The content of the letter criticized us for seizing a Chinese man (*hain*), whom they said must be returned to them. It demanded that he be repatriated, that we send back three officials who had fled across the frontier but had been captured, return Qing horses that were stolen and recovered, and dispatch beautiful women from the homes of the three state councilors (*samgong*), the six ministries (*yukkyŏng*), and the capital elite for [the khan] to wed.

After leaving the mountain fortress, we strengthened Kok Fortress on the peaks of Mangwŏltae at Namhan, adding it to the mountain defenses. A barbarian envoy was dispatched to examine it, and then we were required to pull it all down. Also, we were forced to erect a victory monument (*sŭngbi*) at Samjŏndo.[8] We set up little bright chambers (*ch'aegak*) on top of the various levels and in each one placed steles. We were forced to surround it with a wall.[9] The work was conscripted and quite ruthless. Grand Academic (*taejehak*) Yi Kyŏngsŏk inscribed the epitaph, and Vice-Minister (*ch'amp'an*) O Chun wrote the content. Vice-Minister Yŏ Ijing composed a letter in both Chinese seal script characters and Qing and Mongol barbarian scripts about the same monument.[10] This letter read:

In the great Qing founding year *chongde*, in the winter of the twelfth lunar month, His Imperial Highness grew extremely angry and shocked because our country broke the peace agreement, and thus he assumed a military stance to punish us in the east. There was no one who could resist. At that time, our king was in Namhan Mountain, a cold and pitiful place. It was like trampling on the melting ice of early spring and waiting for the daytime to arrive. Conquered in fifty days, the troops reinforcing from the southeast provinces were defeated one after another. Troops from the northwest were packed into the mountain gorges and could not advance even one step. The provisions in the mountain fortress were also running low. At this time, His Imperial Highness drew near the mountain fortress with his great forces. They came as though they were a gust of wind, or a column of frost that blew up the fallen leaves. It was as though a stove fire had burned through feathers [they advanced so quickly]. But His Imperial Highness had not intended to kill with his military posturing. He was only allowing his virtue to spread. Consequently, he unfolded his imperial orders and said, "Ah, I will fulfill your destiny (chŏn). If not, I will massacre you." Unceasingly, one after another, Ing, Ma, and the other generals received the orders of His Imperial Highness.

Then, our king assembled all the civilian and military officials and said, "It has been ten years of contented peace with the great country [of the Qing] and now we have reached this point. Because of my own stupidity and confusion, I [the king] deserved this heavenly suppression. As a result, all the people have become fish and meat. I am the one who committed this crime. Also, His Imperial Highness did not bear to massacre the people in this way and had his imperial decree inscribed as such upon this monument. How could I dare to not follow? This is to secure my ancestors and preserve our lives." The ministers all consented. Finally, they followed the king with scores of cavalries and arrived at the frontlines to humbly apologize. His Imperial Highness welcomed them with courtesy and pacified them with grace. At first sight, he treated them as trusted confidants (simbok) and bestowed gifts upon them, extending his grace to all of our envoys. With the cessation of the rites, he had our king return to the capital. He immediately withdrew his soldiers that had marched south and moved them westward. He prohibited them from inciting violence against the people and encouraged agricultural production. From far and wide, the people, who had been scattered around, all returned to their places, like the return of migrating birds. The mountains and rivers for several thousand *li* in the Eastern Land appeared as before. The frost and snow turned into luminous spring. The withering drought turned into timely rain. That which had died was now alive, and that which had ended now reemerged. This truly is a rarity since ancient times. Up the Han River (*hansu*), north of Samjŏndo, was the place His Imperial Highness resided. There was an altar (*tan*) and an open space (*chang*) here. Our sovereign ruler (*kwagun*) ordered the water agency (*subu*) to heighten and enlarge the altar. They quarried rock and erected this monument to disseminate the emperor's everlasting achievements and virtue, together with his good fortune and sharing nature (*tong*). How much our small country (*sobang*) particularly depends on him throughout the ages and forever! As for the humanness and power of the great imperial court (*taejo*), no matter how remote the people are, there would be none who would not follow. This is based on all of these reasons. Given the vastness of heaven and earth, or the brightness of the sun and the moon, it is not even one out of ten thousand. There is not enough space here to record this in detail.

The inscription on the monument read,

Heaven descends frost and dew, as it conveys respect and
    birth.
Only the emperor can imitate these, and he spreads powerful
    benevolence.
The emperor brought a punitive crusade east, and his army
    had ten thousand soldiers.
They were powerful, roaring like tigers and leopards.
They conquered the desolate Mongols in the west and
    incorporated them in this battle.

Holding weapons and marching forward, his army displayed
the greatest power ever.
The emperor was extremely humane. His words were always
kind.
He wanted us to alter our minds; even though he spoke with
strictness, he was kind.
We at first were in deep confusion and seeking trouble.
The emperor issued his bright orders, wakening us from
slumber.
We then surrendered and followed His Highness with all of
our hearts.
We were not surrendering out of fear of the emperor's force,
but because of his virtue.
The emperor considered this auspiciously and was pleased
with our propriety and excellence.
With affection, he smiled, and he ended our disagreement.
He even presented us with fine horses and soft furs.
The people in the capital, men and women, all celebrated
with song.
That our ruler returned to the capital is because the emperor
bestowed his favor.
The emperor took pity on the misery of our common people
and encouraged agricultural production.
The royal buildings were recovered, and the shrine altars
were restored.
Those bones became flesh again; the cold root found rebirth.
Here we established this monument at the source of the Han
River.
The emperor rests forever in the Three Hans (Samhan).[11]

When the enemy returned, two of them, Kong Youde and
Geng Zhongming, stayed behind, joined our two countries
together [Chosŏn and the Qing], and occupied Kado Island.[12]
Youde and Zhongming were originally generals from the Ming

and skilled at naval warfare. Before they held the Shangdong Peninsula, they had been attacked by the Ming, and then defected to the side of the enemy [the Qing]. Our country appointed Yu Im as commander (*chujang*) and Im Kyŏngŏp as battalion commander (*pujang*), and they traveled to Kando, following Kong and Geng. Kando Island is in the middle of the sea. Boat landing is rather difficult, and was more so because the island perimeter was ringed with cannons. Thus, even after several days had passed, the enemy was unable to attack. The enemy requested a plan from our two commanders that would threaten the Ming Chinese troops on the island or lure them out. Kyŏngŏp said, "On one side of the island, there is a mountain that blocks the way. The seawater immediately below the mountain can be passed through. The inhabitants of the island have not established any defenses there. If you take a boat at night, circumvent the mountain, and secretly cross over and enter from there, then you will be able to occupy it." The enemy said that it was a brilliant plan. They invaded the island exactly as Kyŏngŏp had described. Im Kyŏngŏp deliberately said he was going to stay behind as an excuse, and he killed many enemy soldiers. Im was the sole originator of the plan to capture the island. When they landed on the island, our forces killed more Ming Chinese than enemy Manchu soldiers. The native inhabitants of the island climbed into five or six boats and escaped across the water. The area commander [of the Ming dynasty] Shen Shikui led several hundred men and ascended a mountain top.[13] The enemy attempted to lure him out, saying, "If you can come down and surrender, then you will gain wealth and honor." Shen Shikui sent an envoy with his reply: "By nature, I am a minister of the Great Ming. If I am doomed to die, then I shall die. How could I surrender to dogs and goats?" The enemy used everything at their disposal to besiege the mountain and attack him. Everyone died by the sword of the enemy, and no one surrendered. Originally, Shen Shikui was a low merchant. But in the end, he established himself with great fidelity. He was a true patriotic martyr. When the enemy first decided to assault the island, our court planned to inform the Ming secretly ahead of time, but because the power of the enemy was frightening, they could not make it in time. So, these events unfolded like this. The Khan and his men all crossed the river [Yalu] in the fourth lunar month. Im Kyŏngŏp was rewarded for attacking the island several times, and he even received the rank of enemy nobility (chŏkchak).

When the barbarian envoy arrived, Chief State Councilor (yŏngŭijŏng) Hong Sŏbong, Minister from the Ministry of Personnel (ijo p'ansŏ) Yi Hyŏnyŏng, and others were appropriated by Ingguldai at Mansang [Ŭiju], so they could not dispute any of the issues. As for our commoners and the Chinese people who had fled but returned, as well as those who used to establish their homes on our soil where they raised their sons and grandsons, they were all sent back [to the Qing]. Without identifying the legitimate or the false, the magistrates and governors from the eight provinces aimed to dispatch more and more people to avert the anger [of the Qing]. As they underwent inspection at the Border Defense Command, for the farewell between fathers and sons and between brothers, the people who remained severed their fingers and exchanged them with the people who were about to depart. The entire garden was covered with flowing blood. Throughout the world in ancient and modern times, could there have been such a horrendous affair? The people who heard this felt bitter and shed tears. The three kinds of people that the barbarian Ingguldai obtained could have been in the hundreds and thousands.[14] But his desire was hardly satisfied. He ordered the dispatch of one hundred additional people, telling them to put this promise into writing. The chief state councilor, a minister from the Ministry of Personnel (ijo p'ansŏ), Imperial Greeting Envoy (wŏnjŏpsa) Yi Kyŏngjŭng, and others thought one hundred was too many, but they promised to send as many as they could find, placing their seals on the promissory letter. After that, the enemy always urged that more people be sent. Their demands were abusive and had grown endless. This was truly pathetic.

Originally, Kyŏng Myŏngsu was an elderly statesman from Kwansŏ in Ŭnsan. The Border Defense Command submitted a petition to His Highness and appointed him to the level of third minister (*chisa*). A royal edict (*kyoji*) came down to him. Myŏngsu responded, "Heavenly favor is immeasurable. Reverently, I must properly pay respects and thank you for this favor. But the surroundings make it troublesome. Late at night, I will choose a clean and quite place, kowtow facing east, and repay the kindness."

In the *sinsa* year [1641], the Qing again ordered one thousand arquebus soldiers (*p'osu*), five hundred horses, and five hundred cavalry troops, along with Yu Im appointed as general, to be dispatched to Mukden on the twentieth day of the third lunar month. Thereafter, Yu Im quickly took charge of the troops. The provisions and military equipment continued to be delivered from our country. Im Kyŏngop and his troops withdrew from Haizhou Command in Manchuria and returned. Yu Im travelled to Mukden and attacked the Jinzhou Command that Zu Dashou of the Middle dynasty [Ming China] protected. He seized the outer city wall and besieged the fortress for several months when skirmishes broke out with Ming troops who had come from Songshan Station. At that time, one of the arquebus soldiers, Yi Saryong, who lived in Sŏngju, packed forty slugs into his pockets. He pretended to discharge his weapon when he was discovered and killed by the barbarian general (*hojang*).[15] Saryong was only a common soldier, originally the secondary son from a highborn family. Whatever occupation he had, it was different from the commoners. When he departed, he announced to his family, "If you hear of war against the Middle dynasty, then you know that will be my day of death." What he meant was that the outcome of his life had already been determined. When people heard about the notice of his death, everyone grew sad. It was said that Magistrate Ch'oe

Yuŏn personally appeared at his residence, wrote out the funeral oration, and performed service to him.[16]

In the fifth lunar month, the enemy asked for a rotation of troops, but they requested that another five hundred arquebus soldiers be dispatched and that the general must be a young military officer. Naval Commander Yu Chŏngik was appointed as general. The arquebus troops from the royal guard in the vicinity of the capital were sent in the sixth lunar month.

The enemy heard that many Chinese boats (*tangchuan*) were being sent toward our country. Ingguldai and another general were to each lead one thousand soldiers, supplemented by our troops, and attempt to protect Kado Island from them. The Border Defense Command petitioned in return, asking for approval. His Highness did not consent. With the pretense that no boats were available, they replied to Mukden. Yi Kyŏngjŭng was appointed imperial meeting envoy (*wŏnjŏpsa*). No further news was heard from Ingguldai about this matter, so he did not depart.

A person from the Middle dynasty called Wang Dushi brought two boats, came to Yongch'ŏn, and anchored them, explaining that he was there to deliver the emperor's imperial orders (*ch'iksŏ*), the imperial robes (*myŏnbok*), and the imperial seal (*insin*). P'yŏngan Provincial Governor Chŏng T'aehwa and Army Officer (*pyŏngsa*) Yi Hyŏndal encamped along the river and fired a number of cannons at him. Wang Dushi turned back and headed out to sea. Former chief royal secretary (*tosŭngji*) Sim Yŏn was appointed the Yangsa governor (*Tosun ch'alsa*). Im Kyŏngŏp was made a white-clothed special commander (*paegŭi pyŏlchang*). Yi Nae was assigned as a staff officer (*chongsagwan*). They defended the area against Chinese vessels to prevent them from landing. Sim Yŏn finished his court duty but was led to see His Highness. He petitioned to fight [against the Middle dynasty], but at the time, His Highness commanded him to follow the circumstances of the situation.

Imperial Horse-Breeding Officer (*taipuqing*) Zhang Chun from the Middle dynasty was born in the *imsul* year [1562].[17] In the *sinmi* year [1631], he came to our frontier as the imperial secretary supervising the army (*jianjunyushi*). The enemy swept in and took him as prisoner. He was humiliated and insulted badly but would not submit. He was then placed somewhere that was uninhabited, but for years he did not die. Later, even the enemy admired his loyalty and relocated him to Mukden, at a site very close to the khan's residence. They built up a school (*qingshe*) with several rooms and had two young monks attending.[18] They provided him with everything he needed. Sometimes, someone would threaten him to surrender, while placing the blade of a sword against his neck. But this was put to a stop when the barbarians returned. Zhang Chun always sat facing north, and he did not speak a word to anybody, or step on the ground with his feet. He woke every morning at dawn, constantly bowed, and invoked one line from a poem titled "The Welcome of Spring Attached to the Gate" ("Ch'unch'uk ch'ŏpch'emun"): "As for hardened fidelity, it should resemble the bamboo trees that break through frost; as for a crimson heart, it should resemble sunflowers who forever face the sun." His physique was small, but his appearance was agile and brave, along with his heart. When he was eighty-two years old, he died of illness in Mukden on the eighth day of the third lunar month of the *sinsa* year [1641]. Because the barbarian custom was cremation, they placed him over a fire and burned him. He was truly a patriotic martyr of heaven and earth, and a person who left his name for all eternity, along with Su Wu and Wen Shan.[19] Although he was not someone from our country, I still record him here.

Ŭiju Government Official (*p'umgwan*) Ch'oe Hyoil sold all of his paddy fields and household goods. He purchased a boat and sailed to the Middle dynasty, where he became a captain (*p'ach'ong*). The barbarian who heard about this sent a Chinese spy to Guanxi, where Hyoil's family was living.[20] The spy, who was alleged to have carried Hyoil's forged letter, pretended to come from the Middle dynasty and secretly conveyed a message for them. Everyone believed him, and no one doubted a thing. In his letter, in vernacular Korean, he had written in detail about everything. One of the items in the letter relayed that the former Ŭiju City Governor (*puyun*) Hwang Irho was impressed by some of Hoyil's work and was going to offer protection to his family.

In the *chiwŏl* month of the *sinsa* year, the bastards directed two men named Tan to go directly to the palace.[21] They spurned the royal secretary (*sŭngji*) and the staff officer (*sagwan*), and whispered directly to His Highness, submitting the Korean letter of Ch'oe Hyoil's family to him. Thus, all of Hyoil's relatives had their names in the letter. They were all arrested and subjected to criminal questioning. The barbarian envoys wanted them to be put to death according to the laws of our country.

Right State Councilor Kang Sŏkki ordered them exiled to a remote island. Chief State Councilor (*yŏngŭijŏng*) Yi Sŏnggu and Left State Councilor Sin Kŏngjin said they must be decapitated. Kang Sŏkki would not argue with them, so he stood up and left. On the ninth day of this month, two barbarians and Chŏng Myŏngsu walked outside the Southern Annex Palace (Nambyŏlgung) and sat on folding stools (*sŭngsang*).[22] The chief state councilor had the government officials below him stand in a single file line. The nephew of Ch'oe Hyoil, eleven relatives, and Third Minister of the Military (*ch'amji*) Hwang Irho were beheaded. Blood flowed and covered the roads. Since our ancient history, there has never been such an unprecedented occurrence. This outraged us. Hwang Irho was very quiet and did not display any fear.

The Minister of Personnel Yi Tŏksu was beside him when Irho said, "Yŏsuk, please come here. Throughout my life, I have only intended to work for the country. Now, this is a useless death and a ridiculous affair. However, it is better for me to die so that you can live."[23] Irho had a seventy-year-old widowed mother. Everyone wept as though they had lost a relative. Hwang Irho's courtesy name was Ikchwi, and he was the adopted son of the late minister Hwang Sin. His nature was fervent, and he took it upon himself to be responsible for the country. Because of this, people begrudged his loss more.

Last year, His Highness ordered the arrest of Ch'oe Hyoil's remaining relatives. Former chief state councilor Hong Sŏbong secretly submitted a letter to His Highness, requesting their release. When the barbarian envoy learned of this, he summoned Sŏbong out into the courtyard and insulted him profusely. When Chief State Councilor Yi Sŏnggu and Chŏng Myŏngsu spoke, Myŏngsu said, "As for the words that come out of Your Excellency's mouth, they are not as good as the sound that comes out of my ass." Sŏnggu did not consider this an insult in the least. He said, "My son will leave for Mukden as a hostage (*injil*) before long. Please love him." Chŏng Myŏngsu made an excuse that his concubine (*panggi*) was not that beautiful, and this was why her parents wanted her to leave his home and look for the gate of a commoner's residence. Sŏnggu bribed Myŏngsu with one thousand *nyang* silver to please his heart. The treatment this time was ten times more generous than the previous occasion.

A barbarian envoy returned and told the king, "I come this time because there is a matter to be handled. Please have one staff member from the prison for official offenders (*kŭmbu tangsang*) accompany me." Pak No was appointed to this location and followed him. The barbarian envoy reached Guanxi. For Hyoil's relatives, whether they were close or distant, fifteen more of them were killed before the envoy departed.

When the incident passed, Chang Yŏhŏn Hyŏn'gwang conducted a ritual at a shrine, and he composed a letter that read, "There is my home, but I am unworthy. There is my country, but I am useless. Going far away from the capital, I am thinking of ending my life." He left directly for Ibam Academy, located in a deep mountain valley of Kyŏngju. He did not return to his home again, and he ended his life there. Former minister from the Ministry of Personnel Kim Kyŏngyŏ, making the excuse that his parents were ill, did not take up a government position. Even though he was appointed as the chief of the post station (*ch'albang*) at Kŭmgyo, he did not assume his post. The court argued that he was avoiding his responsibilities, so he was exiled to Ponyŏk.[24] After he was released, he was appointed as a censor (*ajang*) in the Two Offices and the Military Training Administration (Oktang) in Ŭnggyo several times, but would not accept. Sin Ch'ŏnik and Yi P'irhaeng were appointed censors in the Two Offices, but they did not take office.

RECORD OF CH'ŎNGŬM'S SLANDERING

Numerous officials were bestowed awards and had their positions elevated.[1] Kim Sanghŏn rejected awards and submitted a petition to the throne, which read,

> Originally, I was ill, plus I am old and senile. My heart has fallen. I have committed as many crimes as I have hair; it is as though heaven and earth have changed places. My form is alive, but my insides are dead, just like earthen soil and a dead log, with no hope to stand again at the court to serve. I tossed and drifted about, just waiting for death morning and night. Unexpectedly, I heard that the attending officials in Namhan Mountain Fortress all received rewards and had their positions elevated. And I am one of them. I first felt surprised but, in the end, grew ashamed and fearful. As time passed, I felt even more uneasy. When His Highness was stationed in the mountain fortress, the high-ranking ministers carried out their duties. They argued in debate and urged His Highness to come out of the fortress. Should I have dared to venture to my death to tell His Highness to safeguard righteousness and remain [inside the

fortress]? This is my first crime. As for the letter of capitulation, I could not bear to see the characters written on it. I tore up the draft and wept bitterly at the court. This is my second crime. The two palaces (*yanggung*)—His Highness and the crown prince—personally traveled to the camp of the thieves. I did not die next to their horses or follow them because of my illness. This is my third crime. I carry the burden of these three crimes and yet I have escaped punishment. How could I receive the same favors that other officials who constantly stood by your side had? I prostrate myself in front of you and beg Your Highness to urgently rescind this order of award. Please find a way to advise and punish me. For people beside Your Highness who behaved so bad as I, there must be a public regulation that would correct them. I prostrate myself in a remote wilderness. For those people who we heard and saw, but we did not execute, we were even afraid of such annoyances. Is this ridiculous? I prostrate myself and recall these. If the change of winter and summer never ends, we cannot discard our fur coats or hemp cloth. If the enemy state had not been wiped out thoroughly, attacking them and defending against them cannot be neglected. I prostrate myself and beg that Your Highness please make every effort to lie on firewood and taste gall [bitterness], and, Your Highness, please repair the protective wall to let our country escape the humiliation again.[2] Ah! Do not trust a temporary treaty obtained by force. Do not forget your great kindness of previous days. Do not rely on the benevolence of tigers and wolves. Do not destroy the country of our fathers and mothers. Who other than I could warn Your Highness so sincerely? As for the vastness of our country, it is now controlled by our enemy. It is a shame not felt in ancient and modern times. I recalled that every time our previous king spoke, he would say that all streams flowed east.[3] Without noticing, my clothes grow soaked by my tears.

I prostrate myself here and hope His Highness will remember this. I could be presumptuous and confused. Also, I made this happen again. I deserve a death sentence ten thousand times.

O n the twenty-ninth day of the seventh lunar month in the *muin* year [1638], Inspector-General (*changnyŏng*) Yu Sŏk, Pak Kyeyŏng, and others sent a petition to His Highness. It read,

The relationship between a ruler and his ministers has no escape between heaven and earth. Despite life or death and glory or dishonor, it is not right to render them independent. How could they hold two hearts whether one's fate rises or falls while one gains or suffers?[4] The former minister Kim Sanghŏn was once renowned and recognized by the court. For ten years, he was held in good graces, sitting in the army tent. He received royal bounty, including benefit and heavy righteousness from Your Highness. How could he abandon Your Highness at a moment of desperation of life and death? On the day the mountain fortress fell, Your Highness was trapped in unpredictable dangers. All your subjects were extremely sorrowful. Kim Sanghŏn prioritized his own safety over that of Your Highness, and it was not righteous. Kim Sanghŏn, unlike Zheng Yun thrusting a sword, who always shared the same destiny with Your Highness no matter whether it was fortune or misfortune, ran far away without any thought of Your Highness. After things settled, he unexpectedly returned to observe how matters had turned out. He lay resting in a place and looked on the royal household from a distance. While he believed himself clean and loyal, he could not serve [what he thought to be] a disgraceful ruler. He encouraged dissent, disclosed the evils of the country, and confused the will of our people. Ah! The righteousness of a subject is exhausted and at an all-time low. He demands his fame but ruins the country. He gathers factions (*tang*) and harms the country. This is what Sanghŏn has been doing besides his official duties. His crimes are believing he has no king and being immoral. Your Highness should not pardon him. We hope that you send him far away and surround him tightly with thorns to imprison him.

His Highness responded, "This debate over Sanghŏn's crimes is too late. Just leave it as it is."

At this time, Inspector-General (*taesahŏn*) Kim Yŏngjo was dispatched to Mukden as an envoy to present a memorial. In this memorial, he briefly conveyed a message, hoping to save Sanghŏn. Minister of Rites (*yejo p'ansŏ*) Yi Hyŏnyŏng presented a petition (*chaja*), the general content of which was: "Kim Yŏngjo submitted a petition to save Sanghŏn. I prostrate myself here in front of you. I was informed by the royal decree (*kyo*) that it is too late to judge the crimes of Kim Sanghŏn. This is unimaginably upsetting. I suspect that it is Yŏngjo's plan to strip me of my official duties. He actually hoped to save Kim Sanghŏn." His Highness replied, "This official communication does not seem to conform to previous regulations. Were they this way? Inquire into this."

Inspector (*chip'yŏng*) Yi Haech'ang was in the middle of a report about assuming official positions and presenting memorials that request the court remove Yu Sŏk and Pak Kyeyŏng from the government rolls and never to employ them again. His Highness ordered, "Return this memorial to the petitioner. Do not proceed with your current duties and report about this memorial to the court." He added, "With regard to those unprecedented absurd matters, how could the Royal Secretariat Office (Chŏngwŏn) accept them? The royal secretaries (*sŭngji*) acted very oddly." Because of this issue, Yi Haech'ang was finally exiled to remote Yŏngdŏk.

Military Training Administration Special Counselor Yi Mok, Drafter of Royal Decrees (*ŭnggyo*) Hong Myŏngil, Censorate

Officer Yi Haengu, and others submitted a petition, which basically read that the court should deprive Yu Sŏk of his official title and change the position of Pak Kyeyŏng. His Highness replied,

> This person only wants to die to make a name for himself, when, in fact, he did not sacrifice himself in the end. As I see it, it is as though he is not in the least bit innocent. He abandoned his ruler during precarious times and roamed about in peaceful and quiet places. He appears to differ from those who wept to accompany their ruler and sacrificed their lives unconditionally. However, my dear officials excessively praise him. This is nothing but a lack of justice. For the Office of the Inspector General (Hŏnbu), as for these so-called infamously evil words, everything deserves itself.[5] There is no need to be excessively angry. If Yu Sŏk and others commit moral transgressions, then arguments will naturally appear on their own in the remonstrations (taegan). There is no need to be so anxious as to capture the thieves. This action now is quite astonishing. I will consider taking pity on them.

Right State Councilor Ch'oe Myŏnggil submitted a petition to the court. It roughly read,

> Kim Sanghŏn's literary compositions and moral conduct appeared respectful for a period of time. The day Namhan Mountain Fortress came under siege, he stood up and volunteered to help face the difficult situation. He tore apart his books and wept bitterly. He seemed to value integrity and righteousness. He would not alter his integrity even after falling into ditches.[6] If I were to criticize him for leaving the fortress in haste while still seeing the royal temples and shrines of the king, there is no evidence for this behavior. If an official departs the country, then his name becomes unclean. How should he be

viewed in ordinary times? Dying from illness is where the body abides. As for those who were watching but did not witness the event, they point out that his actions were lofty. They worry about the morals of the time and say that his virtue was not shallow. Even though there are traces of that, it is very biased, and the knowledge of the affair is insufficient. At the same time, there was a difference in viewpoints that finally prevailed over this matter, more or less. Thus, he is here today. He did not pass by the officials who fled to the countryside and join them. He passed by them without showing interest. All the more, when one sees the magnanimity of heaven and earth, the charge of "no ruler" and "no morality" crosses over to the law. This makes the people grieve. Then is there no reason to grow two hearts? Yi Haech'ang did not ask his senior officials. His view was only for impeachment. The matter was completely baseless. The instruction to change his official rank was a generous measure. For the other two officials, it is difficult for them to avoid their crimes. In my humble opinion, despite the similarity and dissimilarity in their debate and discussion, they should both be dismissed so this problem does not arise again. This is the path forward to tranquility. I am not with Kim Sanghŏn. Everybody knows this. But considering the morals of the times, I have no other options but this.

His Highness replied, "As for the matter with Yu Sŏk and others, carry out their dismissal in this way."

The court dismissed Inspector-General Kim Yŏngjo and appointed Kim Pan instead. Kim Pan submitted a petition, which read, "Yu Sŏk and Pak Kyeyŏng do not understand the public discussion, and they firmly maintain their personal opinions. That behavior is unacceptable, and everyone is appalled by Yu and Pak. I hope that you dismiss them." His Highness replied, "Concerning your petition, I have already dismissed them. Do not make this troubling argument again." The criminal record states that

Kim Sanghŏn has been exiled to a house surrounded by a thorn hedge at the frontier. The newly appointed inspector Pak Sumun submitted a petition to the throne and was dismissed.

O n the sixth day of the eighth lunar month, Yi Sanghyŏng and Yi Kye became administrators (*changnyŏng*). Kim Chungil became the inspector. Yi Sanghyŏng remained outside, and Yi Kye submitted a petition:

> As for the discussion of Kim Sanghŏn's crimes, although from the beginning the evidence was lacking in detail, this incident related to the illumination of the ruler and minister relationship. It seems as though everyone in the country is familiar with this. There is not one person who speaks privately. Those who wish to save Sanghŏn continuously stand up. They discuss this passionately. They are for supporting the criminals and attacking the critics. The Military Training Administration pronounced a strict decree that they do not think he should be blamed. The inspector-general has no time to look back on precedence and impeach him directly. They only halt the discussion independently as if they were afraid it was insufficient. How can they avoid impeaching him completely? I entreat you to dismiss Special Councilor (*pujehak*) Yi Mok, Drafter of Royal Decrees (*ŭnggyo*) Hong Myŏngil, Censorate Officer (*uch'an*) Yi Haengu, and Inspector-General (*taesahŏn*) Kim Pan.

His Highness relied, "Agreed."

Inspector Kim Chungil avoided arousing suspicion and submitted a petition.[7] It read, "Inspector-General Yi Kye did not avoid suspicion and stirred up trouble again. He relied upon the view of his political faction (*tang*) for his own selfishness. The public sentiment was anger. Learned men were bitterly disappointed. I entreat you to dismiss Inspector-General Yi Kye." His

Highness replied, "The words of one person are not public opinion. As for the matter of breaking the rules, is it right or wrong? Return Yi Kye's petition from whence it came. From now on, do not accept or pass onto me this kind of letter of impeachment."

Because of this petition, Kim Chungil was demoted to assistant commander of Pukch'ŏng. Censor-General Ch'oe Hyegil avoided arousing suspicion and submitted a petition:

Kim Sanghŏn was a well-known man for a period of time. He sought to but failed to die. In the end, he did not come out to present himself in front of Your Highness below the fortress wall. Even though his sentiment is forgivable, it is difficult to avoid public opinion. However, if he is punished strongly [as others have been], then could we say he has been punished fairly? Comparing what Yi Haech'ang was criticized over with what Yu Sŏk and others were attacked for, there is no distance between them. But given that Yi Haech'ang was exiled far away, the severity of these cases is widely different. There is no difference between Kim Chungil's actions and those of Yi Kye. In my humble opinion, if the court does not dismiss Yi Kye and Kim Chungil from office, then we have no custom of punishing those who break the rules or stir up conflict. If Your Highness does not withdraw the order exiling Yi Haech'ang far away, then, like the crime, the punishment will be regrettable in the end. Therefore, I wish to inform His Highness of my opinion. The opinions from my colleagues could be very different. I am but your humble senior official. If my words are not viewed truthfully, I beg you to dismiss me from office.[8]

Censor Chŏng Chiho submitted a petition: "As for punishing Yi Kye, he cannot be punished the same as Kim Chungil. The senior officials do not agree or consent. I am here first to avoid arousing suspicion. I do not dare to report alone. Otherwise, I beg Your Highness to dismiss me from office."

Third Censor Ch'oe Kyehun followed with a petition:

Many of us sat on woven mats (*chejwa*) the other day and expressed our views about the matter concerning the Military Training Administration.[9] Now, I am viewing the report that Censor-General Ch'oe Hyegil submitted. If Inspector-General Yi Kye and Inspector Kim Chungil are independently accused of misconduct, this is not proper. They should both be impeached and removed from their positions. I have already argued about impeaching the members of the Military Training Administration. Now, I am here again to petition for impeaching Yi Kye, but there is no clear evidence. As for the impeachment of Yi Kye, what the palace and the senior officers did stems from public discussion. It is not improper for me to submit this petition alone. Kim Chungil passed through clean posts one after another without corruption or fault. Who caused this? This so-called proof of suspicion was not avoided. This is honestly his own path.[10] My view and those of my colleagues conflict with each other. I beg Your Highness to dismiss me from office.

Military Training Administration Special Councilor Kim Suhyŏn, Drafter of Royal Decrees Chŏng Ch'ihwa, and Censorate Officer Sim Che submitted a petition to the throne. It requested that His Highness dismiss Ch'oe Hyegil and appoint Third Censor Ch'oe Kyehun and Censor Chŏng Chiho. His Highness replied, "Agreed."

O n the nineteenth day of the eighth lunar month, there was a daytime audience with the king. Vice Minister of the Royal Lecturer (*kyŏngyŏn'gwan*) Yi Kyŏngsŏk and military training administration officials Mok Sŏngsŏn and Sim Che met with His Highness. Yi Kyŏngsŏk said, "The discussion about Yu Sŏk is because of private revenge. It is not public opinion." His Highness replied,

> This is not private revenge. You should view both right and
> wrong. Kim Sanghŏn and Chŏng On are one and the same. You
> only raise the issue of Kim Sanghŏn and discuss him. This is
> wrong. However, Sanghŏn did not care about his king. He did
> not weep for his older brother. Does this mean he possesses
> proper human relations? Kim Sanghŏn has the hereditary ben-
> efits of an official and has attended the court as an official for
> more than twelve years. In response to this extreme change,
> he abandoned and ignored his king. He only cared about him-
> self and fled far away. Sanghŏn is the first person to have done
> such a thing. At this moment, although anyone who discusses
> Sanghŏn will be like a phoenix singing toward the rising sun,
> this is improper.[11] You may not talk about him anymore!

Mok Sŏngsŏn informed His Highness, saying, "The plan now
is to establish discipline, so the right and the wrong can be distinguished. Therefore, from Your Highness, the right person will
be recognized, and the wrong person will fall. After this, the right
and the wrong will be decided naturally."

Deputy Minister of War (*pyŏngjo ch'amp'an*) Yi Kyŏngyŏ
submitted a memorial wishing to retire to his hometown. The
memorial read approximately like this:

> I, your humble servant, was in Namhan Mountain Fortress ear-
> lier. I saw that Kim Sanghŏn and Chŏng On nearly lost their
> lives there, but fortunately they survived. They sought to die
> but were unable to do so. This was really pitiful and something
> to sigh over. They were ashamed of themselves. They are not
> the same as what people believe. Up to now, accusing and blam-
> ing Kim Sanghŏn is akin to accusing those strange and vile

people.[12] I sincerely petition for a way to end this. In a country with two hundred years of righteousness and propriety, the persons protecting righteousness for the Heavenly Court are only these two subjects. If we accuse them deeply, then what should we say to the world under heaven and to our future generations? As for the matters of these two subjects, they are sufficient enough to glorify our country. How could they blame them for revealing the fault of our king and deciding their crimes? I have yet to understand this.

On the ninth day of the tenth lunar month, Inspector-General Yi Yŏik and Inspector Yi Tojang told His Highness,

Seeing danger and then turning his back on our king is the greatest crime of an official. If we do not act on the law and govern, then the ensuing harm will make our officials no longer officials and our country no longer a country. How could this not be dreadful? Former minister Kim Sanghŏn sought death but failed to achieve it. He dared not be righteous afterward. He lay down and feigned illness and, in the end, he did not take part in His Highness's retinue. Instead, he wandered far away to Ch'unch'ŏn to search for his family. He spent his time hiking over mountain ranges and chose ease. The reward for his royal attendance was precisely His Highness's favor. He returned the royal order as though it was filthy. Moreover, the crown prince traveled to a foreign land. Sanghŏn's official duty was that of a guest. In the end, he did not bow and see off the crown prince. We should ask him to go follow Sun Fu.[13] How could they fail to meet? We ask that he be detained in a designated area of exile. The duty of an official to serve his king is that he must sacrifice his life at this critical moment and cannot wash his hands of it.[14] Former vice-minister Chŏng On did not die by the edge of his sword. After he recovered from his illness, he did not go and attend his king. He trekked casually to his hometown instead. He felt he was not fondly attached to Your Highness and only demanded his reputation cleansed. He did not consider the importance of proper righteousness. Being a subject to the king, how dare he do this? We beg Your Highness to dismiss Chŏng On from office and never appoint him again.

His Highness replied, "Let's put this aside. Punishment is unnecessary." Among the accusations, returning the royal order, going to Ch'unch'ŏn, and attending to the crown prince were false.

Inspector-General Sŏ Sangni submitted a memorial:

I, your humble servant, prostrate myself before you. I have seen the memorials submitted to the court about Kim Sanghŏn and Chŏng On. They are extremely surprising. Yi Yŏ and others already resubmitted those affairs that have been terminated. They have made a special move to ensnare someone in a trap. How could this be so extreme? Since encountering this, I cannot blindly follow these two. I entreat you to dismiss them from their positions.

Censors Ŏm Chŏnggu and Pak Sumun asked His Highness to punish Yi Tojang, Yi Yŏik, and Sŏ Sangni by stripping them of their posts and to have Second Inspector (*chibŭi*) Kwŏn To appointed to an office. His Highness replied, "Make these suggestions so." Because of this, Sŏ Sangni was demoted to Kyŏngsang post-station chief by royal decree.

Inspector-General Sŏ Kyŏngu submitted a memorial to the throne for him to be dismissed and replaced with Kim Yŏngjo and then with Kim Pan. Kim Pan submitted a memorial, which read:

The court has already been previously informed of my insignificant and humble opinion. Now, why is this argument spinning in circles disrespectfully? As for dismissing the announcement of the king, even one bit of defamation cannot be allowed. At first, he said the undelivered royal letter had been returned. This is a crime of disrespect. He is extremely good at concealing the truth! As for Chŏng On's noteworthy conduct and independent character, Your Highness used to approve them. His aspirations to die by his own blade can clearly be seen. Who would say that this kind of simple, honest, and responsible person behaves this way only to seek fame? They are trying to locate fault in him. I, your servant, do not honestly understand this. It is difficult for me to endure as the inspector-general. I beg you to dismiss me from my post.

His Highness replied, "Kim Sanghŏn was promoted to carry an edict, so why did he not send it? Ask him about this and report it to me." The ministry of military affairs replied, "In general, there are no rules for sending an edict. The scribe from the Ministry of Personnel, Kim Ŭisin, received it. But he did not deliver it because of the distance. The edict was stored with a variety of other documents."

Second Inspector Kwŏn To avoided arousing suspicion, writing,

Honestly, as for Kim Sanghŏn, I am truly not with him. In the autumn, I was summoned and came up to the court. Just at the time when the western matter was most difficult, I do not wish to talk about these past events or otherwise open up trouble.[15] I was transferred to the court, after which I was dispatched to meet my colleagues. Ignorantly, I had not yet received His Highness's permission. Now, I see Inspector-General Kim Pan and avoid meeting him. This is because my view is different from his. How could I sit around comfortably and deal with this? I ask Your Highness to dismiss me.

Censor Pak Sumun wrote, "My humble opinion conflicts with those of the senior officials (*changgwŏn*). I request that you dismiss me." Censor-General Ch'oe Haegil wrote,

As for the matter of Kim Sanghŏn and Chŏng On, the opinion coming out of the Censorate stirs acrimony. How could this be an urgent matter of today? It seems that the true motives of these two officials should not be distinguished. In providing the applicable provisions for the case, they differ widely. I have never known this to be predictable. Inspector-General Kim Pan's punishment could be very different. This is all for calming today's measures. I, your humble servant, make these statements. First, my colleagues should avoid suspicion. Still, I cannot act under false pretenses, and I ask you to dismiss me.

The Military Training Administration reported, "Inspector-General Kim Pan and Second Inspector Kwŏn To should assume their government posts, and we hope that Censor-General Ch'oe Hyegil and the Censor Pak Sumun will be dismissed." His Highness complied with these recommendations. Kim Pan presented a resignation memorial, and Kwŏn expediently assumed his post.

On the twenty-first day of the tenth lunar month, Second Inspector of the Censorate Kwŏn To, Inspector-General Pak Tonbok, Hong Chin, and Inspector Yi Unjae submitted a memorial. It read,

The criminal charges against Kim Sanghŏn have been submitted previously. But all of the royal opinions passed down about this case instruct us to tolerate him. Our bewilderment has increased greatly. We have no choice but to speak out about this. The plan for the royal temples and shrines differs from the beliefs of common men. The righteousness of ministers should be fully enacted for the ruler they serve. Sanghŏn's demands and expectations from Your Highness are higher than those from the grand king and King Wen of Zhou.[16] Taking their own lives are Ji Lang and Sun Fu.[17] Sanghŏn's words do not match his actions. Alas, what extremes! We can roughly imagine what happened on that day. For the lifetime of narrow-minded people, he could never measure the trend of events, but firmly insisted on what he believed. Moving forward, he cannot die for his country; stepping backward, he cannot sacrifice his life. What he knew was only shame and regret, so he grew angry and left the fortress. As a result, he had no sympathy for the king's danger and never collected his older brother's body. He does not know that the crime of forgetting his parents and betraying his country is all due to his actions.

After traveling beyond the mountain ridge, he could not rest in a quiet location nor conceal his wickedness. While he roamed between Ho and Oyŏng, he was so arrogant that he thought he possessed great integrity.[18] This means that he was no different than a poor man without a place to return.[19] His knowledge and experiences were deviant and secretive even if they were insufficient. Given the capacity of a sage is to tolerate error, add forgiveness and we may consider this one kind of method.[20] Popular opinion is unkind, and harsh commentary is widespread. As for Sanghŏn's incident, the debate continues to be intense. The court is not placated. Those who accuse him point out he is immoral (*pulto*). Those who defend him allow for his upright constancy. His immorality is sincerely excessive. His uprightness is nonexistent. As we know, the Duke of Zheng exposed his shoulder and dragged a sheep on a rope, but Zichan received the affairs of the state.[21] Emperor Gaozong neglected his parents and forgot vengeance, whereas Zhu Xi established the court.[22] For a period of several thousand years, the ways the officials coped with the change were all different. As for what Sanghŏn has done, if this could be recorded in a book, he would be comparable to Chen Yizhong.[23] He abandoned his position and fled to occupy an ancient fortress. What Sanghŏn has done is certainly better than what Zichan or Zhu Xi did; rather, he is comparable to Yizhong.

We do not know what Sanghŏn thinks about Yizhong when he reads these works. At first, Sanghŏn was proud of his good name, which became a model for a generation. When this opinion to impeach him arose, the crowds gathered, shouting in opposition to it. They adamantly insisted that Sanghŏn not be wronged. As for the factional opinion of this villain and his plans, they have gone so far as this [to shout opposition]. They may be sincerely disappointed. In general, originally the affairs of heaven and earth do not have two rights. If Sanghŏn is correct, then those sitting in the court today must be wrong. As for the boundary between right and wrong, the people have leaned toward it, and before long they will leave, one after another. They [the people who support Sanghŏn] all feel they are superior to the rest of us. Who is willing to follow His Highness through a calamitous age? This concern plunges us into great fear. But debate about this cannot go on indefinitely. Right and wrong cannot be unclear. We beg you not to make this issue difficult. We urgently request that you detain Sanghŏn in the province (*chungdo puch'ŏ*).

His Highness replied, "Dismiss him from office." This petition was written by Kwŏn To.

Kim Sanghŏn heard that the ancestral tablet (*kweyŏn*) of his deceased older brother, Right State Councilor Kim Sangyong, was sent down from the capital to Naep'o [in Ch'ungnam]. When he reached Ch'ungju, he realized this was just a rumor, so he returned in vain. The so-called rumor of traveling between Ho and Oyŏng actually refers to this. This is all because of what the various officials thought of Yu Sŏk's and Yi Kye's regret. In the *ŭlsa* year, Mok Sŏngsŏn and Yu Sŏk jointly petitioned the king, appealing the death of Prince Insŏng.[24] Kim Sanghŏn was the censor-general at the time. He bitterly refuted them. Because of this, Mok and Yu abandoned government service for ten years. As for Yi Kye, in the Yi Kwal Rebellion of the *kapcha* year [1624], neither the grandfather of Yi Kye, Slave Administration Bureau Chief (*p'an'gyŏlsa*) Yi Tam, nor Yi Kye's father, nor Assistant Minister for the Ministry of Work (*kongjo chwaryang*) Chin Yŏng joined the royal entourage (*hojong*) to Namhan Mountain Fortress. Sanghŏn, as the inspector-general, argued for impeaching them, saying that the three generations of grandfather, son, and grandson had turned their backs on the country. Now, they have assumed important positions, thus building good connections. Moreover, Sanghŏn used to point out that Kwŏn To was not a righteous man. Combining these regrets, it could be expected that some would attack Sanghŏn. This was their conclusion.

Censor (*chŏngŏn*) Yi Tojang petitioned His Highness, writing, "As for the debate from the previous Inquisition Tribunal over Kim Sanghŏn, public defamation is truly widespread. It has also been reported that he did not accept the royal honor. Among the things people utter about him, his written characters are prone to errors. He has been falsely accused and expelled. I beg you to remove me from office." Inspector-General Hong Chin, Pak Tonbok, and Inspector Yi Unjae petitioned His Highness, saying,

The day before yesterday, various subjects sat down outside the court to offer their opinions about the heaviness of Sanghŏn's crimes and the lightness of the law. They talked about these while sitting atop woven mats. Second Inspector Kwŏn To also discussed these things. He joined this petition to avoid confusion, because he had already reported it previously. Today, Inspector Yi Kyŏngsang made the accusation that Kim Sanghŏn's crimes and the law do not correspond with each other, thus we have failed to discuss his crimes correctly. We beg you to reprimand and dismiss Yi Kyŏngsang.

Second Inspector Kwŏn To petitioned the king, saying,

> Bureaucratic colleagues have spoken of the first petition about Kim Sanghŏn, saying his crime was heavy, but the law was light. I responded that if the truth was really like what my colleagues have commented, we should schedule a discussion about it. My colleagues have agreed with this point. After changing the framing of the discussion, they maintain their previous opinion. So, I believe that a debate has been set to distinguish right and wrong and to pacify people's hearts. There is no need to quibble over lightness and heaviness of the law. Yesterday, we gathered again on woven mats. My colleagues withdrew to avoid dealing with this matter. How can I sit feeling content? I beg you to dismiss me from office.

Inspector Yi Kyŏngsang wrote, "After conducting the meeting ritual today, I suggested that Kim Sanghŏn's crimes be discussed through the submission of petitions. Not only did they neglect this suggestion, but my colleagues also were the first to withdraw from the court to avoid this, thus how can I dare remain in office? I entreat you to dismiss me."

Military Training Administration Office Special Councilor (ŭnggyo) Chŏng Ch'ihwa, Junior Fifth Councilor (pugyori) Mok Sŏngsŏn, Yi Kye, and Censorate Officer Sim Che submitted a petition to the king, requesting in general that Censor Yi Tojang, Inspector-General Hong Chin, Pak Panbon, Inspector Yi Unjae, and Second Inspector Yi Kyŏngsang all be appointed to office. His Highness ordered the request carried out. The court reduced

Kyŏngsang's rank and appointed Inspector-General Hong Chin, Pak Panbon, and Inspector Yi Unjae to their posts.

On the twenty-sixth day of the tenth lunar month, memorials previously composed requesting that Kim Sanghŏn be detained in a designated area came into the court continuously. From today, the scholars writing the memorials began asking for more, that he be exiled far away. Chŏng On was dismissed and asked not to be appointed again. His Highness replied, "I have already issued the command. Cease annoying me."

Inspector-General Kim Pan submitted a memorial about dismissing himself. Yi Haengwŏn replaced Kim Pan's in his position. The memorial read,

> Lately, concerning the matter of Kim Sanghŏn and Chŏng On, disorder is spinning out of control, turning round and round. Those who attack them add improper arguments. Those who want to help do not understand the real circumstances. I secretly regret this matter. Now, although those two officials [Kim Sanghŏn and Chŏng On] were freely in the mountain fortress, they sought death but were unable to die. By the time they returned to the capital, the arguments attacking those who advocated war turned severe day by day. Not only does Kim Sanghŏn dare not step forward, but he is also not tolerated by this world. This is pitiful, but not infuriating. Now, those who attacked him did so at first over a royal order that was not sent out. They called this "returning the letter." Before the disorder broke out, he had already changed his government post, but they referred to him as "still carrying" his position as mentor for the crown prince (*pin'gaek*). As soon as he reached Hosŏ, he wept for the loss of his older brother. They called this "wandering aimlessly." When His Highness returned to the capital,

this cannot be compared with Ya Mountain.[25] Hiding and concealing oneself at the foot of a mountain is not the same as arriving at an ancient fortress. It is comparable to Zhang Shijie's escape.[26] His choice of words was crude and confusing. He changed the color of black with the color of white.[27] How could this establish public opinion and turn people into followers? As for the discussion about Chŏng On's crimes, it must not be spoken of. At first, he sought fame. Fortunately, he surrendered his post in a fit of rage. Ah! This is unusual. As I am tired and inferior, I presumptuously assumed a seat of honor. But it is so difficult to control this baseless discussion and ameliorate this moral decadence. I beg you to dismiss me.

Inspector Chŏng T'aeje reported,

These days, discussion on Kim Sanghŏn and Chŏng On has reached its heights at the headquarters. Among these opinions is a belief that if there are those who hold somewhat different views, then they should be expelled immediately. I really feel upset about this. If there ever comes a time when heaven and earth change places, those who still pledge their hearts and do not change will be Kim Sanghŏn and Chŏng On. Although the debate over advocating war has damaged the country, these two officials do not dare to consider themselves innocent and will be the ones who do not enter the capital again. Honestly, they will be miserable. Those who attack them do not understand this and just make up ridiculous words whenever they find an opportunity. To use such means to get others dismissed from office, this is extreme! My view does not meet those of my colleagues. I beg you to dismiss me.

Inspector-General Pak Tonbok, Hong Chin, and Inspector Yi Unjae reported,

As for the discussion about Kim Sanghŏn, the opinions on his crimes all vary. Some rise up to protect him. Some attack him and instruct others not to say a word about the issue. How bewildered we secretly feel! As for the discussion of officials, they argue in their petitions based on the heaviness of the law to exile him far away. Now, Inspector-General Yi Haengwŏn and Inspector Chŏng T'aeje have resigned to avoid this problem. They only want to save Kim Sanghŏn and attack our opinions. Supposing we want to quickly argue about this matter, then we too will grow exhausted.[28] How dare we remain [in office]? We entreat you to dismiss us.

Censor Yi Tojang reported,

Kim Sanghŏn betrayed His Highness many times. When one becomes an official for Your Highness, if he betrays Your Highness, then this is a crime according to the law. In reality, the debate over this offense stems from public discussion. Now, as for the withdrawal and dismissal of Inspector-General Yi Haengwŏn and Inspector Chŏng T'aeje, I am shocked that this is so! Serving as a first-rank senior official is such a great honor. But Kim Sanghŏn hid himself in the home of a lower official for many years. It is a mistake to confer a respectable title on him. This minister has already walked away from his responsibilities. For ten years, he lectured the crown prince, while he sat in his royal lecture chair, and received special favors from him. Before the disorder broke out, his government post had changed.[29] Now, this is the first time I have heard of this. On the day of Ch'angnŭng, the persons who wept and paid respects were not just the officials attached to the crown prince.[30] This is all about the weighted importance of affection and righteousness. Even if you had made Sanghŏn hear this, even he would certainly weep and be convinced. Chŏng On did not present himself to His Highness. He fled far away and did not return, because he did not care about affection and righteousness. Moreover, he had a very spotless reputation. Therefore, his punishment was decided to be slight. This was to prevent the so-called truth from coming out of the mouths of the persons who always feel good about themselves. Surprisingly, Chŏng On and Kim Sanghŏn are always mentioned together, but they ought to be referred to as "two officials, two officials." But if the two are differentiated from each other, then it must be that the court argues this matter as a criminal case. This is still not yet clear. I rashly discuss this matter to stir up trouble. How could I sit by idly and not handle this affair? I beg you to remove me from office.

Censor Im Hyodal wrote,

Kim Sanghŏn received fame for his calligraphy when he was a child. He maintained a poor but simple life. He certainly can be dubbed an upright person. But his inherent nature is extremely opinionated, and he is close-minded. Throughout his life, he presented towering critiques and decried persons with different opinions. One knows his personality. On the day Your Highness left the fortress, he had no loving attachment to you in the end. He fled far away and did not return. In view of his separation, how could he be innocent? He has already been removed from his official duties. Public opinion has already been acted upon, so easing up on this would be the best.[31] I see it this way. How could I deal with those two officials? I beg you to dismiss me.

Censor-General Kim Seryŏm sent a petition that read,

At first, the affair of Kim Sanghŏn was not related to the survival or collapse of the country. But the debate exploded, with petitioners turning violent against one another. The ruler was in danger and the country was dying, and Sanghŏn gave no thought to either of these. I accept the benefits of senior rank (*susŏk*), yet how can I decide right or wrong and calm this baseless debate? I cannot just sit idly by. I beg you to dismiss me.

Censor Hong Myŏngil wrote,

Inspector-General Yi Haengwŏn, Inspector Chŏng T'aeje, Censor Yi Tojang, Im Hyodal, Third Inspector General Hong Chin, Pak Tonbok, Inspector Yi Unjae, and Inspector-General Kim Seryŏm all avoided arousing suspicion and withdrew from the court. Now, as for the opinions on Kim Sanghŏn and Chŏng On in the Inquisition Tribunal, they decide the right or the wrong from among the various disagreements and differentiate the light or the heavy from one person who keeps his words and actions consistent.[32] The so-called royal order and the position as mentor to the crown prince in the tutorial office (*pin'gaek*) were exposed as false accusations.[33] This was all improper. What causes these kinds of breaches? There is already not much difference between the guilt and innocence of these two officials. But the law is twisted, the punishment is exempted, and the message to the king is not direct. For this reason, it is inevitable that the king was deceived, and these people—Kim Sanghŏn and Chŏng On—were framed. Now, the duty of calming this affair lies with the senior rank officials (*susŏk*). If the court removes their judgement, then the others will talk endlessly. This is not worth mentioning. I request that His Highness appoint Yi Haengwŏn and Chŏng T'aeje to official posts. Hong Chin, Pak Tonbok, Yi Unjae, Yi Tojang, Im Hyodal, and Kim Seryŏm should be dismissed.

His Highness granted the request of the petition. But as for Yi Haengwŏn and others, another opinion arose, that they were corrupt and unwise. As such, they were all removed from office.

On the first day of the eleventh lunar month, Inspector-General Nam Iung, Censor-General Kim Pan, Third Inspector-General Yi Kye, Yi Yŏik, Inspector Sin Yu, Censor Chŏng Chiho, and Hwang Wiwŏn submitted a petition to the court, which read,

> As for the opinion of the Office of the Inspector General (Hŏnbu) concerning Kim Sanghŏn's public debate, if we sampled public discussions for a time, then those who blamed Sanghŏn are wrong. Yi Haengwŏn, Chŏng T'aeje, and others protect their political faction (*tang*) and levy their own falsities to have Sanghŏn seem like someone who is not at fault in the least. For those who avoid arousing suspicion, they attack with words. How heinous their discord is! There is nothing more overwhelming than this. Censor (*sagŏn*) Hong Myŏngil did not consider right and wrong. He was only fortunate in that he could handle this situation with his own hands. He seized the opportunity, indulged himself privately, and dismissed many officials, but conveniently omitted these two people. Without the least bit of fear of the consequences, we cannot let this last for long. We beg you to dismiss us.

His Highness granted the request of the petition. Because of this, Hong Myŏngil was specially appointed to Koc'hang county.

On the third day, the court submitted a letter stating that Kim Sanghŏn should be exiled to a remote location. His Highness responded that Kim Sanghŏn should be divested of his position and rank.

On the fourth day, His Highness dismissed Chŏng On and ordered that he not be appointed again. The petitions ceased.

On the fifth day, the court appointed Censor Kwŏn To, Third Inspector Yi Kye, Junior Fifth Councilor Yi Tojang, Censor Im Hyodal, and Censorate Officer Yŏm Chŏnggyu.

On the sixth day, during the morning studies of the Confucian Classics, an official presented the petition from the previous day next to the royal chair.[34] His Highness responded, "His crime need not be severely punished. At first, he asked to be dismissed from office and that has ended. Recently, the younger group intends to help excessively, but their actions are shameful. Because of this, he has been accused of additional crimes. From now on, I will not approve this. End the discussion!"

On the eighth day, Third Inspector General Yi Kye, Inspector Pak Sumun, and Sin Yu petitioned the throne, writing,

These days, concerning the matter about the debate over Kim Sanghŏn's criminality, the sentiment is not positive among the officials at the court. We are not denying that calmness in the court is good, but regarding the essence of court discussion, its lightness or heaviness, its slowness or quickness, all depends on public consensus. Sanghŏn's punishment ended with the removal of his official title (*sakt'al*). It is public opinion that this punishment is too light (*t'aegyŏng*). We need time to send petitions to Your Highness. Today, Inspector-General Nam Iung asked His Highness to expunge the name of the criminal from the records (*chŏnggye*) and delivered a letter to the court. We sent a reply that renewed the debate. Nam Iung sent another letter to say the situation was difficult to take part in. The view of our officials failed to meet with those of the senior officials. How could they dare debate this matter? We beg you to dismiss us.

Inspector-General Nam Iung explained in a memorial that he wanted to resign. His Highness did not grant this. Nam Iung assumed his official post and reported,

These days, concerning the matter of Kim Sanghŏn, the discussion is fierce and things that go on in the court have not been proper. In my presumptuous opinion, Your Highness has already proclaimed his punishment. The amount of time for public debate should be extended slightly. Inflexibly insisting on a certain period of time appears disturbing and disrespectful. I presented a letter that requested an end to the debate. Then all my colleagues replied that this would be in haste, and they tended to avoid my suggestions. How could I dare claim only my opinion is correct? I beg you to dismiss me.

Censor-General Kim Pan petitioned the king, writing, "Because of this issue, I have been accused of supporting the criminal. Without being afraid of any consequences of blame, how could I calmly say this is proper or improper? I beg you to dismiss me." The petition from the court was such:

Second-Inspector Yi Kye, Inspector Pak Sumun, Sin Yu, Inspector-General Nam Iung, and Censor-General Kim Pan all withdrew from their posts to avoid suspicion. The court should stop forcibly removing Kim Sanghŏn from his position (*sakt'al*). This is quite extreme. The lightness of his punishment will not appease the court officials. We want to end this discussion over the matter. As we have been accused over this issue before, the court dare not cope with it. Without the least suspicion of withdrawing, we beg Your Highness to command all of them to resume their individual posts.

On the thirteenth day, Inspector-General Nam Iung petitioned His Highness to remove him from office and appoint Kim Sik instead. He was residing in his hometown. Sim Che was appointed as third censor (*hŏnnap*), Hong Chin as censor, and Im Tam as junior fifth councilor.

On the twenty-third day, a decree was passed about exiling Kim Sanghŏn far away. All the petitions [regarding Sanghŏn] were halted.

In the first month of the *kyŏngjing* year [1640], Censor-General Pak Hwang petitioned His Highness. The general content was such: "Inspector-General Yu Sŏk was devoted when dealing with all kinds of matters. But he did not seem to be a good person or an upright scholar." He asked His Highness to dismiss him, but His Highness did not approve.

Yu Sŏk petitioned the throne, and the petition's content was roughly this:

> I was careless and stupid by nature. I displease many sometimes, and it has been long since many others felt jealous about me. The officer Kim Sanghŏn of the Board of Revenue (Haenghogun) committed the crime of turning his back on the king and betraying the country. I only know that there is king and father, but I never knew that there are powerful officials. In the past, I served

my position and briefly explained my opinions. How could I not know that once discussion about this person began, it would be followed by extreme misfortune? His view of insanity and foolishness has never changed. Today at the court, there is no one but the persons who advocate for Sanghŏn. I gnash my teeth in anger. I certainly want to kill him. Fortunately, with the blessing of heaven and earth and of fathers and mothers, I receive special graces and have survived until this day. For the hidden poison and concealed danger, I alone have expected that there is no way to avoid the reprimand from what I have been planning and doing.[35] Your Highness resides deeply in the palace. How could you know about the conditions of the times? Sanghŏn is entrenched in a power whose brightness has been overwhelming for some time, roughly eighteen years. He has differentiated his followers and opponents by his own judgment and decided, on his own, who would be rich and who would be deprived. I harbor ordinary sentiments. If I were afraid to lose, then there would be no need for me to surrender this beneficial way, provoke his anger, and place myself in a difficult dilemma.[36]

I also heard secretly that a petition from Sanghŏn stated, "From ancient times until now, there has been no immortal person, as there is no everlasting country."[37] He, being an ordinary man, cannot decide alone. But he, with the lower understanding of an ordinary person, compares himself to the views of the king who pays respects at the royal temples and shrines.[38] How evil is that thinking? Because I am a subject of Your Highness, my king is whom I have affections for. Even if I were harshly scolded ten thousand times, I would be unable to keep my righteous mouth closed. I am also saddened. I was already done without being presumptuous.[39] I have been unreasonably accused by other people. How could I force myself to humiliate my peers when standing together with them at court? Please immediately dismiss me, so my dismissal can calm both the public and private sectors.

His Highness replied, "I have inspected your petition and understand it. The dispute [over the impeachment of the inspector-general and censor-general] is not correct. I have already shed light upon this incident. Thus, do not make accusations about this again or ask to resign. Be at ease and resume your duties."

HUMILIATION RECEIVED
FROM THE QING

In the autumn of the *kimyo* year [1639], an enemy envoy arrived, requesting five thousand naval troops to assist them in attacking the Heavenly Court [the Ming]. Our country appointed Im Kyŏngŏp as admiral (*sangjang*). Yi Wan was appointed as deputy admiral (*pujang*). The court mobilized boats from all of the provinces and dispatched them in the first ten days of the twelfth lunar month.

Kim Sanghŏn petitioned His Highness, saying,

As your humble servant, who bears a crime, I prostrate myself here before you. The enormous amount of criticism, for being sent far away, has shattered my bones. But thanks to the graces from heaven, earth, and my parents, I have avoided banishment and have been reappointed to a succession of posts. I may now rest in a rustic house until the end of my life. I will think about old age and disease throughout the rest of my days. I have waited for death every day and night. There has been no means for me to repay even one ten-thousandth of this extremely rare and splendid virtue, so day and night I can shed only tears and do nothing more. A short while ago, I heard that His Highness was unwell and had been unable to recover for a very long time. With all my heart, I have been extremely worried about the king, but I have found no way to help, because I am blind to the medicinal arts (*panggi*). Recently, I heard that the court obeyed the words of the northern envoy to dispatch five thousand naval personnel and assist with Mukden's invasion of the Great Ming. When I heard this, I was shocked and confused and could not believe it was so. When referring to a subject and his master, there is obeying and disobeying. Zilu and Ran Qiu were subjects of the Ji clan. Yet Confucius praised their disobedience.[1] Originally, the power of the country was weak, and its force was bent. Your Highness established a plan for us to survive. With the great aspiration of Your Highness, to evince order out of chaos, Your Highness has lain upon firewood and tasted gall. Up until now, it has already been three years. To expunge this humiliation and take revenge upon the enemy is expected to be achieved within days. How could Your Highness withdraw this original intent and by doing so disobey your heart to obey [the Qing]? The plan could finally reach a place of nowhere or not reach a place at all.[2] From antiquity until now, there has never been someone who has escaped death, and there has never been a country that has not collapsed. We must endure death and collapse, but we cannot disobey our will. If someone were to make this statement to Your Highness, "that a man would assist the enemy and attack his parents," then Your Highness would certainly command that he be punished. Even though this person could be crafty with words and offer excuses, Your Highness would not forgive him and would have to execute the laws upon him. This is the proper way under heaven. Those who are scheming are now unable to defend their propriety and right conduct. But I did not argue with them because of their failure to hold up their propriety and right conduct. I just argued based on the advantages and disadvantages. Being fearful of the momentary violence of a strong neighbor but not afraid of the movement of the emperor's six commands is not grand strategy.

From the *chŏngch'uk* year [1637–1638] onward, the Middle dynasty went out of its way to pardon us for losing, which is unforgivable, knowing that being defeated and switching our allegiance to those barbarians was not what we wanted to do. Even though their troops progressed toward the frontier and the naval forces of the tower ships (*louchuan*) were insufficient for sweeping away the felt and fur coats [the barbarians] and recapturing the vast border, they were more than enough to block our country. If they heard that our country had played the jackal to the tiger, then a punitive force would strike us like lightning and thunder.[3] If the sails are filled with wind, it would take only one day before they reached Ki Island in the West Sea.[4] Therefore, we cannot say that the persecutors are only in Mukden [the Ming could also destroy us if we offend China by assisting the Manchu-Qing]. All of the people say, "Their power [the Ming's] is still strong. To disobey them would be disastrous." I would think that our reputation and righteousness would be of extreme importance, so damaging our reputation would evince calamity. Rather than turning our backs on righteousness to live with inevitable destruction in the end, why would we not defend propriety and wait for orders from heaven? Moreover, waiting for orders from heaven does not mean that we just sit around and wait to die. If we defend propriety, then the minds of the people will be pleased. If the minds of the people are pleased, then the foundation of our country will be stabilized, therefore defending the country will never not be obtained from heavenly blessings.

Our King T'aejo led his righteous army and established his country with a strong foundation for three hundred years. King Sŏnjo served the great Ming to the utmost. In the *imjin* year [1592], Sŏnjo received kind help from the Ming. Now, if we abandon righteousness and forget kindness—as we carry out this deed [to send troops to assist the Qing to attack the Ming]—then we are ignoring the later discussion of our descendants under heaven; how can we face our late kings in the underworld (ŏjiha)? How can we make our subjects exhaust all of their loyalty for the country? I prostrate myself and gaze upon Your Highness. You should please change your plan and immediately decide on this matter of fundamental importance. Your majesty should please not be deprived by a violent power and not be convinced by an evil thought.[5] In so doing, Your Highness can be heir to the aspirations of T'aejo and Sŏnjo and fulfill the hopes of faithful officials and righteous scholars. I have received the generous grace of this country. For a long time, I followed after the senior officials. Nevertheless, now I step back from my post. Now, when I encounter this matter of great importance for the country, my righteousness cannot remain silent. As for the day before yesterday and the actions of Yu Im, it was an urgent matter, and I stayed far away, so I have not offered any words about it. Sorrow and resentment penetrate me to my bones. Up to this day, I still feel it. Now, I dare not avoid this. With my ignorance, I exert myself to the utmost and respectfully wait to die by an axe. I prostrate myself before you and hope Your Highness will examine this.

In the eleventh lunar month of the *kyŏngjing* year [1640], three people—Ingguldai, Omoktu, and Yesha—arrived.[6] Two of them lodged at Mansang, while Omoktu hurried to the capital. Omoktu claimed that twelve tribute items were not fulfilled as originally promised. He said that escaped Tang people, and the people of our country who had fled, should be returned in no time.[7] The hostage sons (*chilcha*) from three councilors (*samgong*) and six chamberlains (*yukkyŏng*) consisted of some secondary sons (*sŏja*) and some distant relatives. The previous troop recruitment was intended to botch military secrets. Now, the naval officials are unable to leave. They are delayed and cannot advance. The court has not banned those who gather ginseng or hunt along the frontier. The boats of Han Chinese arriving at our frontier were not forbidden or announced. The rebuilding of Kanghwa Island and the mountain fortress should not be undertaken on our own initiative. The planned transfer of Yu Im should wait.[8] The court sent him south without permission. As for the troops led by Im Kyŏngŏp, those who were going to join him, as well as the cavalry horses and provisions, were not promptly delivered to the frontline, and there were other issues. Omoktu made repeated threats.

Chief State Councilor Hong Sŏbong, who took part in the treaty of the mountain fortress, and Minister of Personnel Yi Hyŏnyŏng, were responsible for selecting the people: Chief Royal Secretary Sin Tŭkyŏn, who in the previous years protested when Im Kyŏngŏp sent horsemen, and Vice Minister Pak Hwang, who had previously foreseen some occurrence in Mukden. They both were sent away. Therefore, those people below the chief state councilor dashed to Mansang overnight. This so-called foreseeing things by Pak Hwang meant that he predicted the events of Chŏng Noegyŏng. During the disturbance of the *pyŏngja* year [1637], Chŏng Noegyŏng volunteered to go to Mukden as the tutorial officer for the crown prince (*kangwŏn kyŏmgwan*). Our country sent red persimmons, raw pearls, and other items to the Khan. Chŏng Myŏngsu altered the documents and lowered by half the number of persimmons and pearls that were sent. Noegyŏng intended to eliminate Myŏngsu because of this issue. Librarian Kim Chongil and Censorate Official (*wŏlli*) Kang Hyoil met to discuss this confidentially. Moreover, the Chinese people held as prisoners of war felt the same way. They took an oath simultaneously to expose this matter. When the crown prince went to visit the Khan, Kim Chongil accompanied him. Ingguldai and Mafuta learned about this plan. They asked Chongil, "Is it true that you conspire to murder Chŏng Myŏngsu?" Chongil said that he was unaware of this. Ingguldai and Mafuta entered the

Office of the Examination (Kwanso) and asked Chŏng Noegyŏng about it. Noegyŏng replied that this was the case. Ingguldai and Mafuta grew very angry. They imprisoned Noegyŏng somewhere and, after first killing the Chinese people, they rebuked our court.

His Highness dispatched an envoy to clarify this and save Noegyŏng. Minister Ch'ŏe Myŏnggil said,

If this is so, then they would convey their anger even more. This will not benefit Noegyŏng. It is better to dispatch the royal messenger and to order him to commit suicide. The name of Hyowŏn never comes out of the mouths of the barbarians.[9] If this is finally exposed, then it would be better for our country to first have them both commit suicide at the same time. If this is so, then it would be fortunate for Noegyŏng and others to survive.

His Highness adopted these words. He dispatched the royal messenger, and, on the eighth day of the fourth lunar month, Noegyŏng and Hyowŏn were ordered to commit suicide in Mukden. The crown prince personally intended to go to Ingguldai's and Mafuta's residences (*kwanjung*) to save them. Many officials forcefully requested him not to go, but did not stop him. The crown prince at first sent Lecturer (*kanggwan*) Chŏng Chihwa to the Ministry of Justice (C. *xingbu*), but he was insulted there and thus returned. After that, the crown prince had no other alternative but to stop. After the two people were killed, their funerary clothes were paid for by the crown prince. He came to offer libations and to conduct the mourning rituals, which were unifying acts of sincerity. Those who heard of this, both near and far, were all deeply grateful. Chongil was thus brought and exiled to Yŏngdŏk.

Previously, Pak No was sent to the barbarians as an envoy and formed a long-term friendship with Ingguldai, Mafuta, and Chŏng Myŏngsu. When he reached Mukden, he approached

Ingguldai and Mafuta and presented his wife and children to them. Ingguldai and Mafuta came to our country, and he again presented his son to them. Ingguldai and Mafuta proclaimed, "Your son is my son." It was evident that Pak No was on cordial terms with the barbarians. Noegyŏng and Pak No stayed together in the same residence (*kwanjung*). Noegyŏng had seen Pak do many rude and debased things, so he scolded Pak to the utmost and said he could not even live under the same roof with him. When Noegyŏng died, everyone said that Pak No had something to do with it.

The chief state councilor and the minister of personnel had previously visited Mansang [Ŭiju]. On his way to Songgyŏng [Kaesŏng], Sin Tŭkyŏn returned. He submitted the following report to the throne: "As for the arrival of Ingguldai, he came especially because of me on this occasion. I will certainly perish if I go there. I would rather be killed at the court." His Highness ordered him quickly to depart. He submitted another petition to the throne that went as follows: "I, your humble servant, do not have children or nephews. Even if I were to die, there would be nobody who could collect my bones. I wish to take my sister's son Kang Munmyŏng with me." He made this request to the Border Defense Command. Munmyŏng was the son of Right State Councilor Kang Sŏkki. Sin Tŭkyŏn hoped to take advantage of Kang Munmyŏng's influence.

Along the middle road on his journey north, Sin Tŭkyŏn heard sounds of horns. This meant the arrival of barbarian officials and their capture of someone. Sin trekked through woods and crept and traveled through marshes. In a fortnight, they reached Anju, where he submitted a report. "Day and night, we traveled to reach Anju." There was not a person who did not secretly laugh at them. Ingguldai summoned the chief state councilor and the minister of personnel, saying, "There was a person named Kim Sayang in your esteemed country. He did not use the reign year titles of the great country [the Qing]. When your king walked out of

Namhan Mountain Fortress, Kim Sayang did not comply by attending to the king. Kim also did not welcome the coming and going of the crown prince; he did not receive any official rank. In all of the petitions he submitted, he offered advice to the Young faction. Was it thus?" The name Sayang referred to Kim Sanghŏn in the barbarian language. Ingguldai rebuked Kim Sanghŏn immeasurably. Those below the chief state councilor all knew that this matter concerning Kim eventually would be unavoidable and replied, "Kim Sanghŏn is old and feeble and lives a great distance away. Therefore, the official appointment letter cannot be delivered to him. It is not the case that he wouldn't accept an official rank. For the other issues, we have no way to investigate them." Ingguldai and the others said, "Make him come see us quickly." This is because Sanghŏn repeatedly criticized Pak No before this year. The matter was also something Pak No had incited. The Border Defense Command submitted their reply, requesting that the various officials of Mansang deal with it. His Highness said, "I consent. Moreover, the death of this person would be the misfortune of the country." First Minister (*yŏngbusa*) Yi Sŏnggu secretly reported, "Those people said they never would accept official ranks. If the court appoints Kim Sanghŏn as one of two state councilors or two state advisors, he will accept this. This would then eliminate our misfortune."

The Border Defense Command dispatched the government officials (*hari*) separately. They were sent with silver *yang* (*ŭnyang*). It was to be used as bribes in those locations. At first, the thieves did not demand payment. When Sin Tŭkyŏn reached Mansang, he was met by the anger of Ingguldai. He came out, saw Chŏng Myŏngsu, and pleaded with him thousands of times for his advice on how to keep his life. Myŏngsu said, "If a person utters such harsh words, then he can live." Tŭkyŏn immediately wrote letters to three men: Kim Sanghŏn, Cho Hanyŏng, and the illustrious scholar Ch'ae Ihang, his nephew. Sŏnch'ŏn Magistrate Yi Kye urged this. Ingguldai and others heard about this discussion and demanded that these three people be compelled to emerge and depart in haste. Regarding the matter of Tŭkyŏn, the Border Defense Command stated that there was no evidence of this. It was said that "slandering a person for your own life is not righteous. Harming the country is not loyal. This does not anger the Border Defense Command. It only labels it as 'no evidence.' As for the court now, it could even be said that there is no law.'"

Imperial Greeting Envoy Yi Kyŏngjŭng submitted a memorial that went as follows: "After the *chŏngch'uk* year [1637], I was not the imperial greeting envoy but the envoy to escort the imperial envoy. I was not unaware of their complexion (*kisaek*).[10] Now, the state of affairs is rather different from previous days. Kim Sanghŏn certainly understands the inevitability of his situation. He does not come even now. The court will not order him to come?'"

At first, all of the officials of Mansang wanted to save Kim Sanghŏn. When Ingguldai heard Tŭkyŏn's words, every day he urged him to come present himself. Ingguldai was going to dispatch a thousand soldiers to the Yŏngnam region to personally escort him. Moreover, he threatened to seize all of the officials below the chief state councilor and place them in hemp bags.[11] The capital and the surrounding areas were in an uproar about this threat. The various officials of Mansang, quite fearful, petitioned the throne three times in one day. The ones who were most urgent were those who had pressured to immediately dispatch Kim Sanghŏn.

At first, Kim Sanghŏn did not receive any orders from His Highness and hence could not leave on his own. The official order (*kwanja*) of the Border Defense Command arrived at Kyŏngsang Province. On the last day of the eleventh lunar month, he departed from Andong. His words and actions were just like those on normal days. Relatives and old friends from near and far wept as they saw him off. Servants and soldiers also cried intensely. As for Sanghŏn, not even one hair gave away his words or emotions. When he reached the capital, His Highness appointed him the central envoy (*chungsa*), presented him with sable furs, and generously rewarded him with travel expenditures. His Highness said,

> As the old ministers of the former royal dynasty, you have passed many years like I have. Although our relationship is that between ruler and his subject, our affection is like that between a father and a son. Thus, three years passed with nothing to show for it. Unexpectedly, misfortune befell, and we have reached this point. Indeed, it is all because of my stupidity and foolishness. I am sad and ashamed and unconsciously shed tears. I would like to go and see the barbarians, but it seems to be difficult and would not produce any results. I wish you well in beginning negotiations and resolving their anger.

Kim Sanghŏn expressed his profound gratitude and submitted a memorial to the throne, which read,

> I prostrate myself in front of Your Highness. My words did not help at all and my body is about to depart to lands far away. I traveled through the gates of our country. I did not present myself to Your Highness to greet you. My feelings of loyalty and devotion are extreme. Your Highness examines the thoughts of inferior people. Taking their demonstrations of feelings into consideration, you dispatch people to inquire into their thoughts. The words of Your Highness are full of sorrow and grief. I placed my hand on the precious sable furs that you had given me, and my body was warmed as though spring had returned. It was as though I had climbed the hornless dragon head statue and glimpsed the countenance of Your Highness again.[12] Even though this is the day I die, it is as if this is the day I am born.

I, your humble servant, cannot bear to gaze upon heaven or visit the palace. I shed tears of blood and will gallop away as rapidly as I can. I bring it to your attention that I humbly risk my life.

His Highness replied, "I have reviewed your memorial and I am extremely saddened. Make sure you face this situation well and live up to my expectations of your travels."

The five barbarian envoys reached P'yŏngsan, met Kim Sanghŏn , and were the first to leave. The matter was not humiliating in the least. Ingguldai was anxious to return, thus he urged them on somewhat. They traveled day and night, reaching Mansang from P'yŏngsan in only three days. Their appearance and strength were showing no sign of fatigue. This was the eleventh day of the twelfth lunar month. That day, Ingguldai held a feast with various officials from our court. They presented Kim Sanghŏn to Ingguldai and had him sit down above Minister of Personnel Yi Hyŏnyŏng. Sanghŏn wore the plain clothes and hat [of a commoner] and was carried on someone's back to enter. As soon as he entered, he lay down on the floor facing up. The group of barbarians were not angered. Ingguldai said, "We have all heard everything. So, you can speak your mind candidly with no worries." Sanghŏn asked, "What are you questioning me about?" Ingguldai replied, "In the *chŏngch'uk* year [1637], your king emerged below the castle walls. Only you could not come to serve the Qing or attend your ruler. What was the meaning of all this?" Kim Sanghŏn said, "How could I not wish to follow my ruler? It was only because I was old and infirm that I could not go, and that is all." Ingguldai asked again, "It was said that after the *chŏngch'uk* year you did not accept any appointment from your country, and you also returned the royal decrees. Why was this so?" Kim Sanghŏn responded, "Although I was old and infirm, my country did not remove my position. But how could I have known which official position I would take? Thus, I did not accept one. The high and low officers of our country are all here. I do not know where those absurd accusations originate from." Ingguldai inquired, "When we requisitioned your navy, how could you have thwarted us?" Kim Sanghŏn answered, "I maintained my purpose. I told my king about this. The country did not employ my words. How can the attentive details of my words reach another country?" Ingguldai countered, "How can you call us another country?" Kim Sanghŏn replied, "Both are different countries. Each has its own realm and border. How could it not be called another country?" Three military generals talked among themselves and had Sanghŏn carried out. They did not appear angry.

Omoktu said, "The people of Chosŏn speak gracefully. The replies of this person are very direct and very quick. He is a particular old man who is hard to cope with." The attending barbarians clicked their tongues forcefully [in agreement]. The barbarians separated the hardworking and fit men from the others, chose among them, and had them aide Sanghŏn. Moreover, they gave an order to carry him to Mukden by palanquin. Once they had prepared food on the road, they worried about him the most. Cho Hanyŏng and Ch'ae Ihang followed them, and Sin Tŭkyŏn also traveled to Mukden. Pak Hwang presented a great amount of treasure to Ingguldai and Chŏng Myŏngsu. After that, he returned home immediately. In the end, he was recruited again and detained in Mukden. Originally, Pak No was appointed the provincial governor of Kangwŏn, but because of Pak Hwang's argument, he was demoted and dispatched to Mukden. Pak Hwang greatly reprimanded Pak No and ended up loathing him. Moreover, Pak Hwang was fiercely attacked by Kim Sanghŏn. Today, the various matters regarding Kim Sanghŏn and Pak Hwang have been solely incited by Pak No.

At the beginning of the ninth day, the first lunar month of the *sinsa* year [1641], someone named Jirgalang (K. Chilgawang) gathered at the Ministry of Justice (Xingbu) with other officials of the ministry. They asked that after the crown prince and his attending officials come to meet them, the four men—Kim Sanghŏn, Cho Hanyŏng, Ch'ae Ihang, and Sin Tŭkyŏn—have their necks shackled in irons, their two hands bound together, and the men placed outside the gates of the Ministry of Justice. The first to be interrogated was Kim Sanghŏn, whose answers were the same as those he gave at Mansang. At the time he entered the Ministry of Justice, he was carried in on another person's back. Like before, he lay down on his back, and the barbarians did not berate him. Like Kim Sanghŏn, Sin Tŭkyŏn was carried in by other people, but a barbarian flogged him and said, "You bastard (*t'aeja*)! You bastard! You want to act like Kim Sanghŏn?" Secondly, they asked Cho Hanyŏng, "What are you requesting?" He replied, "Our king has been recuperating for a long time. It is rare for him to receive close officials. He frequently calls the high ministers to his bed chamber, where he discusses the way to govern, and that is all. If I had made harsh and unreasonable discussions, then how could I have passed the government examination in the *chŏngch'uk* year [1637], and when I went to the navy, didn't I become a military officer section chief (*pyŏngnang*) to train soldiers? How could this not mean anything else?" Ch'ae Ihang said, "Country folks do not take part in the domestic affairs of the court. Only for the matter of forced labor can they appeal its unfairness." A barbarian asked, "What kind of forced labor are you referring to?" Ihang replied, "After measuring the fields, the forced labor of the land tax and the selection of horses for the horse trade (*swaema*) have become much heavier than they used to be before." The barbarian asked again, "Why are the words of Cho and Ch'ae not the same?" Tŭkyŏn said, "That's all I knew when I served in Mukden. When Ingguldai's general investigated it closely, I just told him what I had heard. As for what was written in the memorial, I actually don't know anything about it." Three men of the Ministry of Justice had Chŏng Myŏngsu convey these words:

> Before the incident in the *pyŏngja* year [1637], Kim Sanghŏn engaged in unreasonable discussions that put the country on the verge of danger. He still does not admit any regret and is acting as he did before. Cho submitted a memorial that petitioned for the frequent reception of court officials. This was certainly not a good matter to suggest. What in the document that Ch'ae submitted spoke of the hardships of forced labor, undoubtedly referring to the local tribute for the Ming Chinese emperor (*sep'ye*) and army provisions. At the time of procuring and sending horses and labor to China, Sin wrote a memorial to the throne to impede this work and inform against Cho Hanyŏng. At this time, they appear in front of us and equivocate. The four should all be put to death.

Ingguldai arrived where the crown prince resided and said, "Concerning the crimes of Kim and others, they were first sentenced to death. The Khan claimed that when I departed for Chosŏn this time, the twelve tribute items had been agreed upon by our country. Kim and others had also been sent to the court immediately upon request. All the previous faults have been dealt with. Therefore, the crimes of these men should be taken into consideration and then they should be sentenced accordingly." The five men in custody were transferred to an annex. Second Inspector Cho Kyŏng boasted to the court, "The matter of Kim Sanghŏn owes to the impeachment controversy of Yu Sŏk and others. This news scattered distantly to the barbarians and has reached this point. The barbarian people are aware of it, yet they still respect and admire them. However, the people of our country still attempt to attack them, acting the same as dogs or sheep."

In the twelfth lunar month of the *sinsa* year [1641], Kim Sanghŏn turned ill, and it seemed like nothing would save his life.

The crown prince informed Ingguldai about this. The Khan requested that the court dispatch Kim and another five men and deliver them to Mansang [Ŭiju]. When they departed, if the road grew difficult, the barbarian general at the lead would dismount and hold onto Kim Sanghŏn, helping him ride the palanquin. Clearly those ugly slaves (*ch'uno*) greatly respected him. The five men arrived in Mansang at the beginning of the third day of the first lunar month of the *imo* year [1642], and they dispatched a memorial. The king said, "The matter of Sin Tŭkyŏn is extremely shocking. Although the officials that receive an order cannot avoid the hatchet and axe [punishment], they can quickly turn back and entrap many other people. Their punishment has still not been carried out because of their relationship with the Qing. Now, strip them of their government titles." Since the barbarian disturbance in the *pyŏngja* year [1637], those who have constantly supported basic human relations have simply been the two men Kim Sanghŏn and Chŏng On. That is all." Chŏng On fell ill from a paralyzing wind (*p'ungbi*) and died on the twenty-first day of the sixth lunar month in the *sinsa* year [1641]. Kim Sanghŏn is still held captive. Hence, the whole course of events from the beginning to the end, along with their intricacies, has been recorded here in detail.

Ah, the misfortunate disaster of the *pyŏngja* year [1637]! How dare I speak about such endurance and suffering! Chaos, like a charging boar, suddenly appeared. Within a ten-day period, the three regions (*samdo*) [the capital, Songdo, and Kanghwa Island] were overturned and ten thousand people became fish and meat. The royal palanquin left the capital, and Kanghwa Island fell. Through looting and burning, the public and private [the government] were all deprived. It was much worse than the upheavals of the *imjin* year [1592]. The two sages [King Injo and the crown prince] left the fortress. The Eastern Palace [the crown prince] and the grand princes (*taegun*) were tied up and taken to foreign lands. The women of the scholarly order (*sajok*) were defiled.[13] The noble and lowborn were equally taken prisoners. Before this, such events had been rare since antiquity. If one experienced such disorder first-hand but did not honestly record it in detail, then how could future generations learn about this? The works about the *imjin* year were written nearly fifty years after the events. There were still many people who had been harmed by the war, but those who [had lived through it and] were still alive were very hard to find. How does it seem that this surpasses the event of ancient times? Ah, as for the books recording the year *imjin*, the *Accounts of the Ming* (*Huangming chuanxinlu*) records the events of the punitive expedition to the east for the Chinese and Chosŏn officers and soldiers. Yu Sŏae's *Book of Corrections* (*Chingbirok*) records the events of his accompanying the king's retinue to the western provinces [Hwanghae and P'yŏngan] and everything that he heard.[14] Sin Sangch'on's surviving manuscript also records a little of what he saw and heard.[15] Out of ten, seven or eight manuscripts have been lost. I regret this. As for the record of the year *pyŏngja*, first I stated the reasons for this disaster to happen. Next, I recorded in detail everything I saw with my own eyes. As for hearsay, I cited the assisting evidence near it. Regardless of whether events were big or little, or the people good or evil, or the matter right or wrong, I have conveyed them all. I did not distinguish between intimate or distant. I recorded them honestly here. I do not dare compare this to an unofficial history (*yasa*). As time moves on and our generations pass, there might be loss. Overlook my arrogance. I have recorded it all here.

Written by the elderly Kup'o [Na Man'gap].

GLOSSARY OF NAMES, TERMS, AND PLACES

alsŏng mun'gwa 謁聖文科
chaesang 宰相
chaesin 宰臣
Chamo 慈母
ch'amŭi 叅議
ch'an 贊
Chang Yu 張維
changgye 狀啓
Ch'angnang chach'wi 蒼浪自取
Ch'angnŭng 昌陵
changnyŏng 掌令
ch'ebu 體府
ch'ech'alsa 體察使
chejwa 齊坐
chin 鎭
chinsin 搢紳
chip'yŏng 砥平
Cho Myŏnguk 曺明勗
Cho Pogyang 趙復陽
Ch'oe Myŏnggil 崔鳴吉
ch'ogun 哨軍
chŏgyun pulbanjigong 隻輪不返之功
ch'ohang 招降

chojŏng 朝廷
chŏkchak 賊爵
chŏkhwa 斥和
chŏkkoek 賊馘
chŏkpyŏng 賊兵
ch'ŏlgi 鐵騎
ch'ŏmji 僉知
Chŏng On 鄭蘊
Chŏngbang 正方
ch'ŏngdae 請對
chŏngmyo horan 丁卯胡亂
chongsagwan 從事官
chongsil 宗室
ch'ongyung taejang 摠戎大將
ch'ŏnjo 天朝
ch'ot'o 草土
ch'ubang 秋防
ch'ugok 推轂
ch'unch'uk ch'ŏpch'emun 春祝帖門日
chunggun 中軍
chungp'ung 中風
ch'ungŭi 忠義
ch'unsinsa 春信使
ch'usal ch'unsaeng 秋殺春生
chwaŭijŏng 左議政
fulao xieyou 扶老携幼
gui 貴
haenggung 行宮
haengjae 行在
haengnang 行廊
hagyu 學諭
hallim 翰林
hambyŏk yŏch'ŭn 衛璧輿櫬
Han Hoeil 韓會一
Han P'irwŏn 韓必遠
Han Yŏjik 韓汝稷
hanin 漢人
hansŏng ch'amgun 漢城參軍
hari 下吏

hoin 胡人
hojang 胡將
hojo p'ansŏ 戶曹判書
hojonggwan 扈從官
Hong Ikhan 洪翼漢
Hong Myŏnggu 洪命耉
Hong Pang 洪霶
Hong Sŏbong 洪瑞鳳
Hongjewŏn 弘濟院
hŏnnap 獻納
hop'aech'ŏng 號牌廳
howi taejang 扈衛大將
Huang Sunmao 黃孫茂
hugun 後軍
huji 後識
Hung Taiji 皇太極
hwagi 火器
Hwang Chŭp 黃緝
hyŏn'gam 縣監
hyŏngjo ch'amŭi 刑曹參議
hyŏngjo p'ansŏ 刑曹判書
Ich'ŏn 利川
ijo ch'amp'an 吏曹叅判
ijo chŏngnang 吏曹正郎
ijo p'ansŏ 吏曹判書
Imjin 壬辰
Ingguldai 龍骨大
Inmok taebi 仁穆大妃
Inyŏl 仁烈
ju (K. ch'wi) 聚
Kado 椵島
kamgun 監軍
kamsa 監司
Kangdo 江都
Kanghwa (island) 江都
kanghwa 講和
Ki Chonghyŏn 奇宗獻
kibok 起服
kijŏn 畿甸

Kim Chajŏm 金自點

Kim Kyŏngjing 金慶徵

Kim Sanghŏn 金尙憲

Kim Sin'guk 金藎國

Kim Tŏkham 金德諴

Kim Yu 金瑬

kŏmch'alsa 檢察使

kŏmyŏl 檢閱

Ku Inhu 具仁垕

Ku Koeng 具宏

Kŭmch'ŏn'gyo 禁川橋

kun'gwan 軍官

kunjŏng 軍情

kunsu 郡守

kwallyangsa 管糧使

kwan 官

Kwangsu 光洙

kwanhak 館學

kwanhak yusaeng 館學儒生

Kwanon insŏng 寬溫仁聖

kwijung chisin 貴重之臣

kwŏl 厥

kyori 校理

Ma Pudae 馬夫大

Mafuta 馬夫大

Mandongmyo 萬東廟

Mangwŏltae 望月臺

manjŏl p'iltong 萬折必東

Manho 萬戶

Mansang 灣上

Mao Wenlong 毛文龍

minp'ye 民弊

Mohwagwan 慕華館

moksa 牧使

munmugwan 文武官

musin tongji 武臣同知

myo 廟

myoak 廟樂

Na Man'gap 羅萬甲

Na Tŏkhŏn 羅德憲
Namdaemullu 南大門樓
namgun 南郡
Namhan sansŏng 南漢山城
Namsŏng 南城
Nan Chao 南朝
nobok 奴僕
noryuk 努戮
Nŭngbongsu 綾峯守
O Talche 吳達濟
ŏgong 御供
ŏjiha 於地下
okch'e 玉體
ŏsŭng 御乘
ŏyŏng pusa 御營副使
paekhong kwanil 白虹貫日
P'aju 坡州
Pak Hwan 朴煥
Pak Nanyŏng 朴蘭英
Pak No 朴簬
pal 跋
panyŏl 班列
piguk 備局
p'ijapkok 皮雜穀
p'ilsa 筆肆
ponbu 本府
pŏnbyŏng 藩屏
ponghwa 烽火
pongmyŏng choyang 鳳鳴朝陽
Pongnim 鳳林
pon'gwan 本貫
p'osu 砲手
puksŏng 北城
p'ungbi 風痺
puro hyuyu 扶老携幼
pusa 副使
puwŏnsu 副元帥
pyŏnggwa 丙科
pyŏngja chiran 丙子之亂

pyŏngjaran 丙子亂
pyŏngjo p'ansŏ 兵曹判書
pyŏngsa 兵使
P'yŏngyang 平壤
P'yŏngyang sŏyun 平壤庶尹
p'yop'ung 飄風
sadaebu 士大夫
samgwŏl 三闕
Samjŏndo 三田渡
Samsa 三司
Samŭisa 三醫司
san'gwan 散官
saŏ ch'wiung 舍魚取熊
sedo chŏngch'i 勢道政治
seja sigangwŏn podŏk 世子侍講院輔德
Shangfangri 尙方釖
sibwangja 十王子
Sim Aek 沈詻
Sim Chip 沈諿
Sim Kiwŏn 沈器遠
Sim Segoe 沈世魁
sin 臣
Sin Kyŏngjin 申景禛
Sin P'unggun 新豊君
Sin Yong 申榕
sinja 臣子
sinyŏ 侍女
siron 時論
sŏin 西人
sŏm (also sŏk) 石
sŏng 城
Songdo 松都
sŏnjŏn'gwan 宣傳官
Sŏsŏng 西城
soyŏk 小譯
such'an 修撰
Sugumun 水口門
sŭnggun 僧軍
suŏsa 守禦使

Suwŏn　水原
Taebodan　大報壇
taebugin　大北人
Taedongbŏp　大同法
taegun　大君
taejehak　大提學
taesagan　大司諫
taesin　大臣
tian　天
todok　都督
togam changgwan　都監將官
togam taejang　都監大將
t'ongdŏngnang　通德郎
tonggung　東宮
tongyangwi　東陽尉
Tongyuanpu　通远堡
towŏnsu　都元帥
ŭidae chungch'an　衣帶中贊
Ŭiju　義州
ŭmgwan　蔭官
ŭmnae　邑內
wasin sangdan　臥薪尝胆
wiri anch'i　圍籬安置
Wŏn Tup'yo　元斗杓
Wŏnp'yŏnggun　原平君
Yanggŭn　楊根
Yangnŭng　兩陵
Yangsŏ　兩西
yangsŏ iltae　兩西一帶
yejo p'ansŏ　禮曹判書
Yi Chik　李稷
Yi Chin'gyŏng　李真卿
Yi Hongju　李弘冑
Yi Hyŏndal　李顯達
Yi Ilsang　李一相
Yi Kwak　李廓
Yi Kyŏngjik　李景稷
Yi Min'gu　李敏求
Yi Myŏng　李溟

Yi Sibaek 李時白
Yi Sik 李植
Yi Sŏ 李曙
Yi Sŏnggu 李聖求
yidai zhongzan 衣帶中贊
Yŏju 驪州
Yonggolsan 龍骨山
Yŏngnam 嶺南
yŏngŭijŏng 領議政
Yŏnso 年少
yudo taejang 留都大將
Yun Chip 尹集
Yun Hwang 尹煌
Zhongdao 中道

Introduction

1. The term scholars used for the Manchu invasions shifted with the times. *Pyŏngja* was simply the term used by the generation that witnessed the invasions. Writers such as Song Chun'gil (1606–1672) and Yi Hyŏnil (1627–1604) used the terms *pyŏngja* or *pyŏngjajiran*. Yi Ik (1681–1763) later adopted the term *pyŏngjaran*. Not until the twentieth century did writers begin referring to the incidents as a "foreign invasion" (*horan*). See Song Chun'gil and Sŏng Nakhun, *Tongch'undang chip* [Collected writings of Tongch'umdang] (Seoul: Tonghwa ch'ulp'an kongsa, 1972), che 6-kwŏn, soch'a; Yi Hyŏnil and Pak Hŏnun, *Kugyŏk Kalam chip* [Collected writings of Kalam], 8 vols. (Seoul: Minjok munhwa ch'ujinhoe, 1999); and Yi Ik and Chŏng Haeryŏm, *Sŏngho sasŏl chŏgsŏn* [Miscellaneous discussions of Sŏngho], 3 vols. (Seoul: Hyŏndae sirhaksa, 1998), che-23 kywŏn, kyŏngsamun ch'oejongjŏngbo.

2. A cyclical year refers to a year in the sexagesimal calendar cycle, a measurement system East Asian societies used for more than two thousand years, until the twentieth century. The year number combines two Chinese characters. The first represents one in a series of ten characters; the second is a zodiacal sign from a list of twelve characters. For more, see Masayuki Sato, "Comparative Ideas of Chronology," *History and Theory* 30, no. 3 (1991): 280.

3. For instance, see Pyŏn T'aesŏp, *Han'guksa t'ongnon* [An introduction to Korean history] (Seoul: Samyŏngsa, 1996), 338. Other scholars argue that the Imjin War stirred Korean nationalism. See JaHyun Kim Haboush, *The Great East Asian War and the Birth of the Korean Nation* (New York: Columbia University Press, 2016). In North Korean history books, chapters on these events are prefaced with a quote from Kim Il Sung's collected works: "Since ancient times, whenever invaders have attacked, Korean people, in fighting with their entire hearts to preserve the country, rise up like one person and strike the invading foreigners to heroically defend the fatherland. This has been the sagacious history of five thousand years." Pak Yŏnghae, Kim Chaehong, and Mun Pyŏngu, *Chosŏn inmin ŭi panch'imnyak t'ujaengsa Ri Chop'yŏn* [The history of Korean people and anti–foreign invasion wars, Chosŏn edition] (P'yŏngyang: Sahoe kwak ch'ulp'ansa, 2010), 298.

4. Also known as *The Diary of 1636 Southern Fortress (Pyŏngja Namhan ilgi)* and *The Diary of Paektŭngnok (Paektŭngnok)*. Chosŏn era sources claim that Na Man'gap left behind a literary collection titled *Collected Works of Kup'o (Kup'o chip)*, but it has never been found.

5. For descriptions of war sources, see Kim Ilhwan, "Han mugwan ŭi chŏnjaeng ch'ehŏm sugiga mandŭrŏ chigi kkaji namhan surok ŭi sŏsa pangsik yŏn'gu" [Narrative method of war experiences by military officers in *Namhan surok*], *Hanminjok munhwa yŏn'gu* 49 (February 2015): 250–51. See also Thomas Quartermain, "Besieged on a Frozen Mountain Top: Opposing Records from the Qing Invasion of Chosŏn, 1636–1637," *Acta Koreana* 21, no. 1 (June 2018): 140.

6. Kim Kyŏngsu, "Chosŏn chŏn'gi yasa p'yŏnch'an ŭi sahaksajŏn koch'al" [A study of historiographical significance of the unofficial book of history in the early Chosŏn dynasty] *Yŏksa hwa sirhak* 19–20 (2001): 151–53.

7. Yi Kŭngik, *Yŏllyŏsil kisul* [Narrative from Yŏllyŏsil] (Seoul: Kyŏngmunsa, 1976), 2:264.

8. Among other aspects, New Qing historians argue that applying the term "Manchu" to the people of this region is problematic and anachronistic. While recognizing these arguments, I am still using the term "Manchu" here to help modern readers, who may be unfamiliar with the intricate scholarly debates, comprehend the events of the diary. See Pamela Crossley, *A Translucent Mirror: History and Identity in Qing Imperial Ideology* (Berkeley: University of California Press, 1999); and Mark

Elliot, *The Manchu Way: The Eight Banners and Ethnic Identity in Late Imperial China* (Stanford, CA: Stanford University Press, 2001).

9. Crossley, *A Translucent Mirror*, 11.

10. Many of Na Man'gap's disputes are recorded in official and unofficial histories and literary collections, such as the *Taedong yasŭng*. See *Taedong yasŭng* [Unofficial transmissions from the great east], 13 vols. (Seoul: Sŏul taehakkyo ch'ulp'anbu, 1968), Mukche *ilgi* [Mukche diary], 6:199; Sin Hŭm, *Sangch'on chip* [Works of Sangch'on], forward by Yun Namhan (Seoul: Han'guk munhŏn yŏn'guhoe, 1981), 678c; Yi Kŭngik, *Kugyŏk Yŏllyŏsil kisul* [Korean translation of Narrative from Yŏllyŏsil] (Seoul: Minjok munhwa ch'ujinhoe, 1967), 6:613–14. Many of these stories about Na provide an important glimpse of Chosŏn scholars and their alignment with political factions.

11. Na Man'gap is buried in Sanadong, Kurisi, Kyŏnggi Province. The family's burial grounds were designated by the Republic of Korea as Tangible Cultural Heritage number 126 in 1985. Na's sons, Na Sŏngdu (1614–1663) and Na Myŏngjwa (1634–1651), are buried there as well. Various officials inscribed Na Man'gap's memorial stones, such as Kim Sanghŏn and Song Chun'gil, the father-in-law of Na Myŏngjwa. A stone stele describing Na's life was erected in 1658. The title of the stele was inscribed by his grandson-in-law, Censor General (*taesagan*) Kim Suhang (1629–1689).

12. Yi Sik, *T'aektang chip* [Collected writings of T'aektang] (Seoul: Kyŏngmunsa, 1982), 143d–44a, 146c–47c.

13. The Royal Visitation Mun'gwa Examination was given in front of the king. See John Duncan et al., *The Institutional Basis of Civil Governance in the Chosŏn Dynasty* (Seoul: Seoul Selection, 2009). *Pyŏnggwa* were the third of three tiers of exam passers. See Choi Byonghyon, trans., *The Annals of King T'aejo: Founder of Korea's Chosŏn Dynasty* (Cambridge, MA: Harvard University Press, 2014), 307.

14. Factional groups were generally not based on ideology, clan relations, or philosophical lineage, though one group, the Namin, looked to the scholar T'oegye, and another group, the Noron, looked to the competing scholar Yulgok, for political guidance.

15. Accusations that Kim Yu's son Kim Kyŏngjing and the official Pak Chŏng were going to kill criminals such as Na were cited in the *Chosŏn wangjo sillok*. *Chosŏn wangjo sillok* [Veritable records of the Chosŏn dynasty] (Seoul: Panp'o T'amgudang, 1955–1958), 34:18; hereafter *CWS* or *Sillok*.

16. See *CWS* 34:588d–89a.

17. *CWS* 34:709a.

18. Na's death is reported in the *Sillok* on the eleventh day in the twelfth lunar month of the cyclical year *imo* (solar date January 30, 1643). *CWS* 35:145a.

19. *CWS* 40:264a.

20. *CWS* 41:653a.

21. Song Siyŏl, *Songja taejŏn* [Collected writings of Songja] (Seoul: Pogyŏng munhwasa, 1985), 6:319c–d.

22. Chŏng Yŏp was an official during the reigns of King Sŏnjo and King Injo. He served at the time of the Imjin War as a diplomat to the Ming, among other high posts. He protested King Kwanghaegun's imprisonment of Queen Inmok in 1618 and did not return to government service until after the 1623 coup brought King Injo to power. His death touched King Injo, who posthumously elevated his rank. Like Song Siyŏl, King Injo also respected Chŏng Yŏp and Kim Sanghŏn, proclaiming that everyone was in awe of their stature. See *CWS* 35:335b.

23. For more on the discrepancies, see Yun Chaeyŏng, *Pyŏngjarok* [The diary of 1636] (Seoul: Myŏngmundang, 1987), 9.

24. A full copy of this version has been reprinted in Yun Chaeyŏng, *Pyŏngjarok*, in literary Chinese (*Han'mun*) and translated into modern vernacular Korean. My work is indebted to this version and Yun's research.

25. Hŏ T'aegu, "Pyŏngja horan Kanghwado hamnak ŭi wŏnin kwa ch'aegimja ch'ŏbŏl Kim Kyŏngjing p'aejŏn ch'aegimnon ŭi chaegŏmt'o ŭi chungsim ŭro" [Military strength and strategic deployment of Chosŏn and Qing troops at the time of the fall of Kanghwa Island during the 1637 Manchu invasion] *Chindan hakpo* 113 (2011):100.

26. As Patricia Thane points out, "Our memory of the distant past is heavily dependent on past oral histories," some written down later to construct a certain political interpretation, especially after times of war when violence prevents the writing of documents. Patricia Thane, "Oral History, Memory and Written Tradition: An Introduction," *Transaction of the Royal Asiatic Society* 9 (1999): 162.

27. Han Myŏnggi and many other scholars have written extensively on the Imjin War. Han Myŏnggi, *Imjin waeran kwa hanjung kwan'gae* [Imjin invasion and Korean-Chinese relations] (Seoul: Yŏksa pibyŏngsa, 2008).

28. See Gari Ledyard, "Confucianism and War: The Korean Security Crisis of 1598," *Journal of Korean Studies* 6, no. 1 (1988–89): 90.

29. Ledyard, "Confucianism and War," 98–99.

30. For additional studies on the Manchu attacks, see Han Myŏnggi, *Chŏngmyo-pyŏngja horan kwa tongasia* [The 1627 and 1637 Manchu invasions of Chosŏn and East Asia] (Seoul: Paekwang, 2013). For an English source, see Quartermain, "Besieged," 137–67.

31. Shelley Rigger, "Voices of Manchu Identity, 1635–1935," in *Cultural Encounters on China's Ethnic Frontiers*, ed. Stevan Harrell (Seattle: University of Seattle Press, 1995), 188.

32. The Ming recognized this obligation in 1619 when they launched a preemptive strike against the capital of the Later Jin, calling upon Chosŏn forces to assist by deploying the request based on the father-son reciprocity of the tributary system and Chosŏn's obligation to repay the debt owed the Ming for their intervention in the Imjin War. See Sun Joo Kim, "Culture of Remembrance in Late Chosŏn Korea: Bringing an Unknown War Hero Back into History," *Journal of Social Theory* 44, no. 2 (2010): 566. Also, Korean casualty figures were very high for this battle. See Sun Joo Kim's *Voice from the North: Resurrecting Regional Identity Through the Life and Work of Yi Sihang* (Stanford, CA: Stanford University Press, 2013), 124.

33. *CWS* 34:167c.

34. *CWS* 34:159d.

35. *CWS* 34:162a.

36. *CWS* 34:163a.

37. *CWS* 34: 91d–92a and *CWS* 34:217c.

38. *CWS* 34:161c–d.

39. *CWS* 34:159d–160a.

40. For instance, see the preparation of grain in the eighth lunar month or the cyclical year *ch'ŏn'gye* (1625). *CWS* 34:22c.

41. *CWS* 34:163b.

42. *CWS* 34:160b.

43. *CWS* 34:161a.

44. *CWS* 34:163a–b.

45. *CWS* 34:163c.

46. *CWS* 34:163c.

47. *CWS* 34:163c.

48. *CWS* 34:163b–c.

49. *CWS* 34:160b.

50. *CWS* 34:163d.

51. *CWS* 34:163d.

52. *CWS* 34:163d.

53. *CWS* 34:163d.

54. *CWS* 34:165d.

55. *CWS* 34:165d.

56. *CWS* 34:166b.

57. *CWS* 34:166b.

58. *CWS* 34:166b–c.

59. *CWS* 34:166c.

60. *CWS* 34:181b.

61. The *Sillok* describes "barbarians" (*hoindŭng*) leading this ritual, collecting the blood and bones of the animals in a vessel before Yi Haengwŏn swore allegiance to the Great Jin. See *CWS* 34:181b. As the only description in the *Sillok* of such acts, this appears to be a Jurchen (Manchu) custom. It is different from another ritual (*saphyŏl*) in which an animal is sacrificed at an altar and its blood drunk or smeared over the lips as an oath.

62. See No Yŏnggu, "Injo ch'o pyŏngja horan sigi chosŏn ŭi chŏnsul chŏn'gae" [Chosŏn military tactics from the early years of King Injo through the second Manchu invasion of 1636], *Han'guk sahakpo* 41 (2010): 203–35.

63. Chang Chŏngsu, "Pyŏngja horan ijŏn Chosŏn ŭi taejŏngŭm (ch'ŏng) pangŏ chŏllak ŭi sulip kwangjŏng kwa kŭ silsang" [Progress and reality of Chosŏn defense strategy against the later Jin (Qing) before the second Manchu invasion], *Chosŏn sidae sahakpo* 81 (2017): 51.

64. Hwisang Cho, "Feeling Power in Early Chosŏn Korea: Popular Grievances, Royal Rage, and the Problem of Human Sentiments," *Journal of Korean Studies* 20, no. 1 (Spring 2015): 24.

65. For studies on the post-1644 period, see Yuanchong Wang, *Remaking the Chinese Empire: Manchu-Korean Relations, 1616–1911* (Ithaca, NY: Cornell University Press, 2018).

66. See Michiel Leezenberg, "The Vernacular Revolution: Reclaiming Early Modern Grammatical Traditions in the Ottoman Empire," *History of Humanities* 1, no. 2 (2016): 252.

67. See Michael Pettid, Gregory Evon, and Chan Park, eds., *Premodern Korean Literary Prose: An Anthology* (New York: Columbia University Press, 2018), 66–67.

68. See James Palais, *Confucian Statecraft and Korean Institutions: Yu Hyongwon and the Late Choson Dynasty* (Seattle: University of Washington Press), 1996.

69. This is reminiscent of Prince Sado's death in the eighteenth century. See JaHyun Kim Haboush, *The Memoirs of Lady Hyegyŏng: The Autobiographical Writings of a Crown Princess of Eighteenth-Century Korea* (Berkeley: University of California Press, 1996).

70. See JaHyun Kim Haboush, "Constructing the Center: The Ritual Controversy and the Search for a New Identity in Seventeenth-Century Korea," in *Culture and the State in Late Chosŏn Korea*, ed. JaHyun Kim Haboush and Martina Deuchler (Cambridge, MA: Harvard University Press, 1999): 46–90.

71. For more, see James Palais, *Politics and Policy in Traditional Korea* (Cambridge, MA: Harvard University Press, 1991), 121–23; and Seung B. Kye, "The Altar of Great Gratitude: A Korean Memory of Ming China Under Manchu Dominance, 1704–1894," *Journal of Korean Religion* 5, no. 2 (October 2014): 71–88.

72. For instance, see the works of Kim Ian (1722–1791), Sŏ Yŏngbo (1759–1816), Chŏng Pŏmjo (1723–1801), and Yi Imyŏng (1658–1722).

73. See Im Suyŏn, "Namhan sansŏng 'saengsaeng munhwaje saŏp' ŭi ŭiŭi wa kaesŏng pangan yŏn'gu" [The case study of Namhan Mountain Fortress on the significance and direction of the "vibrant cultural property program"], *Munhwa K'ont'ench'e yŏn'gu* 6 (2015): 123–53.

74. For instance, see the 2007 book *Namhan Sansŏng*, written by Kim Hun, and the 2018 movie *Namhan Sansŏng*, written and directed by Hwang Tonghyŏk. Toy companies have also created diorama puzzles of Namhan Mountain Fortress.

75. Yu T'aru writes that "the year *pyŏngja* is an embarrassing stain on the Korean people." Yu T'aru, *Namhan sansŏng ŭi nunmul* [The tears of Namhan Mountain Fortress] (Kyŏnggi-do, P'aju: Alma, 2010), 140.

76. Numerous popular travel books have been written on Namhan Mountain. For instance, see Ch'oe Chinyŏn, *Uri t'ŏ, uri hon Namhan sansŏng* [Our land, our soul: Namhan Mountain Fortress] (Seoul: Tahal midiŏ, 2010); and Sin Yŏngju and Ch'oe Chinyŏn, *Uri ai ch'ŏt Namhan sansŏng yŏhaeng* [First-time travel for Korean children to Namhan Mountain Fortress] (Seoul: Samsŏngdang, 2011).

77. See Maria O'Donovan and Lynda Carroll, "Going Places: The Historical Archaeology of Travel and Tourism," *International Journal of Historical Archaeology* 15, no. 2 (June 2011): 192.

78. Lauren A. Rivera, "Managing 'Spoiled' National Identity: War, Tourism, and Memory in Croatia," *American Sociological Review* 73, no. 4 (August 2008): 615. A literature review on global cultural heritage helps

explain the formation of sites such as Namhan Mountain as a component of contemporary national identity.

Early Complications

1. Diplomatic envoys were dispatched in the spring (*ch'unsinsa*) and winter (*ch'usinsa*) to the courts of the Ming and Qing dynasties. Mukden (K. Shimyang, C. Shenyang) was the Manchu Jin capital. According to an entry in the *Chosŏn wangjo sillok*, on the twenty-sixth day of the fourth lunar month, 1636, the court was unsettled by reports from Na Tŏkhŏn and Yi Kwak concerning the Manchu leader's adoption of the term "great Qing emperor" (K. *taech'ŏng hwangje*, C. *daqing huangdi*) and Manchu use of inferior language toward the Chosŏn. King Injo was angered by their use of the informal term "your country" (K. *iguk*, C. *erguo*), which denoted junior status and arrogance. *Chosŏn wangjo sillok* [Veritable records of the Chosŏn dynasty] (Seoul: Kuksa Pyŏnch'an wiwŏnhoe: Panp'o T'amgudang, 1955–1958), 34:631d; hereafter *Sillok* or *CWS*. The solar year of this meeting was 1636.

2. Hung Taiji, or Abahai (r. 1626–1643), was the second Manchu leader. As the eighth son of the founder Nurhachi (r. 1616–1626), Hung Taiji expanded Manchu control in Northeast Asia and led the second invasion of Korea in 1637 while challenging the Ming dynasty for supremacy in China. The Manchu initially referred to themselves as the Jin or Later Jin dynasty, in reference to the Jurchen Jin (1115–1234), a powerful Northeast Asian tribe that dominated northeastern China in earlier times. In 1636, Hung Taiji changed the name to Qing, proclaiming a new dynasty.

3. Throughout the diary, Na Man'gap frequently uses the first names of individuals he is describing.

4. Pro-Manchu Chinese officers in the Qing court.

5. By assuming the title emperor (K. *hwangje*, C. *huangdi*), Hung Taiji and the Manchu were directly challenging Ming dynastic rule.

6. Tongyuanpu was a town and military fortress located in Manchu territory, roughly halfway between the Manchu capital Mukden and the Chosŏn frontier.

7. A parallel entry in the *Sillok* relates this story of the letter. *CWS* 34:632a.

8. Shangfang (K. Sangbanggŏm, C. Shangfangjian) is a reference to the minister Zhu Yun of the Former Han dynasty (206 BCE–8 CE). It is also a literary allusion used in a number of court discussions during King Injo's

reign, especially regarding apparent traitors of the Manchu wars. In classical text, Zhu Yun risked his life when he asked the emperor for a sword to execute the evil minister Zhang Yu. This classical allusion, found in the *Han shu*, was a subject that Ming dynasty–era poets examined in their works. See Tian Yuan Tan, *Songs of Contentment and Transgression: Discharged Officials and Literati Communities in Sixteenth-Century North China* (Cambridge, MA: Harvard University Press, 2010), 73. Beheading was a punishment based on the Great Ming Code and meant as a deterrent to others.

9. The Border Defense Command, also known as *pibyŏnsa*, the government organ in charge of national security, was established in the middle of the sixteenth century to control Japanese piracy along the coast but later expanded to deal with all threats to the dynasty.

10. The Three Offices included the Office of Special Counselors, the Office of the Censor General, and the Office of the Inspector General.

11. *Kwanhak yusaeng* refers to an elite Confucian scholar of the Royal Confucian Academy (Sŏnggyun'gwan) and the Four Schools (Sahak) in the capital.

12. Most likely this refers to the Young Westerners faction. The Young Westerners were active in government politics and factional fighting at the court. Kim Yu was a member of the Elder Westerners (Nosŏ), an opposing political party.

13. Following the 1627 Manchu attack, King Injo was forced to sever relations with the Ming in favor of "good relations" (K. *hwaho*) with the Manchu on the third day of the third lunar month. *CWS* 34:181b.

14. Queen Inyŏl (1594–1635) was an influential force on her husband, King Injo, assisting him in the consolidation of power. Upon her passing, Injo lavished her with titles. See Kim Insuk, "Injobi Inyŏl wanghu ŭi naejo wa silp'aehan yuga" [The help and infant loss of King Injo's Queen Inyŏl], *Han'guk inmulsa yŏn'gu* 18 (2012): 225–57. According to the *Manzhou shi lu*, the tenth prince of the Jin dynasty is most likely Dodo (1614–1649), the fifteenth son of Nurhachi, the Manchu founder. *Manzhou shi lu* [Veritable records of the Manchu], 8 vols. (Shenyang: Liaoling tong zhi guan, 1934).

15. Queen Dowager Inmok (1584–1632) was the consort of King Sŏnjo (r. 1567–1608).

16. Kŭmch'ŏn Bridge was located at the outer walls of Ch'angdŏk Palace.

17. Soldiers armed with arquebus firearms. This secret training session was unusual because the large garden behind the palace was reserved for women of the court and was off-limits to men.

18. *Chaesin* most likely refers to the chancellors and other courtiers of equal rank. In other words, more than one officer attempted to convince the Manchu to stay.

19. Mansang was located near Ŭiju in North P'yŏngan Province, along the frontier on the Yalu River. Mansang was an important location between Chosŏn and the Manchu. It served as a market for the transportation of grain to the Manchu beginning in 1628. *CWS* 34:255a. It was the location where orders (*kyŏk*) from the Manchu khan were delivered to the Chosŏn king in the summer of 1636. *CWS* 34:635c. It also served as the way station for the comings and goings of Manchu soldiers and envoys, as well as Chosŏn envoys, who sometimes rested there before heading north to Mukden. On one occasion, Ch'oe Myŏnggil stayed behind in Mansang while other officials crossed the Yalu River and proceeded north. *CWS* 35:75c.

20. The king, his royal family members, and other high officials of the capital are known to have withdrawn to Kanghwa Island during foreign invasions, such as the Mongol invasions of the thirteenth century and the first Manchu invasion in 1627. Thus, the burning of the temporary palace on the island would indicate the will to remain on the mainland to fight rather than to flee to relative safety offshore. See the Introduction for more details.

21. Songdo, the capital of the Koryŏ dynasty (936–1392), was located near modern-day Kaesŏng, along the main route from Mansang to Hanyang (Seoul).

22. The shifting of rocks is recorded at various times in the *Sillok*. Earlier in the same year (1636), on the eighth day of the second lunar month, King Injo inquired about the connection between the movement of rocks and extraordinary events. Yun Pang replied that the *Spring and Autumn Annals* (K. *Ch'unch'u*, C. *Chunqiu*) records the spontaneous movement of rocks at the time of Emperor Xuan of Han (91–49 BCE). Yun Hwang followed by explaining that omens suggest the decline (*mang*) of a country. *CWS* 34:623b–c. The *Sillok* records a number of memorials to the throne describing battles between frogs as examples of inauspicious events.

23. The phrase "white rainbow threaded the sun" (K. *paekhong kwanil*, C. *baihong guanri*) is a classical expression used when anticipating inauspicious events. For instance, see *Xinxu* [New prefaces] and *Shuoyuan* [Garden of examples] by Liu Xiang (77–6 BCE).

24. The supreme commander of war was a high-ranking official appointed on a temporary basis during times of national crisis, such as

an invasion or a rebellion. Collective family punishment included the wives and children of accused criminals.

25. *Ch'ubang* was an autumn activity that entailed preparing the military fortresses by taking care of weapons and training the troops.

26. *Ch'ŏnjo* (heavenly court) was a term referring to the Ming dynasty.

27. Pak Inbŏm, an interpreter of Manchu from the middle class (*chungin*), was selected for this assignment. Pak was familiar with the Manchu, having spent time in Mukden carrying messages from the khan to Chosŏn in 1631 and from King Injo to Mukden in the ninth lunar month in the solar year of 1636. *CWS* 34:463b and *CWS* 34:648b–c.

28. Kanghwa Island, a refuge for the king and the court in times of foreign invasion, was small and isolated from the mainland. Also, the Manchu by this time had already witnessed the Chosŏn court fleeing to Kanghwa Island during the 1627 invasion. By asking the question "Can you turn this small island into a country?" Hung Taiji was implying the Chosŏn government would be unable to function on the island, since it was isolated from the mainland.

29. Paengma, Chamo, and Chŏngbang were mountain fortresses. Paengma was located roughly twelve kilometers south of Ŭiju, Chamo was more than fifty kilometers northeast of P'yŏngyang, and Chŏngbang was roughly eight kilometers south of Hwangju. Changsu was the final defensive mountain fortress Kim Yu and Kim Chajŏm fortified with troops that were originally stationed in towns for their protection. It was roughly two kilometers north of P'yŏngsan.

30. The two western regions included Hwanghae and P'yŏngan provinces in the northwest.

31. Kado served as a strategic island of North P'yŏngan Province. The Manchu attacked it in 1627 before invading south.

32. Huang Sunmao (?–1637) was a eunuch of the Ming court. As army supervisor, he led a force of twenty thousand soldiers to Kado in 1634 and requested the use of ships. Later, he returned to Kado with a message from the Ming to resist the Manchu. The Border Defense Command approved his request of boats but could not agree on an appropriate fee. On yet another occasion, Huang asked for sixty warhorses. *CWS* 34:571c–d, *CWS* 34:573d, and *CWS* 34:652a.

33. Kwansŏ was located in an area north of Pyŏngan and Hwanghae provinces.

34. *Ch'ugok* is another expression for supreme field commander (*towŏnsu*).

35. An entry in the *Sillok* in 1436 describes fire beacons as a system adopted from China and the best method for communicating uprisings and incursions along the frontier. These beacons were built on the highest peaks and constantly manned by a fire beacon guard (*ponghwa iin*). From the Yalu River to the Yŏyŏn and Chasŏng commanderies in the northwest, there were approximately six or seven beacons, fully staffed from the fourth to the seventh lunar months. Some troops were stationed nearby for ambushing thieves and enemy troops crossing the Yalu River. *CWS* 4:3b. However, in 1600, following the Imjin War, the Border Defense Command criticized the condition of the fire beacons throughout the country. Recognizing that there was no faster way to communicate than by fire beacons and reiterating the legal requirement for them, Board Defense Command officials expressed concern that the fire beacons were unmanned and no longer functioning, despite the constant threat of the enemy along the frontier. The system should be expanded, they argued, including in the south. *CWS* 24:38a.

36. Sunan is a northwestern county in South P'yŏngan Province, roughly three hundred kilometers from the capital.

Daily Records After Urgent Reports from the Frontier

1. The solar date was January 7, 1637.
2. An official who removed himself from office after the death of a parent but was later reinstated before the end of the mourning period.
3. Sim Kiwŏn was promoted to capital defense general.
4. Sugumun was the southeast gate of Hanyang (Seoul), or what was referred to as the Mouth of the Water Gate. Namhan Mountain Fortress was a castle and compound south of the capital and was considered a temporary capital at times of war when the king withdrew from Hanyang. See the Introduction for more information.
5. *Kangdorok* (*Record of Kanghwa Island*) notes that communication between the Namhan Mountain Fortress and Kanghwa Island had been cut off on the twenty-third day of the twelfth lunar month. Nam Kŭp, ed., *Namhan ilgi* [Diary of Namhan], trans. Sin Haejin (Seoul: Pogosa, 2012), 222.
6. Grand Prince Pongnim (1619–1659) was the second son of King Injo and Queen Inyŏl (1594–1635). He ruled as King Hyojong from 1649 until 1659. Grand Prince Inp'yŏng (1622–1658) was the third son of King Injo and Queen Inyŏl.

7. This was Crown Prince Sohyŏn.

8. *Nyang* was a unit of silver coins in the Chosŏn. Determining its modern-day value is hard. For an overview on pricing of the *nyang*, see Sunglim Kim, *Flowering Plums and Curio Cabinets: The Culture of Objects in Late Chosŏn Korean Art* (Seattle: University of Washington Press, 2018), 244n39.

9. Cutting off the body parts of an enemy was not an uncommon practice throughout history, from antiquity to the present. Ancient Egyptians cut off the tongues and hands of thousands in one battle "as proof of their success." See John Gardner Wilkinson, *Topography of Thebes and General Views of Egypt* (London: John Murray, 1835), 69. During the American Revolutionary War, Maryland officials offered rewards for the right ears of Native Americans. See Andrew McFarland Davis, "The Indians and the Border Warfare of the Revolution," in *Narrative and Critical History of America*, ed. Justin Winsor (Boston: Houghton-Mifflin, 1888), 682. The French also used this strategy in their wars in the fifteenth century and in Indochina in the twentieth century. Richard Gabriel, *The Culture of War: Invention and Early Development*, Contributions in Military Studies, no. 96 (New York: Greenwood Press, 1990), 133. After the Imjin invasion of Korea, the Japanese constructed an "ear mound" from Korean victims. The Chinese character for "gather" or "collect," *ju* (K. *ch'wi*), originally meant "the cutting off of the left ear of captives and presenting them to the officer in command; this was evidence of the number of captives taken." See George D. Wilder, J. H. Ingram, and F. W. Baller, *Analysis of Chinese Characters* (New York: Dover, 1974), 258.

10. *Sŏm* was a unit of measuring the weight of rice and other grain.

11. Chŏng Myŏngsu (?–1653) was born in Ŭnsan, P'yŏngan Province. He served as a soldier in the reinforcements when the Ming and Chosŏn, under Kang Hongnip, attacked the Jin on the Liaodong Peninsula in 1618. In 1629, he and Kang were taken prisoners at the Battle of Fuche. He remained behind after all other Chosŏn prisoners had been released, lived with the Manchu, learned the Manchu language, and came to act as a liaison between the Manchu leaders and the Chosŏn court. He was assassinated in Mukden by individuals from the Chosŏn.

12. *Li* was a unit of distance. Eighty *li* was approximately thirty kilometers.

13. Agogae was located in the district of Ahyŏndong, which is part of west Seoul today.

14. Samgak Mountain is another name for Pukhan Mountain, located on the northern edge of Seoul.

15. Kwangnŭng is just west of Yangju, Kyŏnggi Province, south of Seoul, and is the location of the tombs of King Sejo (r. 1453–1468), the seventh ruler of the Chosŏn dynasty, and his wife, Queen Chŏnghŭi (1418–1483). Yanggŭn is the earlier name for Yangp'yŏng in central Kyŏnggi Province.

16. Chuksan Mountain Fortress was located in the area east of what is Ansŏng today.

17. Kwangnaru is in the Kwangjin district along the northeastern shores of the Han River in Seoul; Map'o is the district along the northwestern shores; and Hŏllŭng is located southwest of Namhan Mountain Fortress. Hŏllŭng was also a sensitive area for the court as the tombs of King T'aejong (r. 1400–1499), the third ruler of the dynasty, and his wife, Queen Wŏn'gyŏng (1365–1420), were (and still are) located there.

18. This lunar date is equivalent to the solar date January 26, 1637.

19. "This fiendishness" refers to the Qing assuming imperial status and pushing out the Ming, which Koreans took as an affront because of their own relations with the Ming.

20. Here is one example of the epistolary battle between the Manchu and Korea. There are others in the diary. For more details, see the Introduction.

21. The Mongol word "Uriankhai" (K. Ollyangha, C. Wuliangha) refers to the region from western Manchuria to eastern Mongolia and to the tribes living there. "Originally [the Uriankhai were] a Mongol tribe located northwest of Chosŏn. In the Chosŏn period . . . the term was also used to refer to Jurchen living to the north of the Korean peninsula." See Eun Kyung Min, "Chengde and the Barbarians: Reading Ethnicity and Difference in Pak Chiwŏn's *Yŏrha ilgi*," *Seoul Journal of Korean Studies* 26, no. 2 (December 2013): 322.

22. This letter refers to the Chinese generals Kong Youde (?–1652) and Geng Zhongming (?–1649), who defected to the Manchu in the 1630s. Both fought against the Ming dynasty. See Nicola Di Cosmo, *Diary of a Manchu Soldier in Seventeenth-Century China* (New York: Routledge, 2006), 7.

23. The Mongol Yuan dynasty (1271–1368) ruled China and had an in-law relationship with the Koryŏ dynasty. In other words, the various princes were of direct Mongol descent.

24. The dynasty referred to here would have been the Koryŏ dynasty (918–1392) rather than the Chosŏn.

25. All three, the Khitan Liao (916–1125), the Jurchen Jin (1115–1234), and the Mongol Yuan dynasties, ruled over parts of northern China or, in the case of the Yuan, conquered all of China. Each dynasty forced Koryŏ to enter into tributary relations, much as the Manchu were doing to Chosŏn in 1637.

26. To "not face north" refers to the subordinate status of Korea. The emperor of China sat north, facing south, while subordinates pleaded to the emperor when they sat south, facing north.

27. Put differently, King Injo's actions to take revenge for the 1627 attack have only brought greater destruction to the Chosŏn.

28. King Injo now takes on a humbled air because of the invasion and presence of the Manchu army.

29. King Onjo (?–28 CE) was a well-known ruler of the kingdom of Paekche (?–660 CE), one of the four early tribal kingdoms on the Korean peninsula. He was also known as the first ruler of Paekche. See Jonathan Best, *The History of the Early Korean Kingdom of Paekche: Together with an Annotated Translation of the Paekche Annals of the* Samguk sagi (Cambridge, MA: Harvard University Press, 2006), 11–15.

30. *Kip'yŏng* is a merit title given to Yu Paekchŭng after his participation in the 1623 coup, in which he supported King Injo.

31. Kwanggyo Mountain is north of Suwŏn, Kyŏnggi Province, and twenty-two kilometers southwest of Namhan Mountain Fortress.

32. Chik Mountain is in South Ch'ungch'ŏng Province, thirty kilometers south of Suwŏn.

33. Tongsŏn is in Tongsŏnmyŏn, Pongsangun, in Hwanghae Province.

34. As three generals were appointed, the strategy was to put weight on the general taking the middle route, rather than the left or right wings of the attack, to defeat the enemy.

35. The *Sillok* records a conversation between King Injo and Na Man'gap concerning the military rations remaining in the fortress. Na responded that the level was less than half of the original amount. Another major issue that concerned the king was the inability of Korean infantry soldiers to engage the more powerful Manchu cavalry. He saw this as the main reason why they were unable to break the siege. *Chosŏn wangjo sillok* [Veritable records of the Chosŏn dynasty] (Seoul: Kuksa Pyŏnch'an wiwŏnhoe: Panp'o T'amgudang, 1955–1958), 34:664a–b; hereafter *Sillok* or *CWS*.

36. The *Sillok* indicates that the king agreed on this day to dispatch an envoy to the Manchu following the advice of Kim Yu, Hong Sŏbong, and Ch'oe Myŏnggil over the protests of Yi Kyŏngjik. *CWS* 34:664b.

37. These halos appearing around the sun were an inauspicious sign for the kingdom, one of several omens appearing in the diary. During the Chosŏn, double halos and other preternatural events were recorded throughout the *Sillok* and the *Sŭngjŏngwŏn ilgi* [Daily record of the royal secretariat].

38. To "suck pus from carbuncles" was an expression implying an individual was currying favors with the elite.

39. Some historians argue that King Injo suffered poor health as a result of the time he spent in Namhan Mountain Fortress.

40. *P'il* is a unit to measure the length of cloth.

41. In ancient Chinese lore, *kiun* (vapors or fog) signify a coming battle. This was yet another omen to the people of the fortress.

42. Sungŭn Palace was the name for the building that housed the portrait of the father of the king of Chosŏn.

43. Prince Chŏngwŏn (1580–1619) was the father of King Injo, the fifth son of King Sŏnjo (r. 1567–1608). His death was recorded in the *Sillok* on the twenty-ninth day of the twelfth lunar month, 1619, when his name was changed to Wŏnjong *kyŏngdŏginhŏn chŏngmokchanghyo taewang*, or simply Grand Prince Wŏnjong (Wŏnjong *taewang*). Following the death of his son, Grand Prince Nŭngch'ang (1599–1615) worried excessively and drank heavily, and it was suggested that this led to his poor health and death. *CWS* 33:289c–d.

44. The only other reference to Kaewŏn Monastery in the *Sillok* was on the twenty-first day, the twelfth lunar month, 1636. Three monks from the monastery presented a horse and an ox to the king, who then ordered a feast for the soldiers. *CWS* 34:659c. The consumption of horse was not unpopular. Dried horsemeat was a delicacy on Cheju Island that was sent to the court as tribute. That the government repeatedly passed laws against the consumption of horse meat attests to its popularity at least among the elite.

45. *Shijing* (*Book of Songs*) and *Shujing* (*Book of Classics*) are major Confucian classical texts. In other words, the dynasty stressed scholarship over military skills.

46. "The crisis of Imjin" refers to the Japanese invasion of Korea, 1592–1598. Emperor Shenzong served as the Ming Wanli emperor from 1572 to 1620.

47. This humble language to appease Hung Taiji is suggesting that the Manchu invasion helped convince Chosŏn of its errors. Withdrawing troops will save the country from further destruction.

48. In other words, the invasion has helped appease the anger of Hung Taiji. By continuing to campaign in Korea, the Manchu would waste their military strength, threaten the brotherly friendship between the two countries, and negatively impact how other countries deal with the Qing.

49. *Ch'usal ch'unsaeng* is a classical Chinese expression originally from "Hesha zeibiao," a poem by the Tang dynasty scholar and official Bai Juyi (772–846).

50. *Hop* is a unit of measurement for food. These quantities add up to a very small amount of food each day.

51. That is, the defenders would run out of food before knowing whether or not they could have defeated the Manchu.

52. Kangnŭng and T'aerŭng were the royal tombs of King Myŏngjong (r. 1545–1567) and his royal concubine, Insun Wanghu (1532–1575), and of King Chungjong's wife, Queen Munjŏng Wanghu (1501–1565), which were (and still are) located in Tongdaemun, Seoul.

53. The troops led by generals Kong and Keng were *Tangbyŏng* (Tang soldiers).

54. Mangwŏl Peak is located east of Namahan Mountain Fortress.

55. The Ch'unsinsa and Ch'usinsa envoys were O Sinnam (1575–1632), Pak Nanyŏng (1575–1637), Na Tŏkhŏn (1573–1640), and Pak No (1584–1643), who were all dispatched to Mukden at various times between 1629 and 1637. For their reports, see various *Sillok* entries, such as *CWS* 34:655d–656a.

56. The defeat of Ming and Chosŏn armies is recorded in CWS 33:217a–c. For a brief account in English, see James B. Palais, *Confucian Statecraft and Korean Institutions: Yu Hyongwon and the Late Choson Dynasty* (Seattle: University of Washington Press, 1996), 93.

57. In other words, no help had come from foreign lands.

58. Using the characters for "subject" and "courtier" indicated Chosŏn's inferior status to the Manchu.

59. In other words, the water is frozen and ships are unable to cross to attack, so the defenders of the island should be safe.

60. "Taking one's heart and placing it into another person's breast" (K. *chŏksim ch'iin pokchung*, C. *chixin zhiren fuzhong*) is a phrase from the *History of Later Han* (*Hou Hanshu*). "The prince of Xiao took his sincere heart and placed it in the breast of another person." Fan Ye, *Hou Hanshu* [History of Later Han] (Beijing: Zhonghua shuju, 2000). It means "to show the greatest confidence in another."

61. Here, a thousand *li* means a great distance.

62. King Injo is suggesting that the Manchu no longer need to capture the fortress because he has already admitted his mistake of breaking the 1627 oath.

63. Crushing bamboo takes a powerful force; here it alludes to the Manchu army.

64. *Tanji* is an act of demonstrating filial piety to one's parents or the king by cutting off pieces of one's flesh, here a finger, to consume or present as an example of one's love and loyalty. See Young Kyun Oh, *Engraving Virtue: The Printing History of a Premodern Korean Moral Primer* (Boston: Brill, 2013), 174.

65. "Not even a single wheel of a war wagon will return" (*chŏgyun pulbanjigong*) is an idiomatic expression describing conquest. In other words, "annihilation of the enemy will be a military success for us."

66. *Chŏnggisan* is an herbal medicine used to treat abdominal pain. *Chŏp* is a small amount of medicine, about a handful.

67. The phrase "celestial troops" (*ch'ŏnbyŏng*) refers to Qing soldiers.

68. The arrival of the Qing to fight the troops that Chosŏn has deployed pressures Chosŏn into accepting the Manchu. These and other humble words are offering apologies and submission to Hung Taiji.

69. A *kyŏng* is a period of time of approximately two hours.

70. Mangwŏn Fortress was east of Namhan Mountain.

71. Kok Fortress was in the valley leading to Namhan Mountain Fortress.

72. The grand prince brothers were Grand Prince Pongnim and Grand Prince Inp'yŏng, King Injo's sons. The crown princess consort was Crown Princess Consort Minhoebin of the Kang family (1611–1646), then wife of Crown Prince Sohyŏn. She was twenty-six years old at the time of the invasion.

73. "Robe and belt praise" (K. *ŭidae chungch'an*, C. *yidai zhongzan*) is a reference to the Song dynasty poet Wen Tianxiang (1236–1283). He was a political and literary figure praised for resisting the Mongol invasion of the 1270s.

74. Witnessing a moon halo signifies an ominous situation, another one of the many omens that appear in the diary.

75. "To discard a fish and take a bear" (*saŏ ch'wiung*) is a statement derived from a Chinese proverb, with roots in Mencius's works. It literally means, "You cannot have fish and bear claw at the same time" because fish and bear claw were both traditional delicacies. Here, Vice-Minister

of Personnel Chŏng On mentioned this, as he wanted to make a final choice.

76. *Ch'obin* is a funeral tradition where the dead body is left outside for one to three years until it has completely decomposed. After this process, the bones are placed in a shroud and buried. See Chu Young Chon, "Transforming Indigenous Performance in Contemporary South Korea: The Case of Sohn Jin Ch'aek's Madangnori" (PhD diss., Ohio State University, 2014), 273.

77. *Changgunsŏk* is a reference to Shi Yong, a fictional character in classical Chinese literature, also known as "the stone general." *Changgunsŏk* may also refer to the landscape in the southern tip of Cheju Island, a well-known geographic landmark.

78. Here, and over the next several pages, the Chosŏn officials are debating how to deal with the Qing suggestions for surrender.

79. Kim Yu is arguing that O Talche and Yun Chip did no wrong, so should not be sent.

80. *Hambyŏk yŏch'ŭn* (C. *xianbi yuchen*) was a surrender ritual described in such classics as the *Zizhi tongjian*. Sima Guang, *Zizhi tongjian* [Comprehensive mirror in aid of governance] (Beijing: Gu ji chu ban she, 1956). The defeated performs courtesy rituals to the victorious.

81. Blue clothes (*ch'ŏngŭi*) represented low or inferior status.

82. Here is another example of the epistolary warfare between the Manchu and Korea over the surrender terms.

83. Cinnabar trees (*Toxicodendron vernicifluum*) were used for medicinal purposes.

84. Prince Hoeŭn, or Yi Tŏgin, was a relative through marriage of King Injo.

85. A similar story is found in the *Sillok*. Pak No and Sin Tŭkyŏn, two envoys returning from Mukden in 1639, informed the court about Prince Hoeŭn's daughter—who was fifteen at the time she was captured on Kanghwa Island—and her service to the emperor as an attendant girl (*sinyŏ*) and her later marriage into the Pipai Bo clan. See *CWS* 35:47a–b.

86. Based on early Chosŏn legal codes, the Ministry of Rites demanded officials of lesser rank stand to the left side of the road and prostrate themselves when passing superiors in the vicinity of the capital. Here this is a rhetorical device to express the writer's sincerity and devotion to the king.

87. Nam Iung (1575–1648) was a high official who reached the level of left state councilor and was given the title *ch'unsŏng* by the court as a distinction for his actions during the Yi Kwal rebellion.

88. The *chobo* referred to in this diary is the handwritten newsletter compiled and distributed daily by the royal secretariat (*sŭngjŏngwŏn*).

89. The term *namyungbok* can be found in the *Kangxi Dictionary* (*Kangxi Zidian*), meaning "barbarian clothes."

90. The crown princess consort referred to here is Crown Princess Minhoebin of the Kang clan (1611–1646).

91. The family members referred to included Grand Prince Pongnim, the future king Hyojong (1619–1659; r. 1649–1659), and his wife the future queen Insŏn (1619–1674) of the Chang clan. They spent eight years in Mukden, from the age of eighteen until they were twenty-six.

92. *Kisaeng* were female entertainers of the scholarly elite.

93. Chŏn'gwan is now part of the eastern section of Seoul at Sagŭndong.

94. The Taegwangt'ong and Sogwangt'ong bridges crossed the Ch'ŏnggye River in Seoul, which lead north to the palace.

95. Ch'abi Gate (*Ch'abimun*) was the side entrance of the royal palace.

96. This is either Dorgon, the son of Nurhachi (rather than the son of Hung Taiji), or an unnamed younger son of Hung Taiji. Most likely it is Dorgon.

97. *Tongyangwi* and *hallim* are high-ranking merit titles.

98. The year referred to here is when Na Man'gap was reworking this portion of the diary, presumably 1638 or 1639.

Record of Loyalists Everywhere

1. Ch'ŏrong Fortress was located in South Hamgyŏng Province. Originally built during the Koryŏ era, it was later fortified and expanded. See No Sasin and Haeng I, *Kugyŏk sinjŭng Tongguk yŏji sŭngnam* [Augmented survey of the geography of Korea] (Seoul: Minjok munhwa ch'ulinhoe, 1969), 6:180a.

2. The military officer who superintends the soldiers in the barracks of all the garrisons in each province is the *manho* (chief of ten thousand households). See Pyŏn Kwangsŏk, "Ŏmo changgun chŏn Manho Chŏng Ŭnggap myo chisŏk kwa kwallyŏ inmul kirok" [Records related to the epitaph stone of General Uno, the former Manho Chŏng Ŭnggap], *Ulsan sahak* 12 (1999): 129. The position began during the Mongol era of control over Korea and evolved in the late Koryŏ dynasty. See Yi Kanghan, "Koryŏ hugi Manhobu ŭi 'chiyŏk tanwijŏk' sŏnggyŏk kŏmt'o" [End of Koryŏ Manhobu], *Yŏksa wa hyŏnsil* 100 (2016): 241–80.

3. Tongsŏn was located in Pongsangun, Hwanghae Province, a strategic point for travel to nearby areas. It was also the site of an important Koryŏ battle in 1231 against Mongol forces led by Sartai (?–1232). While both sides suffered heavy casualties, under the command of Yi Chasŏng (?–1251), Koryŏ troops stopped the advance of Sartai's army along this route. For instance, see Minjok munhwa ch'ujinhoe, eds., *Sinp'yŏn kugyŏk Yŏnhaengnok sŏnjip* [Anthology of travelogues]. 17 vols. (P'aju-si: Han'guk haksul chŏngbo, 2008), 4:289–90; and Kim Chongsŏ, *Kugyŏk Koryŏsa chŏlyo* [Essentials of the Koryŏ dynasty] (Seoul: Minjok munhwa ch'ujinhoe, 1976), 2:652.

4. Monastic fighters served for Yi Sibang and Sim Yŏn, alongside local righteous soldiers (*ŭibyŏng*) and the remnants of Huyŏnggun's forces, amounting to roughly three thousand soldiers in total. See *Taedong yasŭng* [Unofficial history of the great east] (Seoul: Sŏul taehakkyo ch'ulp'anbu, 1968), 7:175; hereafter *TDYS*. These monastic troops appear to have been mobilized only in the southern provinces. In 1638, they were also conscripted by the government to reduce the size of Namhan Mountain Fortress, most likely a Manchu demand. The *Sillok* and *TDYS* are silent about a wider mobilization of monastic armies during the 1627 or 1637 Manchu invasions. In 1626, six hundred and fifty monastic troops from four provinces were conscripted to work with soldiers on Kanghwa Island for a period of fifteen days, most likely to fortify defenses. *Chosŏn wangjo sillok* [Veritable records of the Chosŏn dynasty] (Seoul: Kuksa Pyŏnch'an wiwŏnhoe: Panp'o T'amgudang, 1955–1958), 34:93b–c. But it does not appear that there was a nationwide response from the monasteries or a call for mobilization by the central government in defense against the Manchu. This was unlike forty-five years earlier, in 1592, when numerous monastic soldiers fought against Japan, led by such Buddhists as Hyujŏng (1520–1604), Yujŏng (1544–1610), and Ŭiŏm (dates unknown). One explanation for this is that the Manchu were not as great a national threat as the Japanese. The rise of the Qing as a power in Northeast Asia took place over several decades. Their assaults on Korea were anticipated, unlike the Japanese attack in 1592, for which the court dismissed the warning signs. The Manchu were dangerous but displayed reverence for Chinese and Korean worldviews, unlike the Japanese who were seen as even more barbaric. The Manchu, unlike the Japanese, took great pains to deal diplomatically with the Chosŏn court through proper Confucian language and ritual. Therefore, the countryside, including monasteries, seemed to have responded differently.

There is a long tradition of Buddhist armies on the Korean peninsula fighting at times of foreign invasion or domestic upheavals, such as in the 1592 Imjin War or during the military dictatorship era of the Koryŏ dynasty. See Sem Vermeersch, *The Power of the Buddhas: The Politics of Buddhism During the Koryŏ Dynasty (918–1392)* (Cambridge, MA: Harvard University Press, 2008), 178–80. For the contribution of monastic armies to Imjin and the elevation of Buddhist status in the Chosŏn, see Kim Yong-T'ae, "Changes in Seventeenth-Century Korean Buddhism and the Establishment of the Buddhist Tradition in the Late Chosŏn Dynasty," *Acta Koreana* 16, no. 2 (December 2013): 540–44. Monastic armies were found in China and Japan. See Mikael S. Adolphson, *The Teeth and Claws of the Buddha: Monastic Warriors and Sohei in Japanese History* (Honolulu: University of Hawai'i Press, 2007), 21–86.

5. Imp'i was a mountainous district near Kunsan in North Chŏlla Province, an area the illustrious scholar Chŏng Yagyong described in 1817 as a place where "unfilial sons and criminals" could be arrested and executed daily, attesting to its peripheral nature. Chŏng Yagyong, *Kyŏngse yup'yo* [Design for good government] (Seoul: Minjok munhwa ch'ulinhoe, 1977), 1:153. The *Sillok* also records earthquakes, floods, and falling rocks in this area.

6. Chŏng Hongmyŏng (1582–1650) was a poet and scholar. He held a variety of posts, including recruiting official (*somosa*) in 1637. *TDYS* reports that on the seventeenth day of the first lunar month, Chŏng rallied approximately thirty remaining righteous soldiers from the villages around Kongju, but he retreated once the enemy began scouting north of the area.

Kanghwa Island Records

1. *Kŏbin* refers to *sŏnbo kŏbin*, leaving one's original residence. Here, this means the capital, Hansŏng [Seoul]. Kim Kyŏngjing (1589–1638) was promoted as a merit subject (*chŏngsa kongsin*) in 1623 because of his support during King Injo's restoration, the same year he passed the highest civil service exam (*mun'gwa*) and was promoted to chief magistrate of the capital (*Hansŏngbu p'anyun*), among many other posts. In early 1636, Minister Yun Pang argued that the arrival of a Manchu envoy signaled their intention to invade, thus believing the court must be evacuated to Kanghwa. However, Kim Kyŏngjing insisted that the first policy of the court should not be fleeing the capital. Going to Kanghwa Island should be a

second option. *Chosŏn wangjo sillok* [Veritable records of the Chosŏn dynasty] (Seoul: Kuksa Pyŏnch'an wiwŏnhoe: Panp'o T'amgudang, 1955–1958), 34:626b; hereafter *Sillok* or *CWS*. In 1637, during the invasion, as chief censor general (*taesagan*) and then inspector (*kŏmch'alsa*), he was tasked with the defense of Kanghwa Island. *CWS* 34:657c. The court reported the loss of Kanghwa Island and the escape of Kim Kyŏngjing, Chang Sin, and Yi Min'gu. However, his power at the court made him many enemies, and he was hated by some. *CWS* 34:616c. It was General Han Hŭngil, not Kim Kyŏngjing, who remained behind to defend the fortress, resisting Manchu calls to surrender. *CWS* 34:668b–c. On the eleventh day of the second lunar month, 1637, the Two Offices were already calling for the punishment of Kim and these other officials for their crimes on Kanghwa Island. *CWS* 34:674c–d. The court executed Chang Sin, but by the summer of 1637, Kim Kyŏngjing was still alive, prompting a flurry of petitions calling for his immediate execution. For instance, see *CWS* 34:688c–d and *CWS* 34:695b–c. His death was reported on the fifth day of the fifth lunar month of the *chŏngmyo* year [1638]. *CWS* 35:19d.

Understandably, Kim remained a symbol of hatred throughout the Chosŏn court. For the next century, the court criticized him or occasionally compared those accused of crimes to him. Also, other scholars lambasted him in their poetry. Among others of his generation, Kim Ch'anghyŏp (1651–1708) describes Kim Kyŏngjing as the arrogant, drunken inspector of Kanghwa Island. See Kim Chongil, *Noam chip* [Collected writings of Noam] (Seoul: Minjok munhwa ch'ulinhoe, 2006) and Kim Ch'anghyŏp, *Nongam chip* [Collected writings of Nongam] (Ch'ŏlchong 5 kapin [1854]), 8:114. Yun Chŭng (1629–1714) retells the story of Kim's selfish actions on Kanghwa Island. See Yun Chŭng, *Myŏngje sŏnsaeng yugo* [Posthumous work of Myŏngje] (Seoul: Kyŏngon munhwasa, 1973), 2:445c–d. Along with Chang Sin and Yi Min'gu, Kim Kyŏngjing became known as one of the three generals who betrayed the country. See Cho Kyŏng and O Chun, *Yongju yugo* [Collected works of Yongju] (Seoul: Hakchawŏn, 2015), 2:411. Kanghwa Island is located off the west coast of the Korean Peninsula.

2. Kapkok was the harbor leading to Kanghwa Island and the location the court retreated to in times of national crisis. One official described its importance in 1777: "Since time immemorial, it is hard to know what is more important, either Namhan Mountain Fortress or Bukhan Mountain Fortress. But the most strategic sites are Kapkok and Munsu."

Ilsŏngnok [Diary of self-examination] (Seoul: Sŏul taehakkyo tosŏgwan, 1982), 2:450.

3. This may be an allusion to Yi Sunsin (1545–1598), the naval commander who brilliantly helped destroy much of the Japanese navy during the *Imjin waeran* (the Japanese invasion of Korea).

4. *Tongch'a* were small, handmade, wooden play carts fathers made for their children. See Eugene I. Knez, "The Modernization of Three Korean Villages, 1951–1981: An Illustrated Study of a People and Their Material Culture," *Smithsonian Contributions to Anthropology* (1997): 80.

5. Long River (*changgang*) in the original text refers to the Yalu River between China and Korea.

6. *Puwŏn'gun* is a merit title.

7. *Tongyangwi* is a title given to Sin Iksŏng, who married Princess Chŏngsuk (1587–1627), the daughter of King Sŏnjo.

8. In capital punishment cases, death by poison was considered the more honored method to die rather than other forms of execution, such as decapitation. Instead, the king gave Chang Sin the chance to take his own life rather than face a more humiliating death.

Records of Several People Who Rejected Peace Negotiations and Died of Righteousness

1. Tongyuanpu (K. T'ongwŏnbo) is a town halfway between the Chosŏn border to the south and Mukden to the north.

2. *Tapch'ŏngil* is the third day of the third lunar month, a day celebrating the arrival of spring.

3. The Brocade City (K. *Kŭmsŏng*, C. *Jincheng*), refers to Chengdu, China. Yinshan is a mountain in inner China.

4. In other words, O Talche experienced the hardships of traveling far away from his mother.

5. This Mencian teaching refers to the "three withdrawings of Mencius's mother" (K. *samch'ŏn*, C. *sanqian*), a popular though probably questionable account of the dedication of Mencius's mother to her son's upbringing. "The mother of Meng Ke of Zou was called Mother Meng. She lived near a graveyard. During Mencius's youth, he enjoyed playing among the tombs, romping about pretending to prepare the grounds for burials. Mother Meng said, 'This is not the place to raise my son.' She therefore moved away and settled beside the marketplace. But there he liked to play at displaying and selling wares like a merchant. Again,

Mother Meng said, 'This is not the place to raise my son,' and once more left and settled beside a school. There, however, he played at setting out sacrificial vessels, bowing, yielding, entering, and withdrawing. His mother said, 'This, indeed, is where I can raise my son!' and settled there. When Mencius grew up, he studied the six arts (archery, chariot riding, music, writing, arithmetic, Confucian rites), and finally became known as a great classicist." Anne Behnke Kinney, ed. and trans., *Exemplary Women of Early China: The Lienu Zhuan of Liu Xiang* (New York: Columbia University Press, 2014), 18.

Miscellaneous Notes Concerning What Happened After the Upheaval

1. Exile was reserved as punishment for the serious crimes of officials.

2. The queen referred to here is King Injo's wife, Queen Inyŏl *wanghu* of the Han clan, who died in 1635.

3. Huan Wen (312–373) was a powerful military official of the Jin dynasty and is considered one of the most important generals in Chinese history. Fangtou is the location where Huan was eventually defeated in 369, for which Yuan Zhen (?–370) was blamed. Yuan rose up against Huan but died in 370.

4. These were the ancestral shrines and the temple of earth, the most important symbols of the ruling family and government, to which the king conducted ritual regularly. Because of the Manchu attack and the significance of the shrines to the country, the court moved them from the temple compounds in Seoul to Kanghwa Island. Yun Pang's responsibilities included transporting these to Kanghwa Island and defending them.

5. The court recorded them based on their location of birth.

6. The constellations *Shen* (Orion) and *Shang* (Antares) never appear at the same time. The reference to them here implies a permanent difference or disagreement.

7. There were two letters, one with a seal that was surrounded by these characters, the second did not have a seal.

8. The Samjŏndo stele (Samjŏndobi), erected on the site where King Injo surrendered to the Qing, was used by the Manchu to reinforce their rule over Chosŏn. King Injo sent a rubbing of the stele to the Qing in 1639. A handful of Manchu officials visited the stele between 1639 and 1736. The Samjŏndo stele was also strategically located along a few main

roads and a waterway near Namhan Mountain Fortress. Frequented by Chosŏn officials and soldiers, the stele thus served as a reminder to Chosŏn of their defeat to the Manchu. See Pae Usŏng, "Sŏul e on ch'ŏng ŭ ch'iksa Mafuta hwa samjŏndobi" [Study on the Manchu envoy Mafuta who came to Seoul and the Samjŏndo stele], *Sŏul hak yŏn'gu* 38 (2010): 235–37.

9. This elaborate structure built around the monument may have been of Manchu design. Only the inscribed stone monument survives today.

10. The diary mentions Mongol script on the Samjŏndo stele, but it fails to mention the Manchu. One side of the stele is in literary Chinese, while the other side is in Mongol and Manchu script.

11. "Samhan" is another name for the Korean Peninsula, referencing the era before the Three Kingdoms period and unified Silla (668–935).

12. Kong Youde (?–1652) and Geng Zhongming (?–1649) were brilliant army generals who defected to the Manchu and played a vital role in the Qing army. See Nicola Di Cosmo, *Diary of a Manchu Soldier in Seventeenth-Century China* (New York: Routledge, 2006), 7. Kado is a strategic island off the northwestern corner of the peninsula, roughly fifty kilometers from the mouth of the Yalu River, the frontier of the Chosŏn. Kado Island was held by Ming troops during the first decades of the seventeenth century. The Chinese warlord Mao Wenlong (1576–1629) occupied it from 1622 until 1629. After his death, Ming troops remained on the island until 1637. See Yi Kŭngik, *Kugyŏk Yŏllyŏsil kisul* [Stories by Yŏllyŏsil] (Seoul: Minjok munhwa ch'ulinhoe, 1966), 6:530–32.

13. Shen Shikui was a commander of the Ming who fled to nearby Pido Island and was killed by Qing and Chosŏn troops, along with another officer, Chen Hongfan. See Han Ch'iyun, *Haedong yŏksa* [History of Korea] (Seoul: Kyŏngin munhwasa, 1982), 2:375. Chen was assigned the task of saving Chosŏn when Namhan Mountain Fortress first came under siege in 1637.

14. Most likely, this refers to Hung Taiji's demands to send him daughters from the three state councilors, the six ministries, and the capital elite, as well as hostage sons from the elite.

15. By only pretending to take part in the battle, Yi Saryong was refusing to support the Qing against the Ming.

16. In 1681, Yi Saryong was posthumously awarded honors by the court. In the war, he refused to kill Ming soldiers and fired nothing but blanks, shouting "Even if I were to die, how could I shoot bullets in the direction of the Chinese (Hanin)?" The court granted food to his

grandchildren, and they were also excepted from corvée and military service. *Chosŏn wangjo sillok* [Veritable records of the Chosŏn dynasty] (Seoul: Kuksa pyŏnch'an Wiwŏnhoe: Panp'o T'amgudang, 1955–1958), 38:515a.

17. At the Chosŏn court, Zhang Chun was heralded as a Chinese man who was faithful and unyielding and was treated generously by the emperor. King Injo was curious what Zhang had said after meeting the crown prince. Nam Iŭng stated that Zhang called Chosŏn a country of righteousness. For a conversation between Nam Iŭng and King Injo about Zhang Chun, see *Sŭngjŏngwŏn ilgi* [Daily record of the royal secretariat] (Seoul: Minjok munhwa ch'ujinhoe, 2006), 45:172–73. See also Zhang Tingyu, ed., *Ming shi* [History of the Ming dynasty] (Beijing: Zhonghua shu ju, 1974), 237:7453, 7463.

18. A *qingshe* was a place where one could learn Chinese writing and develop one's character.

19. Su Wu (140–60 BCE) was a diplomat of the Han dynasty; he was known for his bravery and loyal service. Here Wen Shan refers to Wen Tianxian, the Song dynasty poet.

20. Guanxi was located north of the frontier, in Manchuria.

21. The *chiwŏl* month of the *sinsa* year would have been the eleventh month of 1641.

22. Portable folding stools were status symbols, built for the royal family and *yangban* elites. See Hong Sŏna, "Han'guk hosang ŭi siwŏn kwa chohyŏng e kwanhan yŏn'gu," [Study on the origins and creative design of folding stools], *Han'guk kagu hakhoeji* 24, no. 2 (April 2013): 180.

23. Yŏsuk was the brush name (*ho*) of Yi Tŏksu.

24. Ponyŏk was what is now Kŭmgyoyŏk, in North Hwanghae Province.

Record of Ch'ŏngŭm's Slandering

1. Ch'ŏngŭm is the brush name (*ho*) of Kim Sanghŏn.

2. "To lie on firewood and taste gall" (*wasin sangdan*) is to suffer patiently with resolve. It is also an allusion to King of Yueh, who was said to have slept on firewood for bedding, underneath gall hung over his bed to remind him of the bitterness of his loss and to help prepare him for a comeback.

3. The previous king referred to here is King Sŏnjo (r. 1552–1608). "All streams flowed east" (*manjŏl p'iltong*) is an allusion to a passage

from the Confucian text *Xunzi* where Confucius has a discussion with his disciple about the flow of water in China, human morality, and the loyalty between king and officials:

> Confucius was gazing intently at a waterway flowing eastward. Zigong asked Confucius, "Why is it that whenever a gentleman sees a large waterway, he is sure to gaze intently at it?" Confucius said, "When the waterway is large, it provides for the various living things in all-encompassing fashion, without any ulterior motive—this resembles virtue. . . . By going into and out of [the water], one uses it to become fresh and clean—this resembles being transformed to goodness. Even though ten thousand turns, it is sure to heard east—this resembles having settled intuitions. For these reasons, whenever a gentleman sees a large waterway, he is sure to gaze intently at it." (Eric Hutton, ed. and trans. *Xunzi: The Complete Text* [Princeton, NJ]: Princeton University Press, 2014], 322.)

4. Their fates are forever interconnected.

5. "Everything deserves itself" (*ch'angnang chach'wi*) is a reference to Mencius: "There is a boy singing, 'When the water of the Ts'ang-lang is clear, it does to wash the strings of my cap; When the water of the Ts'ang-lang is muddy, it does to wash my feet.' Confucius said, 'Hear what he sings, my children. When clear, then he will wash his cap-strings; and when muddy, he will wash his feet with it. This different application is brought by the water on itself." James Legge, *The Chinese Classics, Vol. 1: Confucian Analects, the Great Learning, the Doctrine of the Mean, and the Works of Mencius* (Taipei: SMC Publishing, 1998), 299. In other words, everything has its usage depending on its qualities.

Here, the king is arguing that the Office of the Inspector General erred in calling for an end to petitions about Kim Kyŏngjing, Chang Sin, Yi Min'gu, and others.

6. The act of falling into a ditch is in reference to Confucius's "Xian Wen":

> Zi Gong said, "Guan Zhong, I apprehend, was wanting in virtue. When the duke Huan caused his brother Jiu to be killed, Guan Zhong was not able to die with him. Moreover, he became prime minister to Huan." The Master said, "Guang Zhong acted as prime minister to the duke Huan, made him leader of all the princes, and united and rectified the

whole kingdom. Down to the present day, the people enjoy the gifts which he conferred. But for Guan Zhong, we should now be wearing our hair unbound, and the lappets of our coats buttoning on the left side. Will you require from him the small fidelity of common men and common women, who would commit suicide in a stream or ditch, no one knowing anything about them?" (Legge, *The Chinese Classics*, 282–83.)

7. Na Man'ap is suggesting that these officials took part in the debate by submitting petitions in order to appear innocent.

8. Requests for dismissal from office by petition writers were standard ways of presenting an opinion that the presenter knew would be controversial or would displease the king. It is a formula most such memorials require, yet sometimes the king took them literally and dismissed the petitioner. Such examples appear throughout this diary.

9. Sitting on woven mats while talking indicated that the conversation was a serious topic.

10. In other words, Kim Chungil's earlier petition calling for the dismissal of Yi Kye is really a petition criticizing Kim Chungil himself.

11. *Pongmyŏng choyang* ("when the phoenix sings toward the rising sun") is a metaphor for when a talented person has a rare chance to reveal their talent.

12. Scholar officials who did not risk their lives to help the king, the real offenders of the court.

13. Sun Fu (1078–1128) was the Northern Song dynasty minister of war during the Jurchen Jin invasion. When the Jurchen captured and took Emperor Qinzong (r. 1126–1127) hostage, Sun Fu continued defending the capital, Kaifeng. However, he was taken prisoner—along with the emperor and other members of the imperial family—sent north, and later died.

14. This is in reference to Zhu Xi's commentary in *The Analects of Confucius*: "The man of honor offers his life in times of danger, hence when in the service of a falling state, he has no right to leave it, but he has no call to enter such a service from without. When his state has its laws all disorganized, he washes his hands of it." William E. Soothill, *The Analects if Confucius* (Tokyo: Methodist Publishing House, 1910), 400.

15. "Western matter" (*sŏsa*) is most likely a euphemism for the decline of the Ming and rise of the Jurchen/Manchu found in the *Chosŏn wangjo sillok* beginning in 1611. *Chosŏn wangjo sillok* [Veritable records of the Chosŏn dynasty], 48 vols. (Seoul: Kuksa Pyŏnch'an wiwŏnhoe: Panp'o T'amgudang, 1955–1958).

16. The grand king was the founder of the ancient Zhou state. King Wen of Zhao (r. 1100–1050 BCE) was his grandson and successor.

17. Ji Lang was a Jin dynasty official who killed himself after lamenting his incompetence and lack of bravery, which prevented him from saving the emperor. On the *jiawu* day, Zong Chang arrived at Yao's camp. On the *yiwei* day, Emperor Min appeared in a sheep cart. He was stripped bare, with jade in his mouth, and was carrying a coffin. He came out of the eastern gate and surrendered. His various ministers wept and climbed onto the cart, grabbing his hand. The emperor was unable to control his own grief. Aide to the Censor-in-Chief Ji Lang of Pingyi sighed and said, "I was not wise enough to be able to save us, and I was not brave enough to be able to die. How can I bare to follow my sovereign and his ministers and go north to become a prisoner of the barbarians?" Thus, he killed himself. Sima Guang, *Zizhi tongjian* [Comprehensive mirror in aid of governance] (Beijing: Gu ji chu ban she, 1956), 5:30–31.

18. Ho and Oyŏng are towns located between Kyŏngsang and Ch'ungch'ŏng provinces.

19. This is an allusion to *Mencius*, chapter 9:

> The Tî caused his own children, nine sons and two daughters, the various officers, oxen and sheep, storehouses and granaries, all to be prepared, to serve Shun amid the channeled fields. Of the scholars of the kingdom there were multitudes who flocked to him. The sovereign designed that Shun should superintend the kingdom along with him, and then to transfer it to him entirely. But because his parents were not in accord with him, he felt like a poor man who has nowhere to turn to.
> (Legge, *The Chinese Classics*, 343–44)

20. In other words, one way to consider Kim Sanghŏn's case is to forgive and forget, as a sage would do. But here in the joint memorial, the writers argue that other methods of judgment, such as popular opinion, point to his criminality.

21. Duke Zhuang of Zheng (757–701 BCE) lived during the Warring States period. This action of exposing his shoulder symbolized his surrender: "Baring his flesh and leading a goat, the Liege of Zheng went forward to meet [the victor]." See Stephen W. Durrant, Wai-yee Li, and David Schaberg, "Lord Xuan (608–591 BCE)," in *Zuo Tradition: Zuozhuan Commentary on the "Spring and Autumn Annals"* (Seattle: University of Washington Press, 2016), 641. Zichan (?– 522 BCE), recorded in

Sima Qian's biographies of virtuous officials, was an officer of the Spring and Autumn and the Warring States eras. He was heralded as a wise official who followed the law through proper Confucian practices.

22. Emperor Gaozong was the first emperor of the Song dynasty (r. 1107–1187).

23. Here the diarist directly quotes the book by Ban Zhao (?–120 CE), a historian who critiqued Sima Qian (145–86 BCE) for not fully embracing the virtues of a Confucian sage. Chen Yizhong was a well-known scholar and government official of Song dynasty China during the Mongol invasion of 1276. As the Mongol forces drove south, Chen and the Song court vacillated between war and peace, but finally supported surrender. Sometime during the 1270s, Chen fled to Annam and never returned. See Adam Kessler, "The Last Days of the Song Dynasty: Evidence of the Flight of Song Officials to Southeast Asia before the Mongol Invasions," *Journal of the Royal Asiatic Society* 28, no. 2 (April 2018): 318–19.

24. The original incorrectly refers to the *ŭlsa* year. The correct year is *kisa* [1629]. See Yun Chaeyŏng, *Pyŏngjarok* [The diary of 1636] (Seoul: Myŏngmundang, 1987), 219. Prince Insŏng (1588–1628) was the seventh son of King Sŏnjo and Queen Consort Chŏngbin Min. As a potential threat to King Injo's rule, Prince Insŏng was swept up in the purges in the wake of the coup against King Kwanghaegun. King Injo banished him from the capital and then forced him to commit suicide. However, Prince Insŏng's punishment did not go unchallenged—a number of officials across the political spectrum argued against it. For more information, see Kim Yonghŭm, "Injodae chŏnban chŏngch'ijŏk kaltŭng kwa pungdangnon," *Yŏksa hwa kyŏnggye* 60 (September 2006): 79.

25. Ya Mountain was the site of a large naval battle between the Mongol Yuan and the Southern Song dynasty in 1279. The defeat ended the Southern Song.

26. Zhang Shijie was the Southern Song admiral who commanded the Chinese navy against the invading Mongol fleet. In the last battle of 1279, his forces were defeated. He is rumored to have escaped but died at sea shortly after.

27. Kim Sanghŏn's words were deceptive.

28. The argument for or against Kim Sanghŏn is time-consuming and destructive.

29. The disorder is the war with the Manchu.

30. Ch'angnŭng refers to the location of the royal tombs of King Yejong (r. 1468–1469) and Queen Ansun (1445–1499) in Koyang and the site of one of the earliest Chosŏn defeats to the Manchu recorded in the diary.

31. Debate about Kim Sanghŏn should end.

32. "The light or the heavy" refers to the weight of a punishment.

33. Hong Myŏngil is claiming Kim Sanghŏn and Chŏng On were falsely accused of destroying the royal letter and abandoning the crown prince despite Kim holding the post of tutor to the crown prince.

34. Presenting next to the king underscored the importance of the topic under discussion.

35. Yu Sŏk is making an emotional appeal to the king, rather than a real threat of violence, to convey his disapproval of Kim Sanghŏn and those who support him.

36. In highly emotive language, Yu Sŏk is arguing that he is unafraid of punishment from the court for holding such feelings against Kim Sanghŏn.

37. Yu Sŏk claims Kim Sanghŏn overstepped his bounds by using words that degrade the king and country.

38. Here the observance of temple rites refers to ruling the country.

39. He is ending his arguments.

Humiliation Received from the Qing

1. "Zilu" was the courtesy name of Zhong You (542–480 BCE). Zilu and Ran Qiu (522–462 BCE) were senior disciples of Confucius. Confucius criticized them repeatedly as ordinary ministers seeking careers and fame rather than having an interest in following Confucian practice. But he praised them for not committing the most serious crimes: "The Master said, 'In an act of parricide or regicide, they would not follow [their chief].'" James Legge, *The Chinese Classics, Vol. 1: Confucian Analects, the Great Learning, the Doctrine of the Mean, and the Works of Mencius* (Taipei: SMC Publishing, 1998), 246.

2. A plan against the Qing might not lead to success, but the plan is within reach and can be put into motion. Acting and failing are better than inaction and failure.

3. "Playing the jackal to the tiger" is in reference to the belief that someone devoured by a tiger may become a ghost who then helps the tiger devour others (*ch'anggwi*).

4. Ki Island is near Seoul. Yun Chaeyŏng, *Pyŏngjarok* [The diary of 1636] (Seoul: Myŏngmundang, 1987), 236.

5. Kim Sanghŏn is arguing that King Injo should not be intimidated by Qing military power or listen to the opinions of officials who advocate for peace.

6. Omoktu was the brother of Mafuta. Yesha was a Chinese official from the Ministry of Justice.

7. Tang people were Chinese.

8. Yu Im (1581–1643) was a general famous for resisting and defeating Manchu attacks.

9. The official Kang Hyowŏn (1603–1639) died with Chŏng Noegyŏng in Mukden. In other words, the Manchu held no real feelings about Kang.

10. He noted that the foreign envoys he welcomed looked Chinese or Manchu.

11. Hung Taiji threatened to kidnap them and bring them back by force.

12. The hornless dragon head statue was at the gate of the royal palace.

13. The wives and daughters of the *sadaebu* on Kanghwa Island.

14. Yu Sŏae was in the Office of Supreme Commander (Toch'ech'alsa) during the attack.

15. Sin Sangch'on was a Confucian scholar who also witnessed the Manchu War.

BIBLIOGRAPHY

Primary Sources

Cho Kyŏng and O Chun. *Yongju yugo* [Collected works of Yongju]. 2 vols. Seoul: Hakchawŏn, 2015.

Chŏng Yagyong. *Kyŏngse yup'yo* [Design for good government]. 4 vols. Seoul: Minjok munhwa ch'ulinhoe, 1977.

Chosŏn wangjo sillok [Veritable records of the Chosŏn dynasty]. 48 vols. Seoul: Panp'o T'amgudang, 1955–1958.

Durrant, Stephen W., Wai-yee Li, and David Schaberg. "Lord Xuan (608–591 BCE)." In *Zuo Tradition: Zuozhuan Commentary on the "Spring and Autumn Annals,"* 578–698. Seattle: University of Washington Press, 2016.

Fan Ye. *Hou Hanshu* [History of Later Han]. Beijing: Zhonghua shuju, 2000.

Han Ch'iyun. *Haedong yŏksa* [History of Korea]. 2 vols. Seoul: Kyŏngin munhwasa, 1982.

Hutton, Eric, ed. and trans. *Xunzi: The Complete Text.* Princeton, NJ: Princeton University Press, 2014.

Ilsŏngnok [Diary of self-examination]. 86 vols. Seoul: Sŏul taehakkyo tosŏgwan, 1982.

Kim Ch'anghyŏp. *Nongam chip* [Collected writings of Nongam]. 15 vols. Ch'ŏlchong 5 kapin [1854].

Kim Chongil. *Noam chip* [Collected writings of Noam]. Seoul: Minjok munhwa ch'ulinhoe, 2006.

Kim Chongsŏ. *Kugyŏk Koryŏsa chŏlyo* [Essentials of the Koryŏ dynasty]. 5 vols. Seoul: Minjok munhwa ch'ujinhoe, 1976.

Manzhou shi lu [Veritable records of the Manchu]. 8 vols. Shenyang: Liaoling tong zhi guan, 1934.

Minjok munhwa ch'ujinhoe, eds. *Sinp'yŏn kugyŏk Yŏnhaengnok sŏnjip* [Anthology of travelogues]. 17 vols. P'aju-si: Han'guk haksul chŏngbo, 2008.

No Sasin and Haeng I. *Kugyŏk sinjŭng Tongguk yŏji sŭngnam* [Augmented survey of the geography of Korea]. 6 vols. Seoul: Minjok munhwa ch'ulinhoe, 1969.

Sima Guang. *Zizhi tongjian* [Comprehensive mirror in aid of governance]. 10 vols. Beijing: Gu ji chu ban she, 1956.

———. *Zizhi tongjian* [Comprehensive mirror in aid of governance]. Beijing: Zhonghua shuju, 2007.

Sin Hŭm. *Sangch'on chip* [Works of Sangch'on]. Seoul: Han'guk munhŏn yŏn'guhoe, 1981.

Song Chun'gil and Sŏng Nakhun. *Tongch'undang chip* [Collected writings of Tongch'umdang]. Seoul: Tonghwa ch'ulp'an kongsa, 1972.

Song Siyŏl. *Songja taejŏn* [Collected writings of Songja]. 8 vols. Seoul: Pogyŏng munhwasa, 1985.

Sŭngjŏngwŏn ilgi Injo [Daily record of the royal secretariat from King Injo]. 59 vols. Seoul: Minjok munhwa ch'ujinhoe, 2006.

Taedong yasŭng [Unofficial history from the great east]. 13 vols. Seoul: Sŏul taehakkyo ch'ulp'anbu, 1968.

Yi Hyŏnil and Pak Hŏnun. *Kugyŏk Kalam chip* [Collected writings of Kalam]. 8 vols. Seoul: Minjok munhwa ch'ujinhoe, 1999.

Yi Ik and Chŏng Haeryŏm. *Sŏngho sasŏl chŏgsŏn* [Miscellaneous discussions of Sŏngho]. 3 vols. Seoul: Hyŏndae sirhaksa, 1998.

Yi Kŭngik. *Kugyŏk Yŏllyŏsil kisul* [Stories by Yŏllyŏsil]. 12 vols. Seoul: Minjok munhwa ch'ulinhoe, 1966.

Yi Sik. *T'aektang chip* [Collected writings of T'aektang]. Seoul: Kyŏngmunsa, 1982.

Yun Chaeyŏng. *Pyŏngjarok* [The diary of 1636]. Seoul: Myŏngmundang, 1987.

Yun Chŭng. *Myŏngje sŏnsaeng yugo* [Posthumous work of Myŏngje]. 2 vols. Seoul: Kyŏngon munhwasa, 1973.

Zhang Tingyu, ed. *Ming shi* [History of the Ming dynasty]. 289 vols. Beijing: Zhonghua shu ju, 1974.

Secondary Sources

Adolphson, Mikael S. *The Teeth and Claws of the Buddha: Monastic Warriors and Sohei in Japanese History.* Honolulu: University of Hawai'i Press, 2007.

Best, Jonathan. *The History of the Early Korean Kingdom of Paekche: Together with an Annotated Translation of the Paekche Annals of the Samguk sagi.* Cambridge, MA: Harvard University Press, 2006.

Chang Chŏngsu. "Pyŏngja horan ijŏn Chosŏn ŭi taejŏngŭm (ch'ŏng) pangŏ chŏllak ŭi sulip kwangjŏng kwa kŭ silsang" [Progress and reality of Chosŏn defense strategy against the later Jin (Qing) before the second Manchu invasion]. *Chosŏn sidae sahakpo* 81 (June 2017): 49–108.

Cho, Hwisang. "Feeling Power in Early Chosŏn Korea: Popular Grievances, Royal Rage, and the Problem of Human Sentiments." *Journal of Korean Studies* 20, no. 1 (Spring 2015): 7–32.

Ch'oe Chinyŏn. *Uri t'ŏ, uri hon Namhan sansŏng* [Our land, our soul: Namhan Mountain Fortress]. Seoul: Tahal midiŏ, 2010.

Choi, Byonghyon, trans. *The Annals of King T'aejo: Founder of Korea's Chosŏn Dynasty.* Cambridge, MA: Harvard University Press, 2014.

Chon, Chu Young. "Transforming Indigenous Performance in Contemporary South Korea: The Case of Sohn Jin Ch'aek's Madangnori." PhD diss., Ohio State University, 2014.

Crossley, Pamela. *A Translucent Mirror: History and Identity in Qing Imperial Ideology.* Berkeley: University of California Press, 1999.

Davis, Andrew McFarland. "The Indians and the Border Warfare of the Revolution." In *Narrative and Critical History of America*, ed. Justin Winsor. Boston: Houghton-Mifflin, 1888.

Di Cosmo, Nicola. *Diary of a Manchu Soldier in Seventeenth-Century China.* New York: Routledge, 2006.

Duncan, John, Jung Chul Lee, Jeong-il Lee, Michael Ahn, and Jack A. Davey. *The Institutional Basis of Civil Governance in the Chosŏn Dynasty.* Seoul: Seoul Selection, 2009.

Elliot, Mark. *The Manchu Way: The Eight Banners and Ethnic Identity in Late Imperial China.* Stanford, CA: Stanford University Press, 2001.

Gabriel, Richard A. *The Culture of War: Invention and Early Development*. New York: Greenwood Press, 1990.

Haboush, JaHyun Kim. "Constructing the Center: The Ritual Controversy and the Search for a New Identity in Seventeenth-Century Korea." In *Culture and the State in Late Chosŏn Korea*, ed. JaHyun Kim Haboush and Martina Deuchler, 46–90. Cambridge, MA: Harvard University Press, 1999.

——. *The Great East Asian War and the Birth of the Korean Nation*. New York: Columbia University Press, 2016.

——. *The Memoirs of Lady Hyegyŏng: The Autobiographical Writings of a Crown Princess of Eighteenth-Century Korea*. Berkeley: University of California Press, 1996.

Han Myŏnggi. *Chŏngmyo-pyŏngja horan kwa tongasia* [The 1627 and 1637 Manchu invasions of Chosŏn and East Asia]. Seoul: Paekwang, 2013.

——. *Imjin waeran kwa hanjung kwan'gae* [Imjin Invasion and Korean-Chinese relations]. Seoul: Yŏksa pibyŏngsa, 2008.

Hŏ T'aegu. "Pyŏngja horan Kanghwado hamnak ŭi wŏnin kwa ch'aegimja ch'ŏbŏl Kim Kyŏngjing p'aejŏn ch'aegimnon ŭi chaegŏmt'o ŭi chungsim ŭro" [Military strength and strategic deployment of the Chosŏn and Qing troops at the time of the fall of Kanghwa Island during the 1637 Manchu invasion]. *Chindan hakpo* 113 (2011): 99–128.

Hong Sŏna. "Han'guk hosang ŭi siwŏn kwa chohyŏng e kwanhan yŏn'gu" [Study on the origins and creative design of folding stools]. *Han'guk kagu hakhoeji* 24, no. 2 (April 2013): 156–82.

Hummel, Arthur W. *Eminent Chinese of the Ch'ing Period, 1644–1912*. Washington, DC: U.S. Government Printing Office, 1943.

Im Suyŏn. "Namhan sansŏng 'saengsaeng munhwajae saŏp' ŭi ŭiŭi wa kaesŏng pangan yŏn'gu" [The case study of Namhan Mountain Fortress on the significance and direction of "vibrant cultural property program"]. *Munhwa K'ont'ench'e yŏn'gu* 6 (2015): 123–53.

Kessler, Adam T. "The Last Days of the Song Dynasty: Evidence of the Flight of Song Officials to Southeast Asia Before the Mongol Invasions." *Journal of the Royal Asiatic Society* 28, no. 2 (April 2018): 315–37.

Kim Ilhwan. "Han mugwan ŭi chŏnjaeng ch'ehŏm sugiga mandŭrŏ chigi kkaji namhan surok ŭi sŏsa pangsik yŏn'gu" [Narrative method of war experiences by military officers in *Namhan surok*]. *Hanminjok munhwa yŏn'gu* 49 (February 2015): 249–80.

Kim Insuk. "Injobi Inyŏl wanghu ŭi naejo wa silp'aehan yuga" [The help and infant loss of King Injo's Queen Inyŏl]. *Han'guk inmulsa yŏn'gu* 18 (2012): 225–57.

Kim Kyŏngsu. "Chosŏn chŏn'gi yasa p'yŏnch'an ŭi sahaksajŏn koch'al" [A study of historiographical significance of the unofficial book of history in the early Chosŏn dynasty]. *Yŏksa hwa sirhak* 19–20 (2001): 151–79.

Kim, Sun Joo. "Culture of Remembrance in Late Chosŏn Korea: Bringing an Unknown War Hero Back into History." *Journal of Social Theory* 44, no. 2 (2010): 563–85.

———. *Voice from the North: Resurrecting Regional Identity Through the Life and Work of Yi Sihang*. Stanford, CA: Stanford University Press, 2013.

Kim, Sunglim. *Flowering Plums and Curio Cabinets: The Culture of Objects in Late Chosŏn Korean Art*. Seattle: University of Washington Press, 2018.

Kim Yonghŭm. "Injodae chŏnban chŏngch'ijŏk kaltŭng kwa pungdang-non." *Yŏksa hwa kyŏnggye* 60 (September 2006): 75–101.

Kinney, Anne Behnke, ed. and trans. *Exemplary Women of Early China: The Lienu Zhuan of Liu Xiang*. New York: Columbia University Press, 2014.

Knez, Eugene I. "Modernization of Three Korean Villages, 1951–1981: An Illustrated Study of a People and Their Material Culture." *Smithsonian Contributions to Anthropology* (1997): 1–216.

Kye, Seung B. "The Altar of Great Gratitude: A Korean Memory of Ming China Under Manchu Dominance, 1704–1894." *Journal of Korean Religion* 5, no. 2 (October 2014): 71–88.

Kim, Yong–T'ae. "Changes in Seventeenth-Century Korean Buddhism and the Establishment of the Buddhist Tradition in the Late Chosŏn Dynasty." *Acta Koreana* 16, no. 2 (December 2013): 537–63.

Ledyard, Gari. "Confucianism and War: The Korean Security Crisis of 1598." *Journal of Korean Studies* 6, no. 1 (1988–89): 81–119.

Leezenberg, Michiel. "The Vernacular Revolution: Reclaiming Early Modern Grammatical Traditions in the Ottoman Empire." *History of Humanities* 1, no. 2 (2016): 251–75.

Legge, James. *The Chinese Classics, vol. 1: Confucian Analects, the Great Learning, the Doctrine of the Mean, and the Works of Mencius*. Taipei: SMC Publishing, 1998.

Min, Eun Kyung. "Chengde and the Barbarians: Reading Ethnicity and Difference in Pak Chiwŏn's *Yŏrha ilgi*." *Seoul Journal of Korean Studies* 26, no. 2 (December 2013): 307–34.

No Yŏnggu. "Injo pyŏngja horan sigi chosŏn ŭi chŏnsul chŏn'gae" [Chosŏn military tactics from the early years of King Injo through the second Manchu invasion of 1636]. *Han'guk sahakpo* 41 (2010): 203–35.

O'Donovan, Maria, and Lynda Carroll. "Going Places: The Historical Archaeology of Travel and Tourism." *International Journal of Historical Archaeology* 15, no. 2 (June 2011): 191–93.

Oh, Young Kyun. *Engraving Virtue: The Printing History of a Premodern Korean Moral Primer*. Boston: Brill, 2013.

Pae Usŏng. "Sŏul e on ch'ŏng ŭ ch'iksa Mafuta hwa samjŏndobi" [Study on the Manchu envoy Mafuta who came to Seoul and the Samjŏndo stele]. *Sŏul hak yŏn'gu* 38 (2010): 235–71.

Pak Yŏnghae, Kim Chaehong, and Mun Pyŏngu. *Chosŏn inmin ŭi panch'imnyak t'ujaengsa Ri Chop'yŏn* [The history of Korean people and anti-foreign invasion wars, Chosŏn edition]. P'yŏngyang: Sahoe kwak ch'ulp'ansa, 2010.

Palais, James B. *Confucian Statecraft and Korean Institutions: Yu Hyongwon and the Late Choson Dynasty*. Seattle: University of Washington Press, 1996.

———. *Politics and Policy in Traditional Korea*. Cambridge, MA: Harvard University Press, 1991.

Pettid, Michael, Gregory Evon, and Chan Park, eds. *Premodern Korean Literary Prose: An Anthology*. New York: Columbia University Press, 2018.

Pyŏn Kwangsŏk. "Ŏmo changgun chŏn Manho Chŏng Ŭnggap myo chisŏk kwa kwallyŏ inmul kirok" [Records related to the epitaph stone of General Uno, the former Manho Chŏng Ŭnggap]. *Ulsan sahak* 12 (1999): 127–35.

Pyŏn T'aesŏp. *Han'guksa t'ongnon* [An introduction to Korean history]. Seoul: Samyŏngsa, 1996.

Quartermain, Thomas. "Besieged on a Frozen Mountain Top: Opposing Records from the Qing Invasion of Chosŏn, 1636–1637." *Acta Koreana* 21, no. 1 (June 2018): 137–67.

Rigger, Shelley. "Voices of Manchu Identity, 1635–1935." In *Cultural Encounters on China's Ethnic Frontiers*, ed. Stevan Harrell, 186–214. Seattle: University of Washington Press, 1995.

Rivera, Lauren A. "Managing 'Spoiled' National Identity: War, Tourism, and Memory in Croatia." *American Sociological Review* 73, no. 4 (August 2008): 613–34.

Sato, Masayuki. "Comparative Ideas of Chronology." *History and Theory* 30, no. 3 (1991): 275–301.

Sin Yŏngju and Ch'oe Chinyŏn. *Uri ai ch'ŏt Namhan sansŏng yŏhaeng* [First-time travel for Korean children to Namhan Mountain Fortress]. Seoul: Samsŏngdang, 2011.

Soothill, William E. *The Analects of Confucius*. Tokyo: Methodist Publishing House, 1910.

Tan, Tian Yuan. *Songs of Contentment and Transgression: Discharged Officials and Literati Communities in Sixteenth-Century North China*. Cambridge, MA: Harvard University Press, 2010.

Thane, Patricia. "Oral History, Memory and Written Tradition: An Introduction." *Transaction of the Royal Asiatic Society* 9 (1999): 160–68.

Yi Kanghan. "Koryŏ hugi Manhobu ŭi 'chiyŏk tanwijŏk' sŏnggyŏk kŏmt'o" [End of Koryŏ Manhobu]. *Yŏksa wa hyŏnsil* 100, no. (2016): 241–80.

Yu T'aru. *Namhan sansŏng ŭi nunmul* [The tears of Namhan Mountain Fortress]. P'aju: Alma, 2010.

Vermeersch, Sem. *The Power of the Buddhas: The Politics of Buddhism During the Koryŏ Dynasty (918–1392)*. Cambridge, MA: Harvard University Press, 2008.

Wang, Yuanchong. *Remaking the Chinese Empire: Manchu-Korean Relations, 1616–1911*. Ithaca, NY: Cornell University Press, 2018.

Wilder, George D., J. H. Ingram, and F. W. Baller. *Analysis of Chinese Characters*. New York: Dover, 1974.

Wilkinson, John Gardner. *Topography of Thebes and General Views of Egypt*. London: John Murray, 1835.

Web Resources for Official Titles and Posts

Brother Anthony's list of government offices and posts: http://anthony.sogang.ac.kr/joseontitles.htm.

Harvard University's *Korean History Gloss*: https://projects.iq.harvard.edu/files/gpks/files/korean_history_glossary_201506__1.docx.

Veritable Records of King Sejong from the National Institute of Korean History: http://esillok.history.go.kr/.

and literary Chinese writing, lxiv; and Manchu identity, xvi; and military tactics, lviii; and Mukden envoy incident, 2, 213n11

Crossley, Pamela, xvi

crown prince. *See* Sohyŏn

Major Plays of Chikamatsu, tr. Donald Keene 1961

Four Major Plays of Chikamatsu, tr. Donald Keene. Paperback ed. only. 1961; rev. ed. 1997

Records of the Grand Historian of China, translated from the Shih chi of Ssu-ma Ch'ien, tr. Burton Watson, 2 vols. 1961

Instructions for Practical Living and Other Neo-Confucian Writings by Wang Yang-ming, tr. Wing-tsit Chan 1963

Hsün Tzu: Basic Writings, tr. Burton Watson, paperback ed. only. 1963; rev. ed. 1996

Chuang Tzu: Basic Writings, tr. Burton Watson, paperback ed. only. 1964; rev. ed. 1996

The Mahābhārata, tr. Chakravarthi V. Narasimhan. Also in paperback ed. 1965; rev. ed. 1997

The Manyōshū, Nippon Gakujutsu Shinkōkai edition 1965

Su Tung-p'o: Selections from a Sung Dynasty Poet, tr. Burton Watson. Also in paperback ed. 1965

Bhartrihari: Poems, tr. Barbara Stoler Miller. Also in paperback ed. 1967

Basic Writings of Mo Tzu, Hsün Tzu, and Han Fei Tzu, tr. Burton Watson. Also in separate paperback eds. 1967

The Awakening of Faith, Attributed to Aśvaghosha, tr. Yoshito S. Hakeda. Also in paperback ed. 1967

Reflections on Things at Hand: The Neo-Confucian Anthology, comp. Chu Hsi and Lü Tsu-ch'ien, tr. Wing-tsit Chan 1967

The Platform Sutra of the Sixth Patriarch, tr. Philip B. Yampolsky. Also in paperback ed. 1967

Essays in Idleness: The Tsurezuregusa of Kenkō, tr. Donald Keene. Also in paperback ed. 1967

The Pillow Book of Sei Shōnagon, tr. Ivan Morris, 2 vols. 1967

Two Plays of Ancient India: The Little Clay Cart and the Minister's Seal, tr. J. A. B. van Buitenen 1968

The Complete Works of Chuang Tzu, tr. Burton Watson 1968

The Romance of the Western Chamber (Hsi Hsiang Chi), tr. S. I. Hsiung. Also in paperback ed. 1968

The Manyōshū, Nippon Gakujutsu Shinkōkai edition. Paperback ed. only. 1969

Records of the Historian: Chapters from the Shih chi of Ssu-ma Ch'ien, tr. Burton Watson. Paperback ed. only. 1969

Cold Mountain: 100 Poems by the T'ang Poet Han-shan, tr. Burton Watson. Also in paperback ed. 1970

Twenty Plays of the Nō Theatre, ed. Donald Keene. Also in paperback ed. 1970

Chūshingura: The Treasury of Loyal Retainers, tr. Donald Keene. Also in paperback ed. 1971; rev. ed. 1997

The Zen Master Hakuin: Selected Writings, tr. Philip B. Yampolsky 1971

Chinese Rhyme-Prose: Poems in the Fu Form from the Han and Six Dynasties Periods, tr. Burton Watson. Also in paperback ed. 1971

Kūkai: Major Works, tr. Yoshito S. Hakeda. Also in paperback ed. 1972

The Old Man Who Does as He Pleases: Selections from the Poetry and Prose of Lu Yu, tr. Burton Watson 1973

The Lion's Roar of Queen Śrīmālā, tr. Alex and Hideko Wayman 1974

Courtier and Commoner in Ancient China: Selections from the History of the Former Han by Pan Ku, tr. Burton Watson. Also in paperback ed. 1974

Japanese Literature in Chinese, vol. 1: *Poetry and Prose in Chinese by Japanese Writers of the Early Period*, tr. Burton Watson 1975

Japanese Literature in Chinese, vol. 2: *Poetry and Prose in Chinese by Japanese Writers of the Later Period*, tr. Burton Watson 1976

Love Song of the Dark Lord: Jayadeva's Gītagovinda, tr. Barbara Stoler Miller. Also in paperback ed. Cloth ed. includes critical text of the Sanskrit. 1977; rev. ed. 1997

Ryōkan: Zen Monk-Poet of Japan, tr. Burton Watson 1977

Calming the Mind and Discerning the Real: From the Lam rim chen mo of Tsoṇ-kha-pa, tr. Alex Wayman 1978

The Hermit and the Love-Thief: Sanskrit Poems of Bhartrihari and Bilhaṇa, tr. Barbara Stoler Miller 1978

The Lute: Kao Ming's P'i-p'a chi, tr. Jean Mulligan. Also in paperback ed. 1980

A Chronicle of Gods and Sovereigns: Jinnō Shōtōki of Kitabatake Chikafusa, tr. H. Paul Varley 1980

Among the Flowers: The Hua-chien chi, tr. Lois Fusek 1982

Grass Hill: Poems and Prose by the Japanese Monk Gensei, tr. Burton Watson 1983

Doctors, Diviners, and Magicians of Ancient China: Biographies of Fang-shih, tr. Kenneth J. DeWoskin. Also in paperback ed. 1983

Theater of Memory: The Plays of Kālidāsa, ed. Barbara Stoler Miller. Also in paperback ed. 1984

The Columbia Book of Chinese Poetry: From Early Times to the Thirteenth Century, ed. and tr. Burton Watson. Also in paperback ed. 1984

Poems of Love and War: From the Eight Anthologies and the Ten Long Poems of Classical Tamil, tr. A. K. Ramanujan. Also in paperback ed. 1985

The Bhagavad Gita: Krishna's Counsel in Time of War, tr. Barbara Stoler Miller 1986

The Columbia Book of Later Chinese Poetry, ed. and tr. Jonathan Chaves. Also in paperback ed. 1986

The Tso Chuan: Selections from China's Oldest Narrative History, tr. Burton Watson 1989

Waiting for the Wind: Thirty-Six Poets of Japan's Late Medieval Age, tr. Steven Carter 1989

Selected Writings of Nichiren, ed. Philip B. Yampolsky 1990

Saigyō, Poems of a Mountain Home, tr. Burton Watson 1990

The Book of Lieh Tʒu: A Classic of the Tao, tr. A. C. Graham. Morningside ed. 1990

The Tale of an Anklet: An Epic of South India—The Cilappatikāram of Iḷaṇkō Aṭikaḷ, tr. R. Parthasarathy 1993

Waiting for the Dawn: A Plan for the Prince, tr. with introduction by Wm. Theodore de Bary 1993

Yoshitsune and the Thousand Cherry Trees: A Masterpiece of the Eighteenth-Century Japanese Puppet Theater, tr., annotated, and with introduction by Stanleigh H. Jones Jr. 1993

The Lotus Sutra, tr. Burton Watson. Also in paperback ed. 1993

The Classic of Changes: A New Translation of the I Ching as Interpreted by Wang Bi, tr. Richard John Lynn 1994

Beyond Spring: Tʒ'u Poems of the Sung Dynasty, tr. Julie Landau 1994

The Columbia Anthology of Traditional Chinese Literature, ed. Victor H. Mair 1994

Scenes for Mandarins: The Elite Theater of the Ming, tr. Cyril Birch 1995

Letters of Nichiren, ed. Philip B. Yampolsky; tr. Burton Watson et al. 1996

Unforgotten Dreams: Poems by the Zen Monk Shōtetsu, tr. Steven D. Carter 1997

The Vimalakirti Sutra, tr. Burton Watson 1997

Japanese and Chinese Poems to Sing: The Wakan rōei shū, tr. J. Thomas Rimer and Jonathan Chaves 1997

Breeʒe Through Bamboo: Kanshi of Ema Saikō, tr. Hiroaki Sato 1998

A Tower for the Summer Heat, by Li Yu, tr. Patrick Hanan 1998

Traditional Japanese Theater: An Anthology of Plays, by Karen Brazell 1998

The Original Analects: Sayings of Confucius and His Successors (0479–0249), by E. Bruce Brooks and A. Taeko Brooks 1998

The Classic of the Way and Virtue: A New Translation of the Tao-te ching of Laoʒi as Interpreted by Wang Bi, tr. Richard John Lynn 1999

The Four Hundred Songs of War and Wisdom: An Anthology of Poems from Classical Tamil, The Puṛanāṇūṛu, ed. and tr. George L. Hart and Hank Heifetz 1999

Original Tao: Inward Training (Nei-yeh) *and the Foundations of Taoist Mysticism*, by Harold D. Roth 1999

Po Chü-i: Selected Poems, tr. Burton Watson 2000

Lao Tʒu's Tao Te Ching: A Translation of the Startling New Documents Found at Guodian, by Robert G. Henricks 2000

The Shorter Columbia Anthology of Traditional Chinese Literature, ed. Victor H. Mair 2000

Mistress and Maid (Jiaohongji), by Meng Chengshun, tr. Cyril Birch 2001

Chikamatsu: Five Late Plays, tr. and ed. C. Andrew Gerstle 2001

The Essential Lotus: Selections from the Lotus Sutra, tr. Burton Watson 2002

Early Modern Japanese Literature: An Anthology, 1600–1900, ed. Haruo Shirane 2002; abridged 2008

The Columbia Anthology of Traditional Korean Poetry, ed. Peter H. Lee 2002

The Sound of the Kiss, or The Story That Must Never Be Told: Pingali Suranna's Kalapurnodayamu, tr. Vecheru Narayana Rao and David Shulman 2003

The Selected Poems of Du Fu, tr. Burton Watson 2003

Far Beyond the Field: Haiku by Japanese Women, tr. Makoto Ueda 2003

Just Living: Poems and Prose by the Japanese Monk Tonna, ed. and tr. Steven D. Carter 2003

Han Feizi: Basic Writings, tr. Burton Watson 2003

Mozi: Basic Writings, tr. Burton Watson 2003

Xunzi: Basic Writings, tr. Burton Watson 2003

Zhuangzi: Basic Writings, tr. Burton Watson 2003

The Awakening of Faith, Attributed to Aśvaghosha, tr. Yoshito S. Hakeda, introduction by Ryūichi Abé 2005

The Tales of the Heike, tr. Burton Watson, ed. Haruo Shirane 2006

Tales of Moonlight and Rain, by Ueda Akinari, tr. with introduction by Anthony H. Chambers 2007

Traditional Japanese Literature: An Anthology, Beginnings to 1600, ed. Haruo Shirane 2007

The Philosophy of Qi, by Kaibara Ekken, tr. Mary Evelyn Tucker 2007

The Analects of Confucius, tr. Burton Watson 2007

The Art of War: Sun Zi's Military Methods, tr. Victor Mair 2007

One Hundred Poets, One Poem Each: A Translation of the Ogura Hyakunin Isshu, tr. Peter McMillan 2008

Zeami: Performance Notes, tr. Tom Hare 2008

Zongmi on Chan, tr. Jeffrey Lyle Broughton 2009

Scripture of the Lotus Blossom of the Fine Dharma, rev. ed., tr. Leon Hurvitz, preface and introduction by Stephen R. Teiser 2009

Mencius, tr. Irene Bloom, ed. with an introduction by Philip J. Ivanhoe 2009

Clouds Thick, Whereabouts Unknown: Poems by Zen Monks of China, Charles Egan 2010

The Mozi: A Complete Translation, tr. Ian Johnston 2010

The Huainanzi: A Guide to the Theory and Practice of Government in Early Han China, by Liu An, tr. and ed. John S. Major, Sarah A. Queen, Andrew Seth Meyer, and Harold D. Roth, with Michael Puett and Judson Murray 2010

The Demon at Agi Bridge and Other Japanese Tales, tr. Burton Watson, ed. with introduction by Haruo Shirane 2011

Haiku Before Haiku: From the Renga Masters to Bashō, tr. with introduction by Steven D. Carter 2011

The Columbia Anthology of Chinese Folk and Popular Literature, ed. Victor H. Mair and Mark Bender 2011

Tamil Love Poetry: The Five Hundred Short Poems of the Aiṅkuṟunūṟu, tr. and ed. Martha Ann Selby 2011

The Teachings of Master Wuzhu: Zen and Religion of No-Religion, by Wendi L. Adamek 2011

The Essential Huainanzi, by Liu An, tr. and ed. John S. Major, Sarah A. Queen, Andrew Seth Meyer, and Harold D. Roth 2012

The Dao of the Military: Liu An's Art of War, tr. Andrew Seth Meyer 2012

Unearthing the Changes: Recently Discovered Manuscripts of the Yi Jing *(*I Ching*) and Related Texts*, Edward L. Shaughnessy 2013

Record of Miraculous Events in Japan: The Nihon ryōiki, tr. Burton Watson 2013

The Complete Works of Zhuangzi, tr. Burton Watson 2013

Lust, Commerce, and Corruption: An Account of What I Have Seen and Heard, by an Edo Samurai, tr. and ed. Mark Teeuwen and Kate Wildman Nakai with Miyazaki Fumiko, Anne Walthall, and John Breen 2014; abridged 2017

Exemplary Women of Early China: The Lienü zhuan *of Liu Xiang*, tr. Anne Behnke Kinney 2014

The Columbia Anthology of Yuan Drama, ed. C. T. Hsia, Wai-yee Li, and George Kao 2014

The Resurrected Skeleton: From Zhuangzi to Lu Xun, by Wilt L. Idema 2014

The Sarashina Diary: *A Woman's Life in Eleventh-Century Japan*, by Sugawara no Takasue no Musume, tr. with introduction by Sonja Arntzen and Itō Moriyuki 2014; reader's edition 2018

The Kojiki: *An Account of Ancient Matters*, by Ō no Yasumaro, tr. Gustav Heldt 2014

The Orphan of Zhao *and Other Yuan Plays: The Earliest Known Versions*, tr. and introduced by Stephen H. West and Wilt L. Idema 2014

Luxuriant Gems of the Spring and Autumn, attributed to Dong Zhongshu, ed. and tr. Sarah A. Queen and John S. Major 2016

A Book to Burn and a Book to Keep (Hidden): Selected Writings, by Li Zhi, ed. and tr. Rivi Handler-Spitz, Pauline Lee, and Haun Saussy 2016

The Shenzi Fragments: *A Philosophical Analysis and Translation*, Eirik Lang Harris 2016

Record of Daily Knowledge *and* Poems and Essays: *Selections*, by Gu Yanwu, tr. and ed. Ian Johnston 2017